United States Marine Corps
Medal of Honor Recipients

United States Marine Corps Medal of Honor Recipients

A Comprehensive Registry,
Including U.S. Navy Medical Personnel
Honored for Serving Marines in Combat

Edited by GEORGE B. CLARK

McFarland & Company, Inc., Publishers
Jefferson, North Carolina, and London

To Jeanne J. Clark,
my dear wife of many years
who always helps me

LIBRARY OF CONGRESS CATALOGUING-IN-PUBLICATION DATA

Clark, George B., 1926–
United States Marine Corps Medal of Honor recipients : a comprehensive registry,
including U.S. Navy medical personnel honored for serving Marines in combat /
Edited by George B. Clark.
p.   cm.
Includes bibliographical references and index.

ISBN 0-7864-2271-8 (illustrated case binding : 50# alkaline paper)

1. Medal of Honor.   2. Marines—Medals—United States.
3. United States. Marine Corps—Medals, badges, decorations, etc.
4. United States. Navy—Medical personnel—Medals.   I. Title.
VE495.3C53 2005   359.9'61'0973—dc22   2005010597

British Library cataloguing data are available

On the cover: Photograph ©2005 Corbis Images; Congressional Medal of Honor U.S. Navy

Manufactured in the United States of America

*McFarland & Company, Inc., Publishers
Box 611, Jefferson, North Carolina 28640
www.mcfarlandpub.com*

Contents

Preface

This is, as of May 2003, a complete listing of all Medal of Honor recipients among the United States Marines and their comrades of the United States Navy — corpsmen and doctors, and one chaplain — who served Marines in combat. All told this book lists 296 Marines and 21 Navy medical personnel. Also listed is one who, like most members of the U.S. Coast Guard, was indirectly serving in the U.S. Navy: Douglas A. Munro, the valiant Coast Guardsman who saved many Marines at Guadalcanal. Since he was actively supporting Marines at the time he was selected for the award, he too deserves to be recognized here.

The primary source for this book is *Medal of Honor Recipients 1863–1973*, a report prepared for the Committee on Veterans' Affairs, United States Senate, October 22, 1973 (Washington, D.C.: Government Printing Office, 1973). Other sources of information are the Jane Blakeney book *Heroes, U.S. Marine Corps 1861–1955* (Washington, D.C.: privately printed, 1957), and the U.S. Navy Department's *Medal of Honor 1861–1949, The Navy*, printed in Washington around 1950. The five latest awards listed in this book were drawn from the Web site for the U.S. Army Center for Military History.

The book is divided into periods of military activity, and the honorees are listed alphabetically within those periods. Each entry provides the text of the official Medal of Honor citation. Any additional material of interest that I discovered during my research is included within brackets and *italicized*. An asterisk before a name indicates that the honoree died in the action for which the award was received.

An appendix to the text lists states and nations of origin and shows how many honorees were born in, or accredited to, each one. (An honoree is "accredited to" the state where he enlisted. For various reasons, an honoree's accredited state and his state or nation of origin are not always the same.) A second appendix offers some numerical breakdowns, such as the number of Marines killed earning the Medal in each war, or the numbers of regulars and reservists earning the Medal.

A third appendix lists the Marine Corps honorees (the Navy recipients are excluded) in the official Marine Corps Medal of Honor sequence. The numbers in

1

this sequence are assigned by the Corps. One anomaly in the sequence is the very late World War II award for Corporal (later major general) James L. Day, which was issued in 1998. Medal of Honor records do not make it clear how Day's award has affected the sequence — i.e., whether he has been assigned a number in the same range as the other World War II recipients, which would change the numbers of all the awards that followed.

Over the years, the format of the Medal of Honor citation has changed. The early citations were quite sparse compared to those of recent years. By and large, however, the substance of the citations remains about the same.

The Medal of Honor was authorized for enlisted men of the naval service by an act of the U.S. Congress dated 21 December 1861. It was the authorization for the promotion of "seamen distinguishing themselves in battle or by extraordinary heroism in the line of their profession." Upon being promoted they would be entitled to an honorarium of $100 plus the Medal. The Congress was approached to approve an award for enlisted men of the U.S. Army as well; that approval was dated 12 July 1862. Both, however, were amended on 3 March 1863 to include Army officers. The law was revised yet again on 3 March 1901 to approve the Medal for "any enlisted man of the Navy and Marine Corps who shall have distinguished himself in battle or displayed extraordinary heroism in the line of his profession." Notice here that the naval service award was still only for enlisted men — until the law was amended, effective 3 March 1915, to permit officers of the Navy, Marine Corps, and Coast Guard to receive the award. Prior to that the Navy officers had had little if anything for recognition of service "above and beyond," while Marine officers were at least given brevet promotions. Following World War I, a medal was struck for Marine brevet recipients still living. Because the reasons for receiving this award closely resembled those associated with the Medal of Honor, it quickly became the second most desirable award for Marine officers.

On 4 February 1919 the $100 honorarium was dropped from the award for the enlisted recipients, but $2.00 per month was added to the pay of an enlisted man who earned the Medal.

The actual medal and its ribbon has been altered by each service several times during the approximately 140 years of its existence. Likewise, the justification for approving the award has changed considerably over the years. Since World War I, it has been awarded only for truly outstanding service. In fact, it seems that the qualifications have become more stringent for each war. Many of the later recipients died in the actions for which they were cited. (Many Marines from World War II through Vietnam were awarded their medals because they threw themselves on grenades to save others.) Those who survived their actions were often badly wounded, and some died later in other actions. In World War II and the Korean campaign, especially, many of the recipients were Marine Reservists, officers and enlisted. As could be expected, most men were very young. As the saying goes, "the best and brightest."

In the Civil War, the Medal of Honor was the only medal available; still, those who received it were the best of their crowd. The same could be said of those honored through the period before World War I. Their heroism is evident in their citations — and for those whose achievements may not seem as obvious, perhaps the broadly written citations fail to express the true measure of their performance. I know that is especially true of Daniel J. Daly at Peking, and both John Fitzgerald and John H. Quick at Cuzco Wells, Cuba.

A sad departure from the spirit of the Medal occurred at the end of 1915 when the barrier against awards to Navy and Marine officers was lifted and practically everyone in that group, including the admiral commanding the entire operation at Vera Cruz in 1914 and the Marine ground commander during the first few days, was promptly written up and awarded the Medal. Even the admiral's nephew, mainly because he was his uncle's "aide," was so honored. One Marine officer tried to refuse the award because he felt he hadn't done anything to deserve it. He was suitably chastised and duly accepted his medal.

That sad affair does not detract from the heroism of the other men awarded the Medal, especially during the twentieth century and beyond. They truly deserve the respect and admiration of their fellow Americans. They have mine, and my envy as well.

The Medal is now, justifiably, considered the ultimate sign of courage and devotion "above and beyond the call of duty." Reportedly, several presidents have said that they would rather have that Medal than be president of the United States. Me too, but neither is likely.

George B. Clark

Civil War • 1861–1865

Binder, Richard. Sergeant, U.S. Marine Corps. *Born:* 1840, in Philadelphia, PA. *Accredited to:* Pennsylvania. *Citation:* On board the U.S.S. *Ticonderoga* during the attacks on Fort Fisher, 24 and 25 December 1864, and 13 to 15 January 1865. Despite heavy return fire by the enemy and the explosion of the 100-pounder Parrott rifle which killed 8 men and wounded 12 more, Sergeant Binder, as captain of a gun, performed his duties with skill and courage during the first 2 days of battle. As his ship again took position on the 13th, he remained steadfast as the *Ticonderoga* maintained a well-placed fire upon the batteries on shore, and thereafter, as she materially lessened the power of guns on the mound which had been turned upon our assaulting columns. During this action the flag was planted on one of the strongest fortifications possessed by the rebels.

Denig, J. Henry. Sergeant, U.S. Marine Corps. *Born:* 1839, York, PA. *Accredited to:* Pennsylvania. *G.O. No.:* 45, 31 December 1864. *Citation:* On board the U.S.S. *Brooklyn* during action against rebel forts and gunboats and with the ram *Tennessee,* in Mobile Bay, 5 August 1864. Despite severe damage to his ship and the loss of several men on board as enemy fire raked her decks, Sergeant Denig fought his gun with skill and courage throughout the furious 2-hour battle which resulted in the surrender of the rebel *Tennessee* and in the damaging and destruction of batteries at Morgan.

Fry, Isaac N. Orderly Sergeant, U.S. Marine Corps. *Accredited to:* Pennsylvania. *G.O. No.:* 59, 22 June 1865. *Citation:* On board the U.S.S. *Ticonderoga* during attacks on Fort Fisher, 13 to 15 January 1865. As orderly sergeant of the Marine guard, and captain of a gun, Orderly Sergeant Fry performed his duties with skill and courage as the *Ticonderoga* maintained a well-placed fire upon the batteries to the left of the palisades during the initial phases of the 3-day battle, and thereafter, as she considerably lessened the firing power of guns on the mount which had been turned upon our assaulting columns. During this action the flag was planted on one of the strongest fortifications possessed by the rebels.

Hudson, Michael. Sergeant, U.S. Marine Corps. *Born:* County Sligo, Ireland. *Accredited to:* New York. *G.O. No.:* 45, 31 December 1864. *Citation:* On board the U.S.S. *Brooklyn* during action against rebel forts and gunboats and with the ram *Tennessee* in Mobile Bay, 5 August 1864. Despite severe damage to his ship and the loss of several men on board as enemy fire raked the decks, Sergeant Hudson fought his gun with skill and courage throughout the furious 2-hour battle which resulted in the surrender of the rebel ram *Tennessee.*

Mackie, John F. Corporal, U.S. Marine Corps. *Born:* 1836, New York, NY. *Accredited to:* New York. *G.O. No.:* 17, 10 July 1862. *Citation:* On board the U.S.S. *Galena* in the attack on Fort Darling at Drewry's Bluff, James River, on 15 May 1862. As enemy shellfire raked the deck of his ship, Corporal Mackie fearlessly maintained his musket fire against the rifle pits along the shore and, when ordered to fill vacancies at guns caused by men wounded and killed in action, manned the weapon with skill and courage. (First Marine awarded a Medal of Honor)

Martin, James. Sergeant, U.S. Marine Corps. *Born*: 1826, Derry, Ireland. *Accredited to:* Pennsylvania. *G.O. No:* 45, 31 December 1864. *Citation:* As captain of a gun on board the U.S.S. *Richmond* during action against rebel forts and gunboats and with the rebel ram *Tennessee* in Mobile Bay, 5 August 1864. Despite damage to his ship and the loss of several men on board as enemy fire raked her decks, Sergeant Martin fought his gun with skill and courage throughout the furious 2-hour battle which resulted in the surrender of the rebel ram *Tennessee* and in the damaging and destruction of batteries at Fort Morgan.

Miller, Andrew. Sergeant, U.S. Marine Corps. *Born*: 1836, Germany. *Accredited to:* Washington, D.C. *G.O. No.:* 45, 31 December 1864. *Citation:* As captain of a gun on board the U.S.S. *Richmond* during action against rebel forts and gunboats and with the ram *Tennessee* in Mobile Bay, 5 August 1864. Despite damage to his ship and the loss of several men on board as enemy fire raked her decks, Sergeant Miller fought his gun with skill and courage throughout the furious 2-hour battle which resulted in the surrender of the rebel ram *Tennessee* and in the damaging at Fort Morgan.

Nugent, Christopher. Orderly Sergeant, U.S. Marine Corps. *Born:* 1840, County Cavan, Ireland. *Accredited to:* Massachusetts. *G.O. No.:* 32, 16 April 1864. *Citation:* Serving on board the U.S.S. *Fort Henry,* Crystal River, Florida, 15 June 1863. Reconnoitering on the Crystal River on this date and in charge of a boat from the *Fort Henry,* Orderly Sergeant Nugent ordered an assault upon a rebel breastwork fortification. In this assault, the orderly sergeant and his comrades drove a guard of 11 rebels into the swamp, capturing their arms and destroying their camp equipage while gallantly withholding fire to prevent harm to a woman among the fugitives. On 30 July 1863, he further proved his courage by capturing a boat off Depot Key, Fla., containing two men and a woman with their baggage.

Oviatt, Miles M. Corporal, U.S. Marine Corps. *Born*: 1841, Cattarangus County, NY. *Accredited to:* New York. *G.O. No.:* 45, 31 December 1864. *Citation:* On board the U.S.S. *Brooklyn* during action against rebel forts and gunboats and with the ram *Tennessee* in Mobile Bay, 5 August 1864. Despite severe damage to his ship and the loss of several men on board as enemy fire raked the deck, Corporal Oviatt fought his gun with skill and courage throughout the furious 2-hour battle which resulted in the surrender of the rebel ram *Tennessee.*

Rannahan, John. Corporal, U.S. Marine Corps. *Born*: 1836, County Monahan, Ireland. *Accredited* to: Pennsylvania. *G.O. No.:* 59, 22 June 1865. *Citation:* On board the U.S.S. *Minnesota* in the assault on Fort Fisher, 15 January 1865. Landing on the beach with the assaulting party from his ship, Corporal Rannahan advanced to the top of the sand hill and partly through the breach in the palisades despite enemy fire which killed or wounded many officers and men. When more than two-thirds of the men became seized with panic and retreated on the run, he remained with the balance of the party until dark when it came safely away, bringing its wounded, its arms and its colors.

Roantree, James S. Sergeant, U.S. Marine Corps. *Born:* Dublin, Ireland. *Accredited to:* New York. *G.O. No.:* 45, 31 December 1864. *Citation:* On board the U.S.S. *Oneida* during action rebel forts and gunboats and with the ram *Tennessee* in Mobile Bay 5 August 1864. Despite damage to his ship and the loss of several men on board as enemy fire raked her decks and penetrated her boilers, Sergeant Roantree performed his duties with skill and courage throughout the furious battle which resulted in the surrender of the rebel ram *Tennessee* and in the damaging and destruction of batteries at Fort Morgan.

Shivers, John. Private, U.S. Marine Corp. *Born*: 1830, Canada. *Accredited to:* New Jersey. *G.O. No.:* 71, 15 January 1866. *Citation:* On board the U.S.S. *Minnesota,* in the assault on Fort Fisher, 15 January 1865. Landing on the beach with the assaulting party from his ship, Private Shivers advanced to the top of the sand hill and partly through the breach in the palisades despite enemy fire which killed or wounded many officers and men. When more than two-thirds of the men became seized with panic and retreated on the run, he remained with the party until dark when it came safely away, bringing its wounded, its arms and its colors.

Smith, Willard M. Corporal, U.S. Marine Corps. *Born*: 1840, Allegheny, NY. *Accredited to:* New York. *G.O. No.:* 45, 31 December 1864. *Citation:* On board the U.S.S. *Brooklyn* during action against rebel forts and gunboats, and with the ram *Tennessee* in Mobile Bay, 5 August 1864. Despite severe damage to his ship and the loss of several men on board as enemy fire continued to fall, Corporal Smith fought his gun with skill and courage throughout the furious 2-hour battle which resulted in the surrender of the rebel ram Tennessee.

Sprowle, David. Orderly Sergeant, U.S. Marine Corps. *Born*: 1811, Lisbon, N.Y. *Accredited to:* New York. *G.O. No.:* 45, 31 December 1864. *Citation:* On board the U.S.S. *Richmond* during action against rebel forts and gunboats, and with the ram *Tennessee* in Mobile Bay, 5 August 1864. Despite damage to his ship and the loss of several men on board as enemy fire raked her decks, Orderly Sergeant Sprowle inspired the men of the Marine guard and directed a division of great guns throughout the furious battle which resulted in the surrender of the rebel ram *Tennessee* and in the damaging and destruction of batteries at Fort Morgan.

Thompson, Henry A. Private, U.S. Marine Corps. *Born*: 1841, England. *Accredited to:* Pennsylvania. *G.O. No.:* 59, 22 June 1865. *Citation:* On board the U.S.S. *Minnesota* in the assault on Fort Fisher, 15 January 1865. Landing on the beach with the assaulting party from his ship Private Thompson advanced partly through a breach in the palisades and nearer to the fort than any man from his ship despite enemy fire which killed or wounded many officers and men. When more than two-thirds of the men became seized with panic and retreated on the run, he remained with the party until dark, when it came safely away, bringing its wounded, its arms and its colors.

Tomlin, Andrew J. Corporal, U. S. Marine Corps. *Born*: 1844, Goshen, NJ. *Accredited to:* New Jersey. *G. O. No.*: 59, 22 June 1865. *Citation:* As corporal of the guard on board the U.S.S. *Wabash* during the assault on Fort Fisher, on 15 January 1865. As one of 200 Marines assembled to hold a line of entrenchments in the rear of the fort which the enemy threatened to attack in force following a retreat in panic by more than two-thirds of the assaulting ground forces, Corporal Tomlin took position in line and remained until morning when relief troops arrived from the fort. When one of his comrades was struck down by enemy fire, he unhesitatingly advanced under a withering fire of musketry into an open plain close to the fort and assisted the wounded man to a place of safety.

Vaughn, Pinkerton R. Sergeant, U.S. Marine Corps. *Born*: 1839, Downingtown, PA. *Accredited to:* Pennsylvania. *G.O. No.*: 17, 10 July 1863. *Citation:* Serving on board the U.S.S. *Mississippi* during her abandonment and firing in the action with the Port Hudson batteries, 14 March 1863. During the abandonment of the *Mississippi* which had to be grounded, Sergeant Vaughn rendered invaluable assistance to his commanding officer, remaining with the ship until all the crew had landed and the ship had been fired to prevent its falling into enemy hands. Persistent until the last, and conspicuously cool under the heavy shellfire, Sergeant Vaughn was finally ordered to save himself as he saw fit.

Korean Campaign • 1871

Brown, Charles. Corporal, U.S. Marine Corps. *Born* New York, NY., *Enlisted at*: Hong Kong, China. *G.O. No.*: 169, 8 February 1872. *Citation:* On board the U.S.S. *Colorado* in action against the Korean fort on 11 June 1871. Assisted in capturing the Korean standard in the center of the citadel of the fort.

Coleman, John. Private U S Marine Corps. *Born*: 9 October 1847, Ireland. *Accredited to:* California. *G.O. No.*: 169, 8 February 1872. *Citation:* On board the U.S.S. *Colorado* in action at Korea on 11 June 1871. Fighting hand-to-hand with the enemy, Coleman succeeded in saving the life of [Boatswain's Mate] Alexander McKenzie [USN].

Dougherty, James. Private, U.S. Marine Corps. *Born:* 16 November 1839, Langhash, Ireland. *Accredited* to: Pennsylvania. *G.O. No.*: 169, 8 February 1872. *Citation:* On board the U.S.S. *Carondelet* in various actions of that vessel. Wounded several times Dougherty invariably returned to duty, presenting an example of constancy and devotion to the flag.

McNamara, Michael. Private, U.S. Marine Corps. *Born*: 1841, Clure, Ireland. *Accredited to:* New York. *G.O. No.*: 169, 8 February 1872. *Citation:* On board the U.S.S. *Benicia* during the capture of the Korean forts, 11 June 1871. Advancing to the parapet McNamara wrenched the match-lock from the hands of an enemy and killed him.

Owens, Michael. Private, U.S. Marine Corps. *Born:*(?), New York, NY. *Accredited to:* New York. *G.O. No.:* 169, 8 February 1872. *Citation:* On board the U.S.S. *Colorado* during the capture of Korean forts, 11 June 1871. Fighting courageously in hand-to-hand combat Owens was badly wounded by the enemy during this action.

Purvis, Hugh. Private, U.S. Marine Corps. *Born:* 5 March 1846, Philadelphia, PA. *Accredited to:* Pennsylvania. *G.O. No.:* 169, 8 February 1872. *Citation:* On board the U.S.S. *Alaska* during the attack on and capture of the Korean forts, 11 June 1871. Braving the enemy fire, Purvis was the first to scale the walls of the fort and capture the flag of the Korean forces.

Interim Period • 1872–1898

Morris, John. Corporal, U.S. Marine Corps. *Born:* 25 January 1855, New York, NY. *Accredited to:* New York. *G.O. No.:* 326, 18 October 1884. *Citation:* For leaping overboard from the U.S. Flagship *Lancaster,* at Villefranche, France, 25 December 1881, and rescuing from drowning Robert Blizzard, ordinary seaman, a prisoner, who had jumped overboard.

Stewart, James A. Corporal, U.S. Marine Corps. *Born:* 1839, Philadelphia, PA. *Accredited to:* Pennsylvania. *G.O. No.:* 180, 10 October 1872. *Citation:* Serving on board the U.S.S. *Plymouth,* Stewart jumped overboard in the harbor of Villefranche, France, 1 February 1872 and saved Midshipman [*William B.*] Osterhaus from drowning.

War with Spain • 1898

Campbell, Daniel. Private, U.S. Marine Corps. *Born:* 26 October 1874, Prince Edward Island, Canada. *Accredited to:* Massachusetts. *G.O. No.:* 521, 7 July 1899. *Citation:* On board the U.S.S. *Marblehead* during the cutting of the cable leading from Cienfuegos, Cuba, 11 May 1898. Facing the heavy fire of the enemy, Campbell set an example of extraordinary bravery and coolness throughout this action. [*On that date several boatloads of sailors and Marines were sent ashore to destroy the sea-cable connections Spain had in Cuba. The officers and men from both the* Marblehead *and* Nashville *were landed and set about hauling the cables ashore then, with no other tools, using hacksaws to cut them. All the while the 1,500 Spanish troops within 50 feet, continually fired their weapons directly into the small party. Additionally, both ships 5-inch guns fired over 600 rounds at the Spaniards and caused the landing party much grief, barely missing them. Two men, one sailor and one Marine were killed and ten wounded. Captain Bowman McCalla, USN, under whose command the men were sent ashore later commented "Their work was performed with the utmost coolness and intrepidity under the most trying circumstances, and I shall later have the honor to call special attention to their conduct."*]

Field, Oscar Wadsworth. Private, U.S. Marine Corps. *Born*: 6 October 1873, Jersey City, NJ. *Accredited to:* New York. *G.O. No.:* 521, 7 July 1899. *Citation:* On board the U.S.S. *Nashville* during the operation of cutting the cable leading from Cienfuegos, Cuba, 11 May 1898. Facing the heavy fire of the enemy, Field set an example of extraordinary bravery and coolness throughout this action. [*See Campbell above.*]

Fitzgerald, John. Private, U.S. Marine Corps. *Born*: 17 March 1873, Limerick, Ireland. *Accredited to:* New York. *G.O. No.:* 92, 8 December 1910. *Citation:* For heroism and gallantry in action at Cuzco [Wells], Cuba, 14 June 1898. [*This was for standing upon a hill and signaling to the U.S.S. Dolphin for gunfire, prior to Sergeant John Quick's action. The ship saw Fitzgerald's signaling and was just about to shell Cuzco Wells when Quick followed just as they began.*]

Franklin, Joseph John. Private, U.S. Marine Corps. *Born*: 18 June 1870, Buffalo, N.Y. *Accredited to:* New York. *G.O. No.:* 521, 7 July 1899. *Citation:* On board the U.S.S. *Nashville* during the operation of cutting the cable leading from Cienfuegos, Cuba, 11 May 1898. Facing the heavy fire of the enemy, Franklin set an example of extraordinary bravery and coolness throughout this action. [*See Campbell above.*]

Gaughan, Philip. Sergeant, U.S. Marine Corp. *Born*: 17 March 1865, Belmullet, Ireland. *Accredited to:* Pennsylvania. *G.O. No.:* 521, 7 July 1899. *Citation:* On board the U.S.S. *Nashville* during the operation of cutting the cable leading from Cienfuegos, Cuba, 11 May 1898. Facing the heavy fire of

Harry Lewis MacNeal

the enemy, Gaughan set an example of extraordinary bravery and coolness throughout this action. [*See Campbell above.*]

Kearney, Michael. Private, U.S. Marine Corps. *Born*: 4 October 1874, Newmarket, Ireland. *Accredited to*: Massachusetts. *G.O. No.*: 521, 7 July 1899. *Citation:* On board the U.S.S. *Nashville* during the operation of cutting the cable leading from Cienfuegos, Cuba, 11 May 1898. Facing the heavy fire of the enemy, Kearney set an example of extraordinary bravery and coolness throughout this action. [*See Campbell above.*]

Kuchneister, Hermann William. Private, U.S. Marine Corps. *Born*: Hamburg, Germany. *Accredited to:* New York. *G.O. No.*: 521, 7 July 1899. *Citation:* On board the U.S.S. *Marblehead* during the operation of cutting the cable leading from Cienfuegos, Cuba, 11 May 1898. Facing the heavy fire of the enemy, Kuchneister displayed extraordinary bravery and coolness throughout this action. [*See Campbell above.*]

MacNeal, Harry Lewis. Private, U.S. Marine Corps. *Born*: 22 March 1875, Philadelphia, PA. *Accredited to:* Pennsylvania. *G.O. No.*: 526, 9 August 1899. *Citation:* On board the U.S.S. *Brooklyn* during action at the Battle of Santiago de Cuba, 3 July 1898. Braving the fire of the enemy, MacNeal displayed gallantry throughout this action.

Meredith, James. Private, U.S. Marine Corps. *Born*: 11 April 1872, Omaha, NE. *Accredited to:* Virginia. *G.O. No.:* 521, 7 July 1899. *Citation:* On board the U.S.S. *Marblehead* during the operation of cutting the cable leading from Cienfuegos, Cuba, 11 May 1898. Facing the heavy fire of the enemy, Meredith displayed extraordinary bravery and coolness throughout this action. [*See Campbell above. Name changed to Patrick Ford, Jr.*]

Parker, Pomeroy. Private, U.S. Marine Corps. *Born*: 17 March 1874, Gates County, NC. *Accredited to:* North Carolina. *G.O. No.:* 521, 7 July00 1899. *Citation:* On board the U.S.S. *Nashville* during the operation of cutting the cable leading from Cienfuegos, Cuba, 11 May 1898. Facing the heavy fire of the enemy, Parker displayed extraordinary bravery and coolness throughout this action. [*See Campbell above.*]

Quick, John Henry. Sergeant, U.S. Marine Corps. *Born*: 20 June 1870, Charleston, WV. *Accredited to:* Pennsylvania. *G.O. No.:* 504, 13 December 1898.

John Henry Quick

Citation: In action during the battle of Cuzco [Wells], Cuba, 14 June 1898. Distinguishing himself during this action, Quick signaled the U.S.S. *Dolphin* on three different occasions while exposed to a heavy fire from the enemy. [*Other Navy award: Navy Cross, at Bouresches, France, 6 June 1918; a U.S. Army Distinguished Service Cross and a Silver Star citation while with the 2d Division.*]

Scott, Joseph Francis. Private, U.S. Marine Corps. *Born:* 4 June 1864, Boston, MA. *Accredited to:* Massachusetts. *G.O. No.:* 521, 7 July 1899. *Citation:* On board the U.S.S. *Nashville* during the operation of cutting the cable leading from Cienfuegos, Cuba, 11 May 1898. Facing the heavy fire of the enemy, Scott displayed extraordinary bravery and coolness throughout this action. [*See Campbell above.*]

Sullivan, Edward. Private, U.S. Marine Corps. *Born;* 16 May 1870, Cork, Ireland. *Accredited to:* Massachusetts. *G.O. No.:* 521, 7 July 1899. *Citation:* On board the U.S.S. *Marblehead* during the operation of cutting the cable leading from Cienfuegos, Cuba, 11 May 1898. Facing the heavy fire of the enemy, Sullivan displayed extraordinary bravery and coolness throughout this action. [*See Campbell above.*]

West, Walter Scott. Private, U.S. Marine Corps. *Born:* 13 March 1872, Bradford, NH. *Accredited to:* New Hampshire. *G.O. No.:* 521, 7 July 1899. *Citation:* On board the U.S.S. *Marblehead* during the operation of cutting the cable leading from Cienfuegos, Cuba, 11 May 1898. Facing the heavy fire of the enemy, West displayed extraordinary bravery and coolness throughout this action.[*See Campbell above.*]

Samoa and the Philippine Insurrection •
1899–1906

Bearss, Hiram Iddings. Colonel (Then Captain), U.S. Marine Corps. *Born:* 13 April 1875, Peru, IN. *Appointed from:* Indiana. *Citation:* For extraordinary heroism and eminent and conspicuous conduct in battle at the junction of the Cadacan and Sohoton Rivers, Samar, Philippine Islands, 17 November 1901. Colonel Bearss (then Captain), second in command of the columns upon their uniting ashore in the Sohoton River region, made a surprise attack on the fortified cliffs and completely routed the enemy, killing 30 and capturing and destroying the powder magazine, 40 lantacas (guns), rice, food and cuartels. Due to his courage, intelligence, discrimination and zeal, he successfully led his men up the cliffs by means of bamboo ladders to a height of 200 feet. The cliffs were of soft stone of volcanic origin, in the nature of pumice, and were honeycombed with caves. Tons of rocks were suspended in platforms held in position by vine cables (known as bejuco) in readiness to be precipitated upon people below. After driving the insurgents from their position which was almost impregnable, being covered with numerous trails lined with poison spears, pits, etc., he led his men across the river, scaled the cliffs on the opposite side, and destroyed the camps there. Colonel Bearss and the men under his command overcame incredible difficulties and dangers in destroying positions which, according to reports from old prisoners, had taken 3 years to perfect, were held as a final rallyingpoint, and were never before penetrated by white troops. Colonel Bearss also rendered distinguished public service in the presence of the enemy at Quinapundan River, Samar, Philippine Islands, on 19 January 1902. [*Other awards: Distinguished Service Cross; Army & Navy Distinguished Service Medal: French awards: Legion of Honor, Officer; Croix de Guerre, (2) Palm; (2) Silver, Belgian Croix de Guerre. He retired a colonel in 1919 but received a promotion to brigadier general in January 1936.*]

Buckley, Howard Major. Private, U.S. Marine Corps. *Born*: 23 January 1868, Croton Falls, NY. *Accredited to:* New York. *G.O. No.:* 55, 19 July 1901. *Citation:* For distinguished conduct in the presence of the

Hiram Iddings Bearss

enemy in battle while with the Eighth Army Corps on 25, 27, 29 March, and 4 April 1899. [*He was part of a Marine Colt automatic rapid-fire gun (machine gun) crew in action at Marialo River, Guiguinto, Malolos, and Novaleta. The few were led by Ensign Cleland Davis, USN, and all were highly praised by MajGen Arthur MacArthur, and Col Frederick Funston.*]

Forsterer, Bruno Albert. Sergeant, U.S. Marine Corps. *Born:* 14 July 1869, Koenigsberg, Germany. *Accredited to:* Massachusetts. *G. O. No.:* 55, 19 July 1901. *Citation:* For distinguished conduct in the presence of the enemy at Samoa, 1 April 1899. [*Forsterer, a former officer in the German navy, was the senior non-com when the native Samoans sprung a trap on a Marine rear-guard. He, Sgt Michael J. McNally, and Private Henry L. Hurlbert, fought off the natives to allow the rest of the mixed party, navy and Marines, to find safety.*]

Harvey, Harry. Sergeant, U.S. Marine Corps. *Born:* 4 June 1873, New York, N.Y. *Accredited to:* New Jersey. *G.O. No.:* 55, 19 July 1901. *Citation:* Served in battle against the enemy at Benefictican,* Philippine Islands, 16 February 1900. Throughout this action and in the presence of the enemy, Harvey distinguished himself by meritorious conduct. [*Harvey, leading seven Marines to the rescue of a small*

Henry Lewis Hulbert

David Dixon Porter

squad led by Sgt. Wallace A. Sullivan, was highly commended by Capt Herbert L. Draper, USMC. *Also spelled Banictician.]

Hulbert, Henry Lewis. Private, U.S. Marine Corps. *Born:* 12 January 1867, Kingston-upon-Hull, England. *Accredited to:* California. *G.O. No.:* 55, 19 July 1901. *Citation:* For distinguished conduct in the presence of the enemy at Samoa, 1 April 1899. [*See Forsterer above. Other Navy award: Navy Cross, and U.S. Army DSC, at Belleau Wood, France, 6 June 1918. He was killed in action at Blanc Mont, on 4 October 1918 where he had earned a Silver Star and a Croix de Guerre with Palm.*]

Leonard, Joseph. Private, U.S. Marine Corps. *Born:* 28 August 1876, Cohoes, NY. *Accredited to:* New York. *G.O. No.:* 55, 19 July 1901. *Citation:* For distinguished conduct in the presence of the enemy in battles, while with the Eighth Army Corps on 25, 27, and 29 March, and on 4 April 1899. [*See Buckley above; enlisted as Joseph Melvin.*]

McNally, Michael Joseph. Sergeant, U.S. Marine Corps. *Born:* 29 June 1860, New York, NY. *Accredited to:* California. *G.O. No.:* 55, 19 July 1901. *Citation:* For distinguished conduct in the presence of the enemy at Samoa, 1 April 1899. [*See Forsterer above.*]

Porter, David Dixon. Colonel (Then Captain), U.S. Marine Corps. *Born:* 29 April 1877, Washington, D.C. *Appointed from:* District of Columbia. *Citation:* For extraordinary heroism and eminent and conspicuous conduct in battle at the junction of the Cadacan and Sohoton Rivers, Samar, Philippine Islands, 17 November 1901. In command of the columns upon their uniting ashore in the Sohoton Region, Colonel Porter (then Captain) made a surprise attack on the fortified cliffs and completely routed the enemy, killing 30 and capturing and destroying the powder magazine, 40 lantacas (guns), rice, food and cuartels. Due to his courage, intelligence, discrimination and zeal, he successfully led his men up the cliffs by means of bamboo ladders to a height of 200 feet. The cliffs were of soft stone of volcanic origin, in the nature of pumice and were honeycombed with caves. Tons of rocks were suspended in platforms held in position by vines and cables (known as bejuco) in readiness to be precipitated upon people below. After driving the insurgents from their position which was almost impregnable, being covered with numerous trails lined with poisoned spears, pits, etc., Colonel Porter led his men across the river, scaled the cliffs on the opposite side, and destroyed the camps there. He and the men under his command overcame incredible difficulties and dangers in destroying positions which, according to reports from old prisoners, had taken 3 years to perfect, were held as a final rallying post, and were never before penetrated by white troops. Colonel Porter also rendered distinguished public service in the presence of the enemy at Quinapundan River, Samar, Philippine Islands, on 26 October 1901. [*Other Navy awards include: U.S.M.C. Brevet Medal, plus numerous campaign medals. He received a "tombstone" promotion to brigadier general.*]

Prendergast, Thomas Francis. Corporal, U.S. Marine Corps. *Born:* 2 April 1871, Waterford, Ireland. *Accredited to:* Massachusetts. G.O. 55, 19 July 1901. *Citation:* For distinguished conduct in the presence of the enemy in battle while with the Eighth Army Corps, 25, 27, 29 March, and 5 April 1899. [*See Buckley above.*]

China Relief Expedition (The Boxer Rebellion) • 1900

Adams, John Mapes. Sergeant, U.S. Marine Corps. *Born:* 11 October 1871, Haverhill, MA. *Accredited to:* Massachusetts. *G.O. No.:* 55, 19 July 1901. *Citation:* In the presence of the enemy during the battle near Tientsin, China, 13 July 1900, Adams distinguished himself by meritorious conduct. [*In Co F, the artillery company led by Capt Ben Fuller, Adams, under heavy rifle fire, helped carry the badly wounded 1stLt Henry Leonard to safety.*]

Adriance, Harry Chapman. Corporal, U.S. Marine Corps. *Born:* 27 October 1864 Oswego, NY. *Accredited to:* Massachusetts. *G.O. No.:* 55, 19 July 1901. Citation: In the presence of the enemy during the battle near Tientsin, China, 13 July 1900, Adriance distinguished himself by meritorious conduct. [*See Adams above.*]

Appleton, Edwin Nelson. Corporal, U.S. Marine Corps. *Born:* 29 August 1876, Brooklyn, NY. *Accredited to:* New York. *G.O. No.:* 84, 22 March 1902. *Citation:* In action against the enemy at Tientsin, China, 20 June 1900. Crossing the river in a small boat flotilla while under heavy enemy fire, Appleton assisted in destroying buildings occupied by the enemy. [*Appleton was a member of Capt Bowman H. McCalla's Marine and sailor detachment's from the* Newark *and* Monocacy *which was* *a small part of the ill-fated Seymour Expedition. They provided a "point sniper team" coming back on the Pei Ho River ahead of the main body.*]

Boydston, Erwin Jay. Private, U.S. Marine Corps. *Born:* 22 April 1875, Deer Creek, CO. *Accredited to:* California. *G.O. No.:* 55, 19 July 1901. U.S.S. *Oregon. Citation:* In the presence of the enemy at Peking, China, 21 July to 17 August 1900. Under a heavy fire from the enemy during this period, Boydston assisted in the erection of barricades.

Burnes, James. Private, U.S. Marine Corps. *Born:* 14 January 1870, Worcester, MA. *Accredited to:* California. *G.O. No.:* 84, 22 March 1902. *Citation:* In action against the enemy at Tientsin, China, 20 June 1900. Crossing the river in a small boat with three other men while under a heavy fire from the enemy, Burnes assisted in destroying buildings occupied by hostile forces. [*See Appleton above.*]

Daniel Joseph Daly

Campbell, Albert Ralph. Private, U.S. Marine Corps. *Born:* 8 April 1875, Williamsport, PA. *Accredited to:* Pennsylvania. *G.O. No.:* 55, 19 July 1901. *Citation:* In action at Tientsin China 21 June 1900. During the advance on Tientsin, Campbell distinguished himself by his conduct.[*He and three other men joined with Lt. Butler and Lt. Arthur E. Harding to go back to rescue a wounded Private C.H. Carter and then carried him many miles to the rear.*]

Carr, William Louis. Private, U.S. Marine Corps. *Born:* 1 April 1875, Peabody, MA. *Accredited to:* Massachusetts. *G.O. No.:* 55, 19 July 1901. U.S.S. *Newark. Citation:* In action at Peking, China, 21 July to 17 August 1900. Throughout this action and in the presence of the enemy, Carr distinguished himself by his conduct.

Cooney, James. Private, U.S. Marine Corps. *Born:* 27 July 1860, Limerick, Ireland. *Accredited to:* Massachusetts. *G.O. No.:* 55, 19 July 1901. *Citation:* In the presence of the enemy during the battle near Tientsin, China, 13 July 1900, Cooney distinguished himself by meritorious conduct. [*He and two other men were cited on this date for holding the exposed extreme right flank thereby protecting the allied force against swarming Boxers.*]

Harry Fisher (under the flag)

Dahlgren, John Olof. Corporal, U.S. Marine Corps. *Born:* 14 September 1872, Kahliwar, Sweden. *Accredited to:* California. *G.O. No.:* 55, 19 July 1901. U.S.S. *Oregon. Citation:* In the presence of the enemy during the battle of Peking, China, 20 June to 16 July 1900, Dahlgren distinguished himself by meritorious conduct.

Daly, Daniel Joseph. Private, U.S. Marine Corps. *Born:* 11 November 1873, Glen Cove, Long Island NY. *Accredited to:* New York. *G.O. No.:* 55, 19 July 1901. U.S.S. *Newark. Citation:* In the presence of the enemy during the battle of Peking, China, 14 August 1900, Daly distinguished himself by meritorious conduct. [*Daly stood watch upon the Great Wall by himself and all night, fighting hordes of Chinese until daylight and killing many. Other Awards: Second Medal of Honor, Navy Cross. U.S. Army, Distinguished Service Cross, Silver Star plus French Military Medal and Croix de Guerre w/Palm.*]

*****Fisher, Harry.** Private, U.S. Marine Corps. *Born:* 20 October 1874, McKeesport, PA. *Accredited to:* Pennsylvania. *G.O. No.:* 55, 19 July 1901. U.S.S. *Oregon. Citation:* Served in the presence of the enemy at the battle of Peking, China, 20 June to 16 July 1900. Assisting in the erection of barricades during the action, Fisher was killed by the heavy fire of the enemy.

Foley, Alexander Joseph. Sergeant, U.S. Marine Corps. *Born:* 19 February 1866, Heckersville, PA. *Accredited to:* Pennsylvania. *G.O. No.:* 55, 19 July 1901. *Citation:* In the presence of the enemy in the battle near Tientsin, China, 13 July 1900, Foley distinguished himself by meritorious conduct. [*See Cooney above. Plus he was also cited for carrying messages through heavy enemy fire.*]

Francis, Charles Robert. Private, U.S. Marine Corps. *Born:* 19 May 1875, Doylestown, PA. *Accredited to:* Pennsylvania. *G.O. No.:* 55, 19 July 1901. *Citation:* In the presence of the enemy during the battle near Tientsin, China, 21 June 1900, Francis distinguished himself by meritorious conduct.[*See Campbell above.*]

Gaiennie, Louis Rene. Private, U.S. Marine Corps. *Born:* 9 June 1878, St. Louis, MO. *Accredited to:* Missouri. *G.O. No.:* 55, 19 July 1901.

Charles Robert Francis

U.S.S. *Newark. Citation:* In the presence of the enemy during the action at Peking, China, 21 July to 17 August 1900, Gaiennie distinguished himself by meritorious conduct.

Heisch, Henry William. Private, U.S. Marine Corps. *Born:* 10 June 1872, Latendorf, Germany. *Accredited to:* California. *G.O. No.:* 84, 22 March 1902. *Citation.:* In action against the enemy at Tientsin, China, 20 June 1900. Crossing the river in a small boat while under heavy fire, Heisch assisted in destroying buildings occupied by the enemy. [*See Appleton above.*]

Horton, William Charlie. Private, U. S. Marine Corps. *Born:* Chicago, IL. *Accredited to:* Pennsylvania. *G.O. No.:* 55, 19 July 1901. U.S.S. *Oregon. Citation:* In action against the enemy at Peking, China, 21 July to 17 August 1900. Although under heavy fire from the enemy, Horton assisted in the erection of barricades. [*He was the enlisted man that drove the train from Tientsin to Peking.*]

Hunt, Martin. Private, U.S. Marine Corps. *Born:* 9 July 1873, County Mayo, Ireland. *Accredited to:* Massachusetts. *G.O. No.:* 55, 19 July 1901.U.S.S. *Oregon. Citation:* In the presence of the enemy during the battle of Peking, China, 20 June to 16 July 1900, Hunt distinguished himself by meritorious conduct.

Kates, Thomas Wilbur. Private, U.S. Marine Corps. *Born:* 7 May 1865, Shelby Center, NY. *Accredited to:* New York. *G.O. No.:* 55, 19 July 1901. *Citation:* In the presence of the enemy during the advance on Tientsin China, 21 June 1900, Kates distinguished himself by meritorious conduct.[*See Appleton above.*]

Mathias, Clarence Edward. Private, U.S. Marine Corps. *Born:* 12 December 1876, Royalton, PA. Accredited to: Pennsylvania. *G.O. No.:* 55, 19 July 1901. *Citation:* In the presence of the enemy during the advance on Tientsin, China, 13 July 1900, Mathias distinguished himself by meritorious conduct. [*See Cooney above.*]

Moore, Albert. Private, U.S. Marine Corps. *Born:* 25 December 1862, Merced, CA. *Accredited to:* California. *G.O. No.:* 55, 19 July 1901. U.S.S. *Oregon. Citation:* In the presence of the enemy during the battle of Peking, China, 21 July to 17 August 1900. Although under a heavy fire from the enemy, Moore assisted in the erection of barricades.

Murphy, John Alphonsus. Drummer, U.S. Marine Corps. *Born:* 26 February 1881, New York, NY. *Accredited to:* Washington, D.C. *G.O. No.:* 55, 19 July 1901. U.S.S. *Newark. Citation:* In the presence of the enemy during the action at Peking, China, 21 July to 17 August 1900, Murphy distinguished himself by meritorious conduct.

Murray, William H. Private, U.S. Marine Corps. *Born:* 3 June 1876, Brooklyn, NY. *Accredited to:* New York. *G.O. No.:* 55, 19 July 1901. U.S.S. *Newark. Citation:* In the presence of the enemy during the action at Peking, China, 21 July to 17 August 1900. During this period, Murray distinguished himself by meritorious conduct. [*He served as Henry W. Davis under which name the award was made.*]

Orndoff, Harry Westley. Private, U.S. Marine Corps. Born: 9 November 1872, Sandusky, OH. *Accredited to:* California. *G.O. No.:* 55, 19 July 1901. *Citation:* In action with the relief expedition of the Allied forces in China, 13, 20, 21, and 22 June 1900. During this period and in the presence of the enemy, Orndoff distinguished himself by meritorious conduct. [*He and two other men were especially cited for their actions on 13 June at Langfang against a massive Boxer attack upon the Seymour column. Their marksmanship dropped numerous of the enemy and protected the exposed flank.*]

Phillips, Reuben Jasper. Corporal, U.S. Marine Corps. *Born:* 28 July 1874. Cambria, CA. *Accredited to:* California. *G.O.. No.:* 55, 19 July 1901. *Citation:* In action with the relief expedition of the Allied forces in China during the battles of 13, 20, 21 and 22 June 1900. Throughout this period and in the presence of the enemy, Phillips distinguished himself by meritorious conduct. [*See Orndoff above.*]

Preston, Herbert Irving. Private, U. S. Marine Corps. *Born:* 6 August 1876, Berkeley, NJ. *Accredited to:* New Jersey. *G. O. No:* 55, 19 July 1901. U.S.S. *Oregon. Citation:* In the presence of the enemy during the action at Peking, China, 21 July to 17 August 1901. Throughout this period, Preston distinguished himself by meritorious conduct.

Scannell, David John. Private, U.S. Marine Corps. *Born:* 30 March 1875, Boston, MA. *Accredited to:* Massachusetts. *G.O. No.:* 55, 19 July 1901. U.S.S. *Oregon. Citation:* In the presence of the enemy during the action at Peking, China, 21 July to 17 August 1900. Throughout this period, Scannell distinguished himself by meritorious conduct.

Silva, France. Private, U.S. Marine Corps. *Born:* 8 May 1876, Haywards, CA. *Accredited to:* California. *G.O. No.:* 55, 19 July 1901. U.S.S. *Newark. Citation:* In the presence of the enemy during the action at Peking, China, 28 June to 17 August 1900. Throughout this period, Silva distinguished himself by meritorious conduct.

Stewart, Peter. Gunnery Sergeant, U.S. Marine Corps. *Born:* 17 February 1858, Airdrie, Scotland. *Accredited to:* Washington, D.C. *G.O. No.:* 55, 19 July 1901. *Citation:* In action with the relief expedition of the Allied forces in China during the battles of 13, 20, 21, and 22 June 1900. Throughout this period and in the presence of the enemy, Stewart distinguished himself by meritorious conduct. [*See Orndoff above.*]

Sutton, Clarence Edwin. Sergeant, U.S. Marine Corps. *Born:* 18 February 1871, Middlesex County, VA. *Accredited to:* Washington, D.C. *G.O. No.:* 55, 19 July 1901. *Citation:* In action during the battle near Tientsin, China, 13 July 1900. Although under heavy fire from the enemy, Sutton assisted in carrying a wounded officer [*1stLt Smedley D. Butler*] from the field of battle.

Upham, Oscar J. Private U.S. Marine Corps. *Born:* 14 January 1871, Toledo, OH. *Accredited to:* Illinois. *G.O. No.:* 55, 19 July 1901. U.S.S. *Oregon. Citation:* In the presence of the enemy at Peking, China, 21 July to 17 August 1900. Although under a heavy fire from the enemy during this period, Upham assisted in the erection of barricades.

Walker, Edward Alexander. Sergeant, U.S. Marine Corps. *Born:* 2 October 1864, Huntley, Scotland. *Accredited to:* New York. *G.O. No.:* 55 19 July 1901. U.S.S. *Oregon. Citation:* In the presence of the enemy during the battle of Peking, China 20 June to 16 July 1900. Throughout this period, Walker distinguished himself by meritorious conduct.

Young, Frank Albert. Private, U.S. Marine Corps. *Born.:* 22 June 1876, Milwaukee, WI. *Accredited to:* Wisconsin. *G.O. No.:* 55, 19 July 1901.U.S.S. *Oregon. Citation:* In the presence of the enemy during the battle of Peking, China, 20 June to 16 July 1900. Throughout this period, Young distinguished himself by meritorious conduct.

Zion, William. Private, U.S. Marine Corps. *Born:* 23 October 1872, Knightstown, MD. *Accredited to:* California. *G.O. No.:* 55, 19 July 1901. U.S.S. *Newark. Citation:* In the presence of the enemy during the battle of Peking, China, 21 July to 17 August 1900. Throughout this period, Zion distinguished himself by meritorious conduct.

Interim Period • 1901

Helms, John Henry. Sergeant, U.S. Marine Corps. *Born:* 16 March 1874, Chicago, IL. *Accredited to:* Illinois. *G.O. No.:* 35, 23 March 1901. *Citation:* Serving on board the U.S.S. *Chicago,* for heroism in rescuing Ishi Tomizi, ship's cook, from drowning at Montevideo, Uruguay, 10 January 1901.

Pfeifer, Louis Fred. Private, U.S. Marine Corps. *Born:* 19 June 1876, Philadelphia, PA. *Accredited to:* New Jersey. *G.O. No.:* 85, 22 March 1902. *Citation:* Serving on board the U.S.S. *Petrel;* for heroism and gallantry, fearlessly exposing his own life to danger for the saving of the others on the occasion of the fire on board that vessel, 31 March 1901. [Served as Louis F. Theis during first enlistment.]

Vera Cruz • 1914

Berkeley, Randolph Carter. Major, U.S. Marine Corps. *Born:* 9 January 1875, Staunton, VA. *Appointed from:* Washington, D.C. *G.O. No.:*177, 4 December 1915. *Citation:* For distinguished conduct in battle, engagements of Vera Cruz, 21 and 22 April 1914. Major Berkeley was eminent and conspicuous in command of his battalion; was in the fighting of both days, and exhibited courage and skill in leading his men through action. His cool judgment and courage, and his skill in handling his men in encountering and overcoming the machine gun and rifle fire down Cinco de Mayo and parallel streets account for the small percentage of the losses of Marines under his command. [*Other Navy awards: Navy Cross, Distinguished Service Medal. He retired a major general in 1939.*]

Butler, Smedley Darlington. Major, U.S. Marine Corps. *Born:* 30 July 1881, West Chester, PA. *Appointed from:* Pennsylvania. *G.O. No.:* 177, 4 December 1915.

Smedley Darlington Butler

Randolph Carter Berkeley

Citation: For distinguished conduct in battle, engagement of Vera Cruz, 22 April 1914. Major Butler was eminent and conspicuous in command of his battalion. He exhibited courage and skill in leading his men through the action of the 22d and in the final occupation of the city. [*Other awards: Second Medal of Honor, Brevet Medal, Army & Navy Distinguished Service Medal. He retired a major general 1 October 1931.*]

Catlin, Albertus W. Major, U.S. Marine Corps. *Born:* 1 December 1868, Gowanda, NY. *Appointed from:* Minnesota. *G.O. No.:* 177, 4 December 1915. *Citation:* For distinguished conduct in battle, engagement of Vera Cruz, 22 April 1914. Eminent and conspicuous in command of his battalion, Major Catlin exhibited courage and skill in leading his men through the action of the 22d and in the final occupation of the city. [*Other awards: Two French Croix de Guerre, one with Palm, one Gilt, Legion of Honor. He retired a brigadier general in 1919.*]

Albertus W. Catlin

Dyer, Jesse Farley. Captain, U.S. Marine Corps. *Born:* 2 December 1877, St. Paul, MN. *Appointed from:* Minnesota. *G.O. No.:* 177, 4 December 1915. *Citation:* For distinguished conduct in battle, engagements of Vera Cruz, 21 and 22 April 1914; was in both days' fighting at the head of his company, and was eminent and conspicuous in his conduct, leading his men with skill and courage. [*He retired a brigadier general in 1942.*]

Fryer, Eli Thompson. Captain, U.S. Marine Corps. *Born:* 22 August 1878, Hightstown, NJ. *Appointed from:* New Jersey. *G.O. No.:* 177, 4 December 1915. *Citation:* For distinguished conduct in battle, engagements of Vera Cruz, 21 and 22 April 1914. In both days' fighting

Jesse Farley Dyer

Eli Thompson Fryer

Walter Newell Hill

at the head of his company, Captain Fryer was eminent and conspicuous in his conduct, leading his men with skill and courage. [*He retired a brigadier general in 1942.*]

Hill, Walter Newell. Captain, U.S. Marine Corps. *Born:* 29 September 1881, Haverhill, MA. *Appointed from:* Massachusetts. *G.O. No.:* 177, 4 December 1915. *Citation:* For distinguished conduct in battle, engagements of Vera Cruz, 21 and 22 April 1914. Captain Hill was in both days' fighting at the head of his company, and was eminent and conspicuous in his conduct, leading his men with skill and courage. [*He retired in 1938 but was recalled in January 1942.*]

Hughes, John Arthur. Captain, U.S. Marine Corps. *Born:* 2 November 1880, New York, NY. Accredited to: New York. *G.O. No.:* 177, 4 December 1915. *Citation:* For distinguished conduct in battle, engage-

John Arthur Hughes

ments of Vera Cruz, 21 and 22 April 1914. Captain Hughes was in both days' fighting at the head of his company, and was eminent and conspicuous in his conduct, leading his men with skill and courage. [*Other Navy Award: Navy Cross. He retired with a medical disability in 1919.*]

Neville, Wendell Cushing. Lieutenant Colonel, U.S. Marine Corps. *Born:* 12 May 1870, Portsmouth, VA. *Appointed from:* Virginia. *G.O. No.:* 177, 4 December 1915. *Citation:* For distinguished conduct in battle engagements of Vera Cruz 21 and 22 April 1914. In command of the Second Regiment Marines, Lieutenant Colonel Neville was in both days' fighting and almost continually under fire from soon after landing, about noon on the 21st, until we were in possession of the city, about noon of the 22d. His duties required him to be at points of great danger in directing his officers and men, and he exhibited conspicuous courage, coolness, and skill in his conduct of the fighting. Upon his courage and skill depended, in great measure, success or failure. His responsibilities were great and he met them in a manner worthy of commendation. [*Other Navy award: USMC Brevet Medal, Army & Navy Distinguished Service Medal; French Legion of Honor and six Croix de Guerre; four Palm and two Bronze. Neville was Major General Commandant when he died in office in July 1930.*]

Reid, George Croghan. Major, U.S. Marine Corps. *Born:* 9 December 1876, Lorain, OH. *Appointed from:* Ohio. *G.O.. No.:* 177, 4 December 1915. *Citation:* For distinguished conduct in battle engagements of Vera Crux, 21 and 22 April 1914; was eminent and conspicuous in command of his battalion; was in the fighting of both leading his men through action. His cool judgment and courage and his skill in handling his men in encountering and overcoming the machine gun and rifle fire down Cinco de Mayo and parallel streets account for the small percentage of the losses of Marines under his command. [*He retired a brigadier general in 1930.*]

George Croghan Reid

Haitian Campaign • 1915

Butler, Smedley Darlington. Major, U.S. Marine Corps. *Born:* 30 July 1881, West Chester, PA. *Appointed from:* Pennsylvania. *Citation:* As Commanding Officer of detachments from the Fifth, Thirteenth, Twenty-third Companies and the Marine and sailor detachment from the U.S.S. *Connecticut,* Major Butler led the attack on Fort Riviere Haiti, 17 November 1915. Following a concentrated drive, several different detachments of Marines gradually closed in on the old French bastion fort in an effort to cut off all avenues of retreat for the Caco bandits. Reaching the fort on the southern side where there was a small opening in the wall, Major Butler gave the signal to attack and Marines from the Fifteenth Company poured through the breach, engaged the Cacos in hand-to-hand combat, took the bastion and crushed the Caco resistance. Throughout this perilous action, Major Butler was conspicuous for his bravery and forceful leadership. [*Other awards: See entry above. Butler entered the fort after Iams and Gross.*]

Daly, Daniel Joseph. Gunnery Sergeant, U.S. Marine Corps. *Born:* Glen Cove, Long Island, NY., 11 November 1873. *Accredited to:* New York. *Citation:* Serving with the Fifteenth Company of Marines on 22 October 1915, Gunnery Sergeant Daly was one of the company to leave Fort Liberte, Haiti, for a 6-day reconnaissance. After dark on the evening of 24 October, while crossing the river in a deep ravine, the detachment was suddenly fired upon from three sides by about 400 Cacos concealed in bushes about 100 yards from the fort. The Marine detachment fought its way forward to a good position, which it maintained during the night, although subjected to a continuous fire from the Cacos. At daybreak the Marines, in three squads, advanced in three different directions, surprising and scattering the Cacos in all directions. Gunnery Sergeant Daly fought with exceptional gallantry against heavy odds throughout this action. [*He led one of three squads; Ostermann and Upshur led the other two. He was also instrumental in providing a Colt machine gun and ammunition, from a dead mule, which he brought out of a rapidly rushing river and he hauled up the hill for his CO, Major Butler. The latter has frequently been mistaken as the reason for his second MoH award. Other awards: See entry above. He retired a sergeant major. A destroyer was named for him.*]

Gross, Samuel. Private, U.S. Marine Corps. *Born:* 9 May 1891, Philadelphia, PA. *Accredited to:* Pennsylvania. *Citation:* In company with members of the Fifth, Thirteenth, Twenty-third Companies and the Marine and sailor detachment from the U.S.S. *Connecticut,* Gross participated in the attack on Fort Riviere, Haiti, 17 November 1915. Following a concentrated drive, several different detachments of Marines gradually closed in on the old French bastion fort in an effort to cut off all avenues of retreat for the Caco bandits. Approaching a breach in the wall which was the only entrance to the fort, Gross was the second man to pass through the breach in the face of constant fire from the Cacos and, thereafter, for a 10-minute period, engaged the enemy in desperate hand-to-hand combat until the bastion was captured and Caco resistance neutralized. [*Real name was Samuel Marguiles.*]

Iams, Ross Lindsey. Sergeant, U.S. Marine Corps. *Born:* 5 May 1879, Graysville, PA. *Accredited to:* Pennsylvania. *Citation:* In company with members of the Fifth, Thirteenth, Twenty-third Companies and Marine and sailor detachment from the U.S.S. *Connecticut,* Sergeant Iams participated in the attack on Fort Riviere, Haiti, 17 November 1915. Following a concentrated drive, several different detachments of Marines gradually closed in on the old French bastion fort in an effort to cut off all avenues of retreat for the Caco bandits. Approaching a breach in the wall which was the only entrance to the fort, Sergeant Iams unhesitatingly jumped through the breach despite constant fire from the Cacos and engaged the enemy in a desperate hand-to-hand combat until the bastion was captured and Caco resistance neutralized. [*He was promoted to 1stLt during WWI and retired a captain in 1932. Was recalled as a major in January 1942.*]

Ross Lindsey Iams

Ostermann, Edward Albert. First Lieutenant, U.S. Marine Corps, 15th Company of Marines (mounted). *Place and date:* Vicinity Fort Liberte, Haiti, 24 October 1915. *Entered service at:* OH. *Birth:* Columbus, Ohio. *Citation:* In company with members of the 15th Company of Marines, all mounted, First Lieutenant Ostermann left Fort Liberte, Haiti, for a. 6-day reconnaissance. After dark on the evening of 24 October 1915, while crossing the river in a. deep ravine, the detachment was suddenly fired upon from 3 sides by about 400 Cacos concealed in bushes about 100 yards from the fort. The Marine detachment

Edward Albert Osterman

William Peterkin Upshur

Joseph Anthony Glowin

fought its way forward to a good position, which it maintained during the night, although subjected to a continuous fire from the Cacos. At daybreak, First Lieutenant Ostermann, in command of one of the three squads which advanced in three different directions, led his men forward, surprising and scattering the Cacos, and aiding in the capture of Fort Dipitie. [*He retired as a major general with a medical disability in January 1943.*]

Upshur, William Peterkin. Captain, U.S. Marine Corps. *Born:* 28 October 1881, Richmond, VA. *Appointed from:* Virginia. *Citation:* In company with members of the Fifteenth Company of Marines, all mounted, Captain Upshur left Fort Liberte, Haiti, for a 6-day reconnaissance. After dark on the evening of 24 October 1915, while crossing the river in a deep ravine, the detachment was suddenly fired upon from three sides by about 400 Cacos concealed in bushes about 100 yards from the fort. The Marine detachment fought its way forward to a good position, which it maintained during the night, although subjected to a continuous fire from the Cacos. At daybreak, Captain Upshur, in command of one of the three squads which advanced in three different directions led his men forward, surprising and scattering the Cacos, and aiding in the capture of Fort Dipitie. [*As a major general, he died in a plane crash near Sitka, Alaska on 18 August 1943.*]

Dominican Campaign • 1916–1917

Glowin, Joseph Anthony. Corporal, U.S. Marine Corps. *Born:* 14 March 1892, Detroit, MI. *Accredited to:* Michigan. *G.O. No.:* 244, 30 October 1916. *Citation:* During an engagement at Guayacanas on 3 July 1916, Corporal Glowin participated in action against a considerable force of rebels on the line of march. [*He kept firing his Colt Machine Gun in the advance of the 4th Marines at Guayacanas, even though he had been hit several times, until he was dragged from it. Glowin eventually was promoted to gunnery sergeant, discharged in 1919, became a policeman in Detroit, MI, and died on 23 August 1952.*]

Williams, Ernest Calvin. First Lieutenant, U.S. Marine Corps. *Born:* 2 August 1887, Broadwell, IL. *Accredited to:* Illinois. *G.O. No.:* 289, 27 April 1917. *Citation:* In action against hostile forces at San Francisco de Macoris, Dominican Republic, 29 November 1916. With only a dozen men available, First Lieutenant Williams rushed the gate of the fortress. With eight of his party wounded by rifle fire of the defenders, he pressed on with the four remaining men, threw himself against the door just as it was being closed by the Dominicans and forced an entry. Despite a narrow escape from death at the hands of a rifleman, he and his men disposed of the guards and within a few minutes had gained control of the fort and the hundred prisoners confined there. [*Other Navy award: Navy Cross at Blanc Mont, France, 3 October 1918. Major Williams served in command of 2/6. He received a medical discharge and died on 31 March 1921.*]

Winans, Roswell. First Sergeant, U. S. Marine Corps. *Place and date:* Guayacanas, Dominican Republic, 3 July 1916. *Entered service* at: Washington, D.C.. *Birth:* Brookville, IN. *G.O. No.:* 244, 30 October 1916. *Citation:* During an engagement at Guayacanas on 3 July 1916, First Sergeant Winans participated in action against a considerable force of rebels on the line of march. [*Other awards: two Silver Stars, Croix de Guerre w/Palm. Winans and his gun crew took over after Glowin (see above) was wounded and no longer able to continue. Winans served as a captain in France with the 17th Company, 1/5, and later in Nicaragua and WWII, becoming a brigadier general upon retirement on 1 August 1946.*]

Roswell Winans

World War I • 1918

Balch, John Henry. Pharmacist's Mate First Class, United States Navy. *Place and date:* Vierzy, France, and Somme-Py, France, 19 July and 5 October 1918. *Entered service* at: Missouri. *Birth:* Edgerton, Kansas. *Citation:* For gallantry and intrepidity at the risk of his life above and beyond the call of duty, with the 6th Regiment, United States Marines, in action at Vierzy, on 19 July 1918. Balch unhesitatingly and fearlessly exposed himself to terrific machine gun and high-explosive fire to succor the wounded as they fell in the attack, leaving his dressing station voluntarily and keeping up the work all day and late into the night unceasingly for 16 hours on a field torn by shell and machine-gun fire. Also in the action at Somrne-Py on 5 October 1918, he exhibited exceptional bravery in establishing an advanced dressing station under heavy shellfire. [*Served in 3/6 at Soissons and Blanc Mont.*]

Boone, Joel Thompson. Lieutenant (Medical Corps), United States Navy. *Place and date:* Vicinity Vierzy, France 19 July 1918. *Entered service* at: St. Clair, PA. *Birth:* Pennsylvania. *Citation:* For extraordinary heroism, conspicuous gallantry, and intrepidity while serving with the 6th Regiment, United States Marines, in actual conflict with the enemy at and in the vicinity of Vierzy, France, 19 July 1918. With absolute disregard for personal safety, ever conscious and mindful of the suffering fallen, Surgeon Boone, leaving the shelter of a ravine, went forward onto the open field where there was no protection and, despite the extreme enemy fire of all calibers through a heavy mist of gas, applied dressings and first aid to wounded Marines. This occurred southeast of Vierzy, near the cemetery, and on the road south from that town. When the dressings and supplies had been exhausted, he went through a heavy barrage of large-caliber shell, both high explosive and gas, to replenish these supplies, returning quickly with a sidecar load, and administered them in saving the lives of the wounded. A second trip, under the same conditions and for the same purpose, was made by Surgeon Boone later that day. [*At Soissons; Boone was a dentist.*]

Cukela, Louis. (*Army Medal*). Sergeant, 66th Company, 5th Regiment, U.S. Marine Corps. *Place and date:* Near Villers-Cotterets, France, 18 July 1918. *Entered service* at: Minneapolis, MN. *Birth:* Austria. *G.O. No.:* 34, W.D., 1919. *Citation:* When his company, advancing through a wood, met with strong resistance from an enemy strong point, Sergeant Cukela crawled out from the flank and made his way toward the German lines in the face of heavy fire, disregarding the warnings of his comrades. He succeeded in getting behind the enemy position and rushed a machine gun emplacement, killing or driving off the crew with his bayonet. With German hand grenades he then bombed out the remaining portion of the strong point, capturing four men and two damaged machine guns.

Cukela, Louis. (*Navy Medal*). Sergeant, U.S. Marine Corps. *Born:* 1 May 1888, Sebenes, Austria. *Accredited to:* Minnesota. *Citation:* For extraordinary heroism while serving with the Sixty-sixth Company, Fifth Regiment, during action in the Forest de Retz, near Viller-Cottertes, France, 18 July 1918. Sergeant Cukela advanced alone against an enemy strong point that was holding up his line. Disregarding the warnings of his comrades, he crawled out from the flank in the face of heavy fire and worked his way to the rear of the enemy position. Rushing a machine-gun emplacement, he killed or drove off the crew with his bayonet bombed out the remaining part of the strong point with German hand grenades and captured two machine guns and four men. [*At Soissons. Other awards: Silver Star; France, Military Medal, two Croix de Guerre, w/ Palms, Legion of Honor. He retired as a major in June 1940.*]

Hayden, David E. Hospital Apprentice First Class, United States Navy, serving with the 2d Battalion, 6th Regiment, United States Marines. *Place and date:* Thiaucourt, France, 15 September 1918. *Entered service at:* Texas. *Birth:* Florence, Texas. *Citation:* For gallantry

Louis Cukela

and intrepidity at the risk of his life above and beyond the call of duty in action at Thiaucourt 15 September 1918, with the 2d Battalion, 6th Regiment, United States Marines. During the advance, when Corporal [Carlos Dickson] Creed was mortally wounded while crossing an open field swept by machine-gun fire, Hayden unhesitatingly ran to his assistance and, finding him so severely wounded as to require immediate attention, disregarded his own personal safety to dress the wound under intense machine-gun fire, and then carried the wounded man back to a place of safety. [*At St. Mihiel.*]

Hoffman, Charles F. (*Army Medal*). Gunnery Sergeant, 49th Company, 5th Regiment, 2d Division, USMC [*sic*]. *Place and date:* Near Chateau Thierrv, France, 6 June 1918. *Entered service at:* Brooklyn, NY. *Birth:* New York, NY. *G.O. No.:* 34, W.D., 1919. *Citation:* Immediately after the company to which he belonged had reached its objective on Hill 142, several hostile counterattacks were launched against the line before the new position had been consolidated. Sergeant Hoffman was attempting to organize a position on the north slope of the hill when he saw 12 of the enemy, armed with five light machine guns, crawling toward his group. Giving the alarm, he rushed the hostile detachment, bayoneted the two leaders, and forced the others to flee, abandoning their guns. His quick action, initiative, and courage drove the enemy from a position from which they could have swept the hill with machine gun fire and forced the withdrawal of our troops. [*At Belleau Wood; his name was really Ernest August Janson, see below.*]

Janson, Ernest August. (*Navy Medal*). Gunnery Sergeant, U.S. Marine Corps. *Born:* 17 August 1878, New York, NY. *Accredited to:* New York. *Citation:* For conspicuous gallantry and intrepidity above and beyond the call of duty in action with the enemy near Chateau Thierry, France, 6 June 1918. Immediately after the company to which Gunnery Sergeant Janson belonged, had reached its objective on Hill 142, several hostile counterattacks were launched against the line before the new position had been consolidated. Gunnery Sergeant Janson was attempting to organize a position on the north slope of the hill when he saw 12 of the enemy, armed with five light machine guns, crawling toward his group. Giving the alarm, he rushed the hostile detachment, bayoneted the two leaders, and forced the others to flee, abandoning their guns. His quick action, initiative and courage drove the enemy from a position from which they could have swept the hill with machine-gun fire and forced the withdrawal of our troops. [*At Belleau Wood; see Hoffman above.*]

Kelly, John Joseph. (*Army Medal*). Private, U.S. Marine Corps. 78th Company, 6th Regiment, 2d Division, U.S. Marine Corps. *Place and date:* At Blanc Mont Ridge, France, 3 October 1918. *Entered service at:* Chicago, IL. *Birth:* Chicago, IL. *G.O. No.:* 16. W.D., 1919. *Citation:* Private Kelly ran through our own barrage a hundred yards in advance of the front line and attacked an enemy machine-gun nest, killing the gunner with a grenade, shooting another member of the crew with his pistol, and returning through the barrage with eight prisoners. [*At Blanc Mont.*]

Kelly, John Joseph. (*Navy Medal*). Private, U.S. Marine Corps. *Born:* Chicago, IL. *Accredited to:* Illinois. *Citation:* For conspicuous gallantry and intrepidity above and beyond the call of duty while serving with the Seventy-eighth Company, Sixth Regiment, Second Division, in action with the enemy at Blanc Mont Ridge, France, 3 October 1918. Private Kelly ran through our own barrage a hundred yards in advance of the front line and attacked an enemy machine-gun nest, killing the gunner with a grenade, shooting another member of the crew with his pistol, and returning through the barrage with eight prisoners.

John Joseph Kelly

Kocak, Matej. *(Army Medal).* Sergeant, 66th Company, 5th Regiment, 2d Division, U.S. Marine Corps. *Place and date:* Near Soissons, France, 18 July 1918. *Entered service at:* New York, NY. *Birth:* Austria. *G.O. No.:* 34, W.D., 1919. *Citation:* When the advance of his battalion was checked by a hidden machine-gun nest, he went forward alone, unprotected by covering fire from his own men, and worked in between the German positions in the face of fire from enemy covering detachments. Locating the machine-gun nest, he rushed it and with his bayonet drove off the crew. Shortly after this he organized 25 French colonial soldiers who had become separated from their company and led them in attacking another machine-gun nest, which was also put out of action. [*Soissons.*]

Kocak, Matej. *(Navy Medal).* Sergeant, U.S. Marine Corps. *Born:* Austria. *Accredited to:* New York.

Matej Kocek

Citation: For extraordinary heroism while serving with the Sixty-sixth Company, Fifth Regiment, Second Division, in action in the Viller-Cottertes section, south of Soissons, France, 18 July 1918. When a hidden machine-gun nest halted the advance of his battalion, Sergeant Kocak went forward alone unprotected by covering fire and worked his way in between the German positions in the face of heavy enemy fire. Rushing the enemy position with his bayonet, he drove off the crew. Later the same day, Sergeant Kocak organized French colonial soldiers who had become separated from their company and led them in an attack on another machine-gun nest which was also put out of action.

Lyle, Alexander Gordon. Lieutenant Commander (Dental Corps), U.S. Navy. *Born:* 12 November 1889, Gloucester, MA. *Appointed from:* Massachusetts. *Citation:* For extraordinary heroism and devotion to duty while serving with the Fifth Regiment, United States Marines. Under heavy shellfire, on 23 April 1918, on the French Front, Lieutenant Commander Lyle rushed to the assistance of Corp. Gerald V. Regan, who was seriously wounded, and administered such effective surgical aid while bombardment was still continuing, as to save the life of Corporal Regan. [*At Verdun; Other Navy award: Legion of Merit.*]

*Osborne, Weedon E. Lieutenant, Junior Grade, (Dental Corps), U.S. Navy. *Born.*: 13 November 1892, Chicago, IL. *Appointed from:* Illinois. *Citation:* For extraordinary heroism while attached to the Fifth Regiment, [*sic Sixth Marines*] United States Marines, in actual conflict with the enemy and under fire during the advance on Bouresche, France, on 6 June 1918. In the hottest of the fighting when the Marines made their famous advance on Bouresche at the southern edge of Belleau Wood, Lieutenant, Junior Grade, Osborne threw himself zealously into the work of rescuing the wounded. Extremely courageous in the performance of this perilous task, he was killed while carrying a wounded officer [*Capt Donald F. Duncan*] to a place of safety. [*At Belleau Wood. Duncan died of his wounds that same day.*]

Petty, Orlando Henderson. Lieutenant (Medical Corps), U.S. Navy Reserve. *Born:* 20 February 1874, Harrison, OH. *Appointed from:* Pennsylvania. *Citation:* For extraordinary heroism while serving with the [*2/5*] Fifth Regiment, United States Marines, in France during the attack in the Bois de Belleau, 11 June 1918. While under heavy fire of high explosive and gas shells in the town of Lucy, where his dressing station was located, Lieutenant Petty attended to and evacuated the wounded under most trying conditions. Having been knocked to the ground by an exploding gas shell which tore his mask Lieutenant Petty discarded the mask and courageously continued his work. His dressing station being hit and demolished, he personally helped carry Captain [*Lloyd W.*] Williams, wounded, through the shell-fire to a place of safety. [*At Belleau Wood. Williams died a few days later.*]

Pruitt, John H. (*Army Medal*). Corporal, 78th Company, 6th Regiment, 2d Division. *Place and date*: At Blanc Mont Ridge, France, 3 October 1918. *Entered service at:* Tucson Ariz. *Birth:* Faderville, AR. *G.O. No.:* 62, W.D., 1919. *Citation:* Corporal Pruitt single-handed attacked two machine guns, capturing them, and killing two of the enemy. He then captured 40 prisoners in a dugout nearby. This gallant soldier was killed soon afterward by shellfire while he sniped at the enemy. [*At Blanc Mont.*]

Pruitt, John H. (*Navy Medal*). Corporal, U.S. Marine Corps. *Born:* 4 October 1896, Faderville, AR. *Accredited to:* Arizona. *Citation:* For extraordinary gallantry and intrepidity above and beyond the call of duty while serving with the Seventy-eighth Company, Sixth Regiment, Second Division, in action against the enemy at Blanc Mont Ridge, France,

John H. Pruitt

Robert Guy Robinson

3 October 1918. Corporal Pruitt, single-handed, attacked two machine guns, capturing and killing two of the enemy. He then captured 40 prisoners in a dugout nearby. This gallant soldier was killed soon afterward by shellfire while he was sniping the enemy.

Robinson, Robert Guy. Gunnery Sergeant, 1st Marine Aviation Force, U.S. Marine Corps. *Place and date:* Pittham, Belgium, 14 October 1918. *Entered service at:*

Illinois. *Birth:* New York, NY. *Citation:* For extraordinary heroism as observer in the 1st Marine Aviation Force at the front in France. In company with planes from Squadron 218, Royal Air Force, conducting an air raid on 8 October 1918, Gunnery Sergeant Robinson's plane was attacked by nine enemy scouts. In the fight which followed, he shot down one of the enemy planes. In a later air raid over Pittham, Belgium, on 14 October 1918, his plane and one other became separated from their formation on account of motor trouble and were attacked by 12 enemy scouts. Acting with conspicuous gallantry and intrepidity in the fight which ensued, Gunnery Sergeant Robinson, after shooting down one of the enemy planes, was struck by a bullet which carried away most of his elbow. At the same time his gun jammed. While his pilot maneuvered for position, he cleared the jam with one hand and returned to the fight. Although his left arm was useless, he fought off the enemy scouts until he collapsed after receiving two more bullet wounds, one in the stomach and one in the thigh. [*He retired a second lieutenant, for medical disability, May 1923, but was later promoted to first lieutenant.*]

***Stockham, Fred W.** Gunnery Sergeant, 96th Company, 2d Battalion, 6th Regiment, U.S. Marine Corps. *Place and date:* In Bois-de-Belleau, France, 13–14 June 1918. *Entered service at:* New York, NY. *Birth:* Detroit, MI. *G.O. No.:* (?). *Citation:* During an intense enemy bombardment with high explosive and gas shells which wounded or killed many members of the company, Sergeant Stockham, upon noticing that the gas mask of a wounded comrade was shot away, without hesitation, removed his own gas mask and insisted upon giving it to the wounded man, well knowing that the effects of the gas would be fatal to himself. Despite the fact that he was without protection of a gas mask, he continued with undaunted courage and valor to direct and assist in the evacuation of the wounded in an area saturated with gas and swept by heavy artillery fire, until he himself collapsed from the effects of gas, dying as a result thereof a few days later. His courageous conduct undoubtedly saved the lives of many of his wounded comrades and his conspicuous gallantry and spirit of self-sacrifice were a source of great inspiration to all who served with him. [*At Belleau Wood. Late award.*]

Talbot, Ralph. Second Lieutenant, U.S. Marine Corps. *Bern:* 6 January 1897, South Weyrnouth, MA. *Appointed from:* Connecticut. *Citation:* For exceptionally meritorious service and extraordinary heroism while attached to Squadron C, First Marine Aviation Force, in France. Second Lieutenant Talbot participated in numerous air raids into enemy territory. On 8 October 1918, while on such a raid, he was attacked by nine enemy scouts, and in the fight

Ralph Talbot

that followed shot down an enemy plane. Also, on 14 October 1918, while on a raid over Pittham, Belgium, Lieutenant Talbot and another plane became detached from the formation on account of motor trouble, and were attacked by 12 enemy scouts. During the severe fight that followed, his plane shot down one of the enemy scouts. His observer [Robinson] was shot through the elbow and his gun jammed. Second Lieutenant Talbot maneuvered to gain time for his observer to clear the jam with one hand, and then returned to the fight. The observer fought until shot twice, once in the stomach and once in the hip. When he collapsed, Lieutenant Talbot attacked the nearest enemy scout with his front guns and shot him down. With his observer unconscious and his motor failing, he dived to escape the balance of the enemy and crossed the German trenches at an altitude of 50 feet, landing at the nearest hospital to leave his observer, and then returning to his aerodrome. [*Not long after the above fight, on 25 October 1918 he was killed in a plane crash.*]

Haitian Campaign • 1919

Button, William Robert. Corporal, U.S. Marine Corps. *Born:* 3 December 1895, St. Louis, MO. *Accredited to:* Missouri. *G.O. No.:* 536, 10 June 1920. *Citation:* For extraordinary heroism and conspicuous gallantry and intrepidity in actual conflict with the enemy near Grande Riviere, Republic of Haiti, on the night of 31 October–1 November 1919, resulting in the death of Charlemagne Peralte, the supreme bandit chief in the Republic of Haiti, and the killing, capture and dispersal of about 1,200 of his outlaw followers. Corporal William R. Button not only distinguished himself by his excellent judgment and leadership but also unhesitatingly exposed himself to great personal danger when the slightest error would have forfeited not only his life but the lives of the detachments of

William Robert Button

Gendarmerie under his command. The successful termination of his mission will undoubtedly prove of untold value to the Republic of Haiti.

Hanneken, Herman Henry. Sergeant, U. S. Marine Corps. *Place and date:* Near Grande Riviere, Republic of Haiti, 31 October–1 November 1919. *Entered service at:* Missouri. *Birth:* St. Louis, MO. *G.O. No.:* 536, 10 June 1920. *Citation:* For extraordinary heroism and conspicuous gallantry and intrepidity in actual conflict with the enemy near Grande Riviere, Republic of Haiti, on the night of 31 October–1 November 1919, resulting in the death of Charlemagne Peralte, the supreme bandit chief in the Republic of Haiti, and the killing, capture, and dispersal of about 1,200 of his outlaw followers. Second Lieutenant Hanneken not only distinguished himself by his excellent judgment and leadership but also unhesitatingly exposed himself to great personal danger when the slightest error would have forfeited not only his life but the lives of the detachments of gendarmerie under his command. The successful termination of his mission will undoubtedly prove of untold value to the Republic of Haiti. [*Other Navy awards: Silver Star, Legion of Merit, and Bronze Star w/Combat V. He retired a brigadier general July 1948.*]

Herman Henry Hanneken

Christian Frank Schilt

Second Nicaraguan Campaign • 1927–1932

Schilt, Christian Frank. First Lieutenant, U. S. Marine Corps. *Place and date:* Quilahi, Nicaragua, 6, 7, and 8 January 1928. *Entered service at:* Illinois. *Birth:* Richland County, IL. *Citation:* During the progress of an insurrection at Quilahi, Nicaragua, 6, 7, and 8 January 1928, Lieutenant Schilt, then a member of a Marine expedition which had suffered severe losses in killed and wounded, volunteered under almost impossible conditions to evacuate the wounded by air and transport a relief commanding officer to assume charge of a very serious situation. First Lieutenant Schilt bravely undertook this dangerous and important task and, by taking off a total of 10 times in the rough, rolling street of a partially burning village, under hostile infantry fire on each occasion succeeded in accomplishing his mission, thereby actually saving three lives and bringing supplies and aid to others in desperate need. [*Other Navy awards: Legion of Merit, Silver Star, Bronze Star. He retired a lieutenant general in 1957.*]

Truesdell, Donald Leroy. Corporal, U. S. Marine Corps. *Place and date:* Vicinity Constancia, near Coco River, northern Nicaragua, 24 April 1932. *Entered service at:* South Carolina. *Birth:* Lugoff, SC. *Citation:* Corporal Truesdale was second in command of a Guardia Nacional Patrol in active operations against armed bandit forces in the vicinity of Constancia, near Coco River, northern Nicaragua, on 24 April 1932. While the patrol was in formation on the trail searching for a bandit group with which contact had just previously been made, a rifle grenade fell from its carrier and struck a rock, igniting the detonator. Several men close to the grenade at the time were in danger. Corporal Truesdale, who was several yards away, could easily have sought cover and safety for himself. Knowing full well the grenade would explode within 2 or 3 seconds he rushed for the grenade, grasped it in his right hand, and attempted to throw it away from the patrol. The grenade exploded in his hand, blowing it off and inflicting serious multiple wounds about his body. Corporal Truesdale, in taking the full shock of the explosion himself, saved the members of the patrol from loss of life or serious injury. [*Name was officially changed to Truesdale after this incident. He retired a warrant officer in May 1946.*]

Donald Leroy Trusdell (Truesdale)

Interim Period • 1921

Smith, Albert Joseph. Private, U. S. Marine Corps. *Place and date:* Marine Barracks, Naval Air Station, Pensacola, FL., 11 February 1921. *Entered service at:* Michigan. *Birth:* Calumet City, MI. *G.O. No.:* 72, 29 September 1921. At about 7:30 a.m. on the morning of 11 February 1921, Private Smith, while on duty as sentry, rescued Plen M. Phelps, late Machinist Mate 2d Class, U.S. Navy, from a burning seaplane which had fallen near his post, gate No. 1, Marine Barracks, Naval Air Station, Pensacola, Fla. Despite the explosion of the gravity gasoline tank, with total disregard of personal safety, he pushed himself into a position where he could reach Phelps, who was pinned beneath the burning wreckage, and rescued him from the burning plane, in the performance of which he sustained painful burns about the head, neck, and both hands.

World War II • 1941–1945

***Agerholm, Harold Christ.** Private First Class, U.S. Marine Corps. *Born:* 29 January 1925, Racine, WI. *Accredited to:* Wisconsin. *Citation:* For conspicuous gallantry and intrepidity at the risk of his life above and beyond the call of duty while serving with the Fourth Battalion, Tenth Marines, Second Marine Division, in action against enemy Japanese forces on Saipan, Marianas Islands, 7 July 1944. When the enemy launched a fierce, determined counter-attack against our positions and overran a neighboring artillery battalion, Private First Class Agerholm immediately volunteered to assist in the efforts to check the hostile attack and evacuate our wounded. Locating and appropriating an abandoned ambulance jeep, he repeatedly made extremely perilous trips under heavy rifle and mortar fire and single-handedly loaded and evacuated approximately 45 casualties, working tirelessly and with utter disregard for his own safety

Agerholm, Harold Christ

during a grueling period of more than 3 hours. Despite intense, persistent enemy fire, he ran out to aid two men whom he believed to be wounded Marines but was himself mortally wounded by a Japanese sniper while carrying out his hazardous mission. Private First Class Agerholm's brilliant initiative, great personal valor and self-sacrificing efforts in the face of almost certain death reflect the highest credit upon himself and the United States Naval Service. He gallantly gave his life for his country.

***Anderson, Richard Beatty.** Private First Class, U.S. Marine Corps. *Born:* 26 June 1921, Tacoma, WA. *Accredited to:* Washington. *Citation:* For conspicuous gallantry and intrepidity at the risk of his life above and beyond the call of duty while serving with the Fourth Marine Division during action against enemy Japanese forces on Roi Island, Kwajalein Atoll, Marshall Islands, 1 February 1944. Entering a shell crater occupied by three other Marines, Private First Class Anderson was preparing to throw a grenade at an enemy position when it slipped from his hands and rolled toward the men at the bottom of the hole. With insufficient time to retrieve the armed weapon and throw it, Private First Class Anderson fearlessly chose to sacrifice himself and save his companions by hurling his body upon the grenade taking the full impact of the explosion. His personal valor and exceptional spirit of loyalty in the face of almost certain death were keeping with the highest traditions of the U.S. naval service. He gallantly gave his life for his country.

***Bailey, Kenneth D.** Major, U.S. Marine Corps. *Born.:* 21 October 1910, Pawnee, OK. *Appointed from:* Illinois. *Citation:* For extraordinary courage and heroic conduct above and beyond the call of duty as Commanding Officer of Company C, First Marine Raider Battalion, during the enemy Japanese attack on Henderson Field, Guadalcanal, Solomon Islands, on 12–13 September 1942. Completely reorganized following the severe engagement of the night before, Major Bailey's company, within an hour after taking its assigned position as reserve battalion between the main line and the coveted airport, was threatened on the right flank by the penetration of the enemy into a gap in the main line. In addition to repulsing this threat, while steadily improving his own desperately held position, he used every weapon at his command to cover the forced withdrawal of the main line before a hammering assault by superior enemy forces. After rendering invaluable service to the battalion commander in stemming the retreat, reorganizing the troops and extending the reverse position to the left, Major Bailey, despite a severe head wound, repeatedly led his troops

Kenneth D. Bailey

in fierce hand-to-hand combat for a period of 10 hours. His great personal valor while exposed to constant and merciless enemy fire, and his indomitable fighting spirit inspired his troops to heights of heroic endeavor which enabled them to repulse the enemy and hold Henderson Field. He gallantly gave his life in the service of his country. [*Other Navy award: Silver Star Medal.*]

Basilone, John. Sergeant, U.S. Marine Corps. *Born:* 4 November 1916, Buffalo, NY. *Accredited to:* New Jersey. *Citation:* For extraordinary heroism and conspicuous gallantry in action against enemy Japanese forces, above and beyond the call of duty, while serving with the First Battalion, Seventh Marines, First Marine Division in the Lungs Area, Guadalcanal, Solomon Islands, on 24 and 25 October 1942. While the enemy was hammering at the Marines' defensive positions, Sergeant Basilone, in charge of two sections of heavy machine guns, fought valiantly to check the savage and determined assault. In a fierce frontal attack with the Japanese blasting his guns with grenades and mortar fire, one of Sergeant Basilone's sections, with its gun crews, was put out of action, leaving only two men able to carry on. Moving an extra gun into position, he placed it in

John Basilone

action, then, under continual fire, repaired another and personally manned it, gallantly holding his line until replacements arrived. A little later, with ammunition critically low and the supply lines cut off, Sergeant Basilone, at great risk of his life and in the face of continued enemy attack, battled his way through hostile lines with urgently needed shells for his gunners, thereby contributing in large measure to the virtual annihilation of a Japanese regiment. His great personal valor and courageous initiative were in keeping with the highest traditions of the United States Naval Service. [*Other Navy award: Navy Cross. He was killed in action on 19 February 1945, at Iwo Jima. A destroyer was named for him.*]

Bauer, Harold William. Lieutenant Colonel, U.S. Marine Corps. *Born:* 20 November 1908, Woodruff, KS. *Appointed from:* Nebraska. *Citation:* For extraordinary heroism and conspicuous courage as Squadron Commander of Marine Fighting Squadron Two Hundred Twelve in the South Pacific Area during the period 10 May to 14 November 1942. Volunteering to pilot a fighter plane in defense of our positions on Guadalcanal, Colonel Bauer participated in two air battles against enemy bombers and fighters outnumbering our force more than two to one, boldly engaged the enemy and destroyed one Japanese bomber in the engagement of 28 September and shot down four enemy fighter planes in flames on 3 October, leaving a fifth smoking badly. After successfully leading 26 planes on an over-water ferry flight of more than 600 miles on 16 October, Colonel Bauer, while circling to land, sighted a squadron of enemy planes attacking the U.S.S. *McFarland*. Undaunted by the formidable opposition and with valor above and bezzzyond the call of duty, he engaged the entire squadron and, although alone and his fuel supply nearly exhausted, fought his plane so brilliantly that four of the Japanese planes were destroyed

Harold William Bauer

before he was forced down by lack of fuel. His intrepid fighting spirit and distinctive ability as a leader and an airman exemplified in his splendid record of combat achievement, were vital factors in the successful operations in the South Pacific Area.

***Bausell, Lewis Kenneth.** Corporal, U.S. Marine Corps. *Born:* 17 April 1924, Pulaski, VA. *Accredited to:* District of Columbia. *Citation:* For conspicuous gallantry and intrepidity at the risk of his life above and beyond the call of duty while serving with the First Battalion, Fifth Marines, First Marine Division, during action against enemy Japanese forces on Peleliu Island, Palau Group, 15 September 1944. Valiantly placing himself at the head of his squad, Corporal Bausell led the charge forward against a hostile pillbox which was covering a vital sector of the beach and, as the first to reach the emplacement, immediately started firing his automatic into the aperture while the remainder of his men closed in on the enemy. Swift to act, as a Japanese grenade was hurled into their midst, Corporal Bausell threw himself on the deadly weapon, taking the full blast of the explosion and sacrificing his own life to save his men. His unwavering loyalty and inspiring courage reflect the highest credit upon Corporal Bausell and the United States Naval Service. He gallantly gave his life for his country.

*****Berry, Charles Joseph.** Corporal, U.S. Marine Corps. *Born:* 10 July 1923, Lorain, OH. *Accredited to:* OH. *Citation:* For conspicuous gallantry and intrepidity at the risk of his life above and beyond the call of duty as member of a machine-gun crew, serving with the First Battalion, Twenty-sixth Marines, Fifth Marine Division, in action against enemy Japanese forces during the seizure of Iwo Jima in the Volcano Islands, on 3 March 1945. Stationed in the front lines, Corporal Berry manned his weapon with alert readiness as he maintained a constant vigil with other members of his gun crew during the hazardous night tours. When infiltrating Japanese soldiers launched a surprise attack shortly after midnight in an attempt to overrun his position, he engaged in a pitched hand-grenade duel, returning the dangerous weapons with prompt and deadly accuracy until an enemy grenade landed in the foxhole. Determined to save his comrades, he unhesitatingly chose to sacrifice himself and immediately dived on the deadly missile, absorbing the shattering violence of the exploding charge in his own body and protecting the others from serious injury. Stout-hearted and indomitable, Corporal Berry fearlessly yielded his own life that his fellow Marines might carry on the relentless battle against a ruthless enemy and his superb valor and unfaltering devotion to duty in the face of certain death reflect the highest credit upon himself and upon the United States Naval Service. He gallantly gave his life for his country.

*****Bonnyman, Alexander, Jr.** First Lieutenant, U.S. Marine Corps Reserves. *Born:* 2 May 1910, Atlanta, Ga. Accredited to: New Mexico. *Citation:* For conspicuous

Lewis Kenneth Bausell

Charles Joseph Berry

gallantry and intrepidity at the risk of his life above and beyond the call of duty as Executive Officer of the Second Battalion Shore Party, Eighth Marines, Second Marine Division, during the assault against enemy Japanese-held Tarawa in the Gilbert Islands, 20–22 November 1943. Acting on his own initiative when assault troops were pinned down at the far end of Betio Pier by the overwhelming fire of Japanese shore batteries, First Lieutenant Bonnyman repeatedly defied the blasting fury of the enemy bombardment to organize and lead the besieged men over the long, open pier to the beach and then, voluntarily obtaining flame throwers and demolitions, organized his pioneer shore party into assault demolitionists and directed the blowing of several hostile installations before the close of D–day. Determined to effect an opening in the enemy's

Alexander Bonnyman

strongly organized defense line the following day, he voluntarily crawled approximately 40 yards forward of our lines and placed demolitions in the entrance of a large Japanese emplacement as the initial move in his planned attack against the heavily garrisoned, bombproof installation which was stubbornly resisting despite the destruction early in the action of a large number of Japanese who had been inflicting heavy casualties on our forces and holding up our advance. Withdrawing only to replenish his ammunition, he led his men in a renewed assault, fearlessly exposing himself to the merciless slash of hostile fire as lie stormed the formidable bastion, directed the placement of demolition charges in both entrances and seized the top of the bombproof position, flushing more than 100 of the enemy who were instantly cut down, and effecting the annihilation of approximately 150 troops inside the emplacement. Assailed by additional Japanese after he had gained his objective, he made a heroic stand on the edge of the structure, defending his strategic position with indomitable determination in the face of the desperate charge and killing three of the enemy before lie fell, mortally wounded. By his dauntless fighting spirit, unrelenting aggressiveness and forceful leadership throughout 3 days of unremitting, violent battle, First Lieutenant Bonnyman had inspired his men to heroic effort, enabling them to beat off the counterattack and break the beck of hostile resistance in that sector for an immediate gain of 400 yards with no further casualties to our forces in this zone. He gallantly gave his life for his country.

*Bordelon, William James.** Staff Sergeant, U.S. Marine Corps. *Born:* 25 December 1920, San Antonio, TX. *Accredited to:* Texas. *Citation:* For valorous and gallant conduct above and beyond the call of duty as a member of an assault engineer platoon of the First Battalion, Eighteenth Marines, tactically attached to the Second Marine Division, in action against the Japanese-held atoll of Tarawa in the Gilbert Islands on 20 November 1943. Landing in the assault waves under withering enemy fire which killed all but four of the men in his tractor, Staff Sergeant Bordelon hurriedly made demolition charges and personally put two pillboxes out of action. Hit by enemy machine gun fire just as a charge exploded in his hand while assaulting a third position, he courageously remained in action and, although out of demolition, provided himself with a rifle and furnished fire coverage for a group of men scaling the seawall. Disregarding his own serious condition, he unhesitatingly

William James Bordelon

went to the aid of one of his demolition men, wounded and calling for help in the water, rescuing this man and another who had been hit by enemy fire while attempting to make the rescue. Still refusing first aid for himself, he again made up demo-lition charges and single-handedly assaulted a fourth Japanese machine gun position but was instantly killed when caught in a final burst of fire from the enemy. Staff Sergeant Bordelon's great personal valor during a critical phase of securing the limited beachhead was a contributing factor in the ultimate occupation of the island, and his heroic determination throughout 3 days of violent battle reflects the highest credit upon the United States Naval Service. He gallantly gave his life for his country.

Boyington, Gregory. Major. U.S. Marine Corps Reserve, Marine Squadron 214. *Place and date:* Central Solomons area, from 12 September 1943 to 3 January 1944. *Entered service at:* Washington. *Birth:* Coeur D'Alene, Idaho. *Citation:* For extraordinary heroism and valiant devotion to duty as commanding officer of Marine Fighting Squadron 214 in action against enemy Japanese forces in the Central Solomons

Gregory Boyington

Area from 12 September 1943 to 3 January 1944. Consistently outnumbered throughout successive hazardous flights over heavily defended hostile territory, Major Boyington struck at the enemy with daring and courageous persistence, his squadron into combat with devastating results to Japanese shipping, shore installations, and aerial forces. Resolute in his efforts inflict crippling damage on the enemy, Major Boyington led a formation of 24 fighters over Kahili on 17 October and, persistently circling the airdrome where 60 hostile aircraft were grounded, boldly challenged the Japanese to send up planes. Under his brilliant command, our fighters shot down 20 enemy craft in the ensuing action without the loss of a single ship. A superb airman and determined fighter against over-whelming odds, Major Boyington personally destroyed 26 of the many Japanese planes shot down by his squadron and, by his forceful leadership, developed the combat readiness in his command which was a distinctive factor in the Allied aerial achievements in this vitally strategic area. [*Other Navy award: Navy Cross. He retired as a colonel in August 1947.*]

Bush, Richard Earl. Corporal, U.S. Marine Corps Reserve, 1st Battalion, 4th Marines, 6th Marine Division. *Place and date:* Mount Yaetake on Okinawa, Ryukyu Islands, 16 April 1945. *Entered service at:* Kentucky. *Birth:* Glasgow, KY. *Citation:* For conspicuous gallantry and intrepidity at the risk of his life above and beyond the call of duty as a squad leader serving with the 1st Battalion, 4th Marines, 6th Marine Division, in action against enemy Japanese forces, during the final assault against Mount Yaetake on Okinawa, Ryukyu Islands, 16 April 1945. Rallying his men forward with indomitable determination, Corporal Bush boldly defied the slashing fury of concentrated Japanese artillery fire pouring down from the gun-studded mountain fortress to lead his squad up the face of the rocky precipice, sweep over the ridge, and drive the defending troops from their deeply entrenched position. With his unit, the break through to the inner defense of Mount Yaetake, he relentlessly in the forefront of the action until seriously wounded evacuated with others under protecting rocks. Although prostrate under medical treatment when a Japanese hand grenade landed the midst of the group, Corporal Bush, alert and courageous in extremity as in battle unhesitatingly pulled the deadly missile to himself and absorbed the shat-

Richard Earl Bush

tering violence of the exploding charge in his own body, thereby saving his fellow Marines from severe injury or death despite the certain peril to his own life. By his valiant leadership and aggressive tactics in the face of savage opposition, Corporal Bush contributed materially to the success of the sustained toward the conquest of this fiercely defended outpost of the Japanese Empire. His constant concern for the welfare of his men, his resolute spirit of self-sacrifice, and his unwavering devotion to throughout the bitter conflict enhance and sustain the highest of the United States naval service.

Bush, Robert Eugene. Hospital Apprentice First Class, United States Navy, serving as Medical Corpsman with a rifle company, 2d Battalion, 5th Marines, 1st Marine Division. *Place and date:* Okinawa Jima, Ryukyu Islands, 2 May 1945. *Entered service at:* Washington. *Birth:* Tacoma, WA. *Citation:* For conspicuous gallantry and intrepidity at the risk of his life above and beyond the call of duty while serving as Medical Corpsman with a rifle company, 2d Battalion, 5th Marines, 1st Marine Division, in action against enemy Japanese forces on Okinawa Jima, Ryukyu Islands, 2 May 1945. Fearlessly braving the fury of artillery, mortar, and machine-gun fire from strongly entrenched hostile positions, Bush constantly unhesitatingly moved from one casualty to another to attend the tided falling under the enemy's murderous barrages. As the attack passed over a ridge top, Bush was advancing to administer plasma to a Marine officer lying wounded on the skyline when the Japanese launched a savage counterattack. In this perilously exposed position, he resolutely maintained the flow of life-giving plasma. With the bottle held high in one hand, Bush drew his pistol with the other and fired into the enemy's ranks until his ammunition was expended. Quickly seizing a discarded carbine, he trained his fire on the Japanese charging point-blank over the hill, accounting for six of the enemy despite his own serious wounds and the loss of one eye suffered during his desperate battle in defense of the helpless man. With the hostile force finally routed, he calmly disregarded his own critical condition to complete his mission, valiantly refusing medical treatment for himself until his officer patient had been evacuated, and collapsing only after attempting to walk to the battle aid station. His daring initiative, great personal valor, and heroic spirit of self-sacrifice in service of others reflect great credit upon Bush and enhance the finest traditions of the United States naval service.

*Caddy, William Robert. Private First Class, U.S. Marine Corps Reserve. *Born:* 8 August 1925, Quincy, MA. *Accredited to:* Massachusetts. *Citation:* For conspicuous gallantry and intrepidity at the risk of his life above and beyond the call of duty while serving as a Rifleman with Company I, Third Battalion, Twenty-sixth Marines, Fifth Marine Division, in action against enemy Japanese forces during the seizure of Iwo Jima in the Volcano Islands, 3 March 1945. Consistently aggressive, Private First Class Caddy boldly defied shattering Japanese machine-gun and small-arms fire to move forward with his platoon leader and another Marine during the determined advance of his company through an isolated sector and, gaining the comparative safety of a shell hole, took temporary cover with his comrades. Immediately pinned down by deadly sniper fire from a well-concealed position, he made several unsuccessful attempts to again move forward and then, joined by his platoon leader, engaged the enemy in a fierce exchange of hand grenades until a Japanese grenade fell beyond reach in the shell hole. Fearlessly disregarding all personal danger, Private First Class Caddy instantly dived on the deadly missile, absorbing the exploding charge in his own body and protecting the others from serious injury. Stouthearted and indomitable, he unhesitatingly yielded his own life that his fellow Marines might carry on the relentless battle against a fanatic enemy. His dauntless courage and valiant spirit of self-sacrifice in the face of certain death reflect the highest credit upon Private First Class Caddy and upon the United States Naval Service. He gallantly gave his life for his comrades.

William Robert Caddy

*Cannon, George Ham. First Lieutenant., U.S. Marine Corps. *Born:* 5 November 1915, St. Louis, MO. *Appointed from:* Michigan. *Citation:* For distinguished conduct in the line of his profession, extraordinary courage and disregard of his own condition during the bombardment of Sand Island, Midway Islands, by Japanese forces on 7 December 1941. Lieutenant Cannon, Battery Commander of Battery H, Sixth Defense Battalion, Fleet Marine Force, U.S. Marine Corps, was at his Command Post when he was mortally wounded by enemy shellfire. He refused to be evacuated from his post until after his men who had been wounded by the same shell were evacuated, and directed the reorganization of his Command Post until forcibly removed. As a result of his utter disregard of his own condition he died from loss of blood. [*In May 1943 a destroyer was named for him.*]

Casamento, Anthony. Corporal, U. S. Marine Corps. *Born:* 16 November 1920,

George Ham Cannon

Manhattan, NY. *Entered service at:* Brooklyn, NY, on 19 August 1940. *Place and date:* Guadalcanal, 1 November 1942. With Company D, First Battalion, Fifth Marines, First Marine Division. *Citation:* For conspicuous gallantry and intrepidity at the risk of his life above and beyond the call of duty while serving with Company D, 1st Battalion, 5th Marines, 1st Marine Division on Guadalcanal, British Solomon Islands, in action against the enemy Japanese forces on 1 November 1942. Serving as a leader of a machine gun section, Corporal Casamento directed his unit to advance along a ridge near the Matanikau River where they engaged the enemy. He positioned his section to provide covering fire for two flanking units and to provide direct support for the main force of his company which was behind him. During the course of this engagement, all members of his section were either killed or severely wounded and he himself suffered multiple, grievous wounds. Nonetheless, Corporal Casamento continued to

Anthony Casamento

provide critical supporting fire for the attack and in defense of his position. Following the loss of all effective personnel, he set up, loaded, and manned his unit's machine gun tenaciously holding the enemy forces at bay. Corporal Casamento single-handedly engaged and destroyed one machine gun emplacement to his front and took under fire the other emplacement on the flank. Despite the heat and ferocity of the engagement, he continued to man his weapon and repeatedly repulsed multiple assaults by the enemy forces, thereby protecting the flanks of the adjoining companies and holding his position until the arrival of his main attacking force. Corporal Casamento's courageous fighting spirit, heroic conduct, and unwavering dedication to duty reflected great credit upon himself and were in keeping with the highest traditions of the Marine Corps and the United States Naval Service. [*A late WWII award.*]

Chambers, Justice M. Colonel, U.S. Marine Corps Reserve, 3d Assault Battalion Landing Team, 25th Marines. 4th Marine Division. *Place and date:* On Iwo Jima,

Justice M. Chambers

Volcano Islands, from 19 to 22 February 1945. *Entered service* at: Washington, D.C. *Birth:* Huntington, WV. *Citation:* For conspicuous gallantry and intrepidity at the risk of his life above and beyond the call of duty as commanding officer of the 3d Assault Battalion Landing Team, 25th Marines 4th Marine Division, in action against enemy Japanese forces on Iwo Jima, Volcano Islands, from 19 to 22 February 1945. Under a furious barrage of enemy machine-gun and small-arms fire from the commanding cliffs on the right, Colonel Chambers (then Lieutenant Colonel) landed immediately after the initial assault waves of his battalion on D-day to find the momentum of the assault threatened by heavy casualties from withering Japanese artillery, mortar, rocket, machine-gun, and rifle fire. Exposed to relentless hostile fire he, he coolly reorganized his battle-weary men, inspiring them to heroic efforts by his own valor and leading them in an attack on the critical, impregnable high ground from which the enemy was pouring an increasing volume of fire directly onto troops ashore as well as amphibious craft in succeeding waves. Constantly in the front lines encouraging his men to push forward against the enemy's savage resistance, Colonel Chambers led the 8-hour battle to carry the flanking ridge top and reduce the enemy's fields of aimed fire, thus protecting the vital foothold gained. In constant defiance of hostile fire while reconnoitering the entire regimental combat team zone of action, he maintained contact with adjacent units and forwarded vital information to the regimental commander. His zealous fighting spirit undiminished despite terrific casualties and the loss of most of his key officers, he again reorganized his troops for renewed attack against the enemy's main line of resistance and was directing the fire of the rocket platoon when he fell, critically wounded. Evacuated under heavy Japanese fire, Colonel Chambers, by forceful leadership, courage, and fortitude in the face. of staggering odds, was directly instrumental in insuring the success of subsequent operations of the 5th Amphibious Corps on Iwo Jima, thereby sustaining and enhancing the finest traditions of the United States naval service. [*Other Navy award: Navy Cross, Silver Star, Legion of Merit. He retired on 1 January 1946. His Medal of Honor was a late World War II award.*]

*Cole, Darrell Samuel. Sergeant, U.S. Marine Corps Reserve. *Born:* 20 July 1920, Flat River, MO. *Accredited to:* Missouri. *Other Navy award:* Bronze Star Medal. *Citation:* For conspicuous gallantry and intrepidity at the risk of his life above and beyond the call of duty while serving as leader of a Machine-gun Section of Company B, First Battalion, Twenty-third Marines, Fourth Marine Division, in action against enemy Japanese forces during the assault on Iwo Jima in the Volcano

Darrell Samuel Cole

Islands, 19 February 1945. Assailed by a tremendous volume of small-arms, mortar and artillery fire as he advanced with one squad of his section in the initial assault wave, Sergeant Cole boldly led his men up the sloping beach toward Airfield No. 1 despite the blanketing curtain of flying shrapnel and, personally destroying with hand grenades two hostile emplacements which menaced the progress of his unit, continued to move forward until a merciless barrage of fire emanating from three Japanese pillboxes halted the advance. Instantly placing his one remaining machine gun in action, he delivered a shattering fusillade and succeeded in silencing the nearest and most threatening emplacement before his weapon jammed and the enemy, reopening fire with knee mortars and grenades, pinned down his unit for the second time. Shrewdly gaging the tactical situation and evolving a daring plan of counterattack, Sergeant Cole, armed solely with a pistol and one grenade, cooly advanced alone to the hostile pillboxes. Hurling his one grenade at the enemy in sudden, swift attack, he quickly withdrew, returned to his own lines for additional grenades and again advanced, attacked, and withdrew. With enemy guns still active, he ran the gauntlet of slashing fire a third time to complete the total destruction of the Japanese strong point and the annihilation of the defending garrison in this final assault. Although instantly killed by an enemy grenade as he returned to his squad, Sergeant Cole had eliminated a formidable Japanese position, thereby enabling his company to storm the remaining fortifications, continue the advance, and seize the objective. By his dauntless initiative, unfaltering courage, and indomitable determination during a critical period of action, Sergeant Cole served as an inspiration to his comrades, and his stout-hearted leadership in the face of certain death sustained and enhanced the highest tradition of the United States Naval Service. He gallantly gave his life for his country. [*Other Navy award: Bronze Star w/Combat V.*]

*Courtney, Henry Alexius, Jr.** Major, U.S. Marine Corps Reserve. *Born:* 6 January 1916, Duluth, MN. *Appointed from:* Minnesota. *Citation:* For conspicuous gallantry and intrepidity at the risk of his life above and beyond the call of duty as Executive Officer of the Second Battalion, Twenty-second Marines, Sixth Marine Division, in action against enemy Japanese forces on Okinawa Shima in the Ryukyu Islands, 14 and 15 May 1945. Ordered to hold for the night in static defense behind Sugar Loaf Hill after leading the forward elements of his command in a prolonged fire fight, Major Courtney weighed the effect of a hostile night counterattack against the tactical value of an immediate Marine assault,

Henry Alexius Courtney, Jr.

resolved to initiate the assault, and promptly obtained permission to advance and seize the forward slope of the hill. Quicky explaining the situation to his small remaining force, he declared his personal intention of moving forward and then proceeded on his way, boldly blasting nearby cave positions and neutralizing enemy guns as he went. Inspired by his courage, every man followed without hesitation, and together the intrepid Marines braved a terrific concentration of Japanese gunfire to skirt the hill on the right and reach the reverse slope. Temporarily halting, Major Courtney sent guides to the rear for more ammunition and possible replacements. Subsequently reinforced by 26 men and an LVT load of grenades, he determined to storm the crest of the hill and rush any planned counterattack before it could gain sufficient momentum to effect a breakthrough. Leading his men by example rather than by command, he pushed ahead with unrelenting aggressiveness, hurling grenades into cave openings on the slope with devastating effect. Upon reaching the crest and observing large numbers of Japanese forming for action less than 100 yards away, he instantly attacked, waged a furious battle and succeeded in killing many of the enemy and in forcing the remainder to take cover in the caves. Determined to hold, he ordered his men to dig in and, coolly disregarding the continuous hail of flying enemy shrapnel to rally his weary troops, tirelessly aided casualties and assigned his men to more advantageous positions. Although instantly killed by a hostile mortar burst while moving among his men, Major Courtney, by his astute military acumen, indomitable leadership and decisive action in the face of overwhelming odds, had contributed essentially to the success of the Okinawa campaign. His great personal valor throughout sustained and enhanced the highest traditions of the United States Naval Service. He gallantly gave his life for his country.

*Damato, Anthony Peter. Corporal, U.S. Marine Corps. *Born:* 28 March 1922, Shenandoah, PA. *Accredited to:* Pennsylvania. Citation: For conspicuous gallantry and intrepidity at the risk of his life above and beyond the call of duty while serving with an assault company in action against enemy Japanese forces on Engebi Island, Eniwetok Atoll, Marshall Islands, on the night of 19–20 February 1944. Highly vulnerable to sudden attack by small, fanatical groups of Japanese still at large despite the efficient and determined efforts of our forces to clear the area, Corporal Damato lay with two comrades in a large foxhole in his company's defense perimeter which had been dangerously thinned by the forced withdrawal of nearly half of the available men. When one of the enemy approached the foxhole undetected and threw in a hand grenade, Corporal

Anthony Peter Damato

Damato desperately groped for it in the darkness. Realizing the imminent peril to all three and fully aware of the consequences of his act, he unhesitatingly flung himself on the grenade and, although instantly killed, as his body absorbed the explosion, saved the lives of his two companions. Corporal Damato's splendid initiative, fearless conduct and valiant sacrifice reflect great credit upon himself and the United States Naval Service. He gallantly gave his life for his comrades. [*He was a member of 2d Bn, 22d Marines, VAC. He had already landed against French forces in North Africa on 8 November 1942.*]

Day, James L. Corporal. U.S. Marine Corps. *Born:* 5 October 1925 at East Saint Louis, IL, *Place and date:* 14–17 May 1945, Okinawa Shima, *Entered service at:* [?] in 1943. *Citation:* For conspicuous gallantry and intrepidity at the risk of his life above and beyond the call of duty as a squad leader serving with the Second Battalion, Twenty-Second Marines, Sixth Marine Division, in sustained combat operations against Japanese forces on Okinawa, Ryukyu Islands from 14 to 17 May 1945. On the first day, Corporal Day rallied his squad and the remnants of another unit and led them to a critical position forward of the front lines of Sugar Loaf Hill. Soon thereafter, they came under an intense mortar and artillery barrage that was quickly followed by a ferocious ground attack by some forty Japanese soldiers. Despite the loss of one-half of his men, Corporal Day remained at the forefront, shouting encouragement, hurling hand grenades, and directing deadly fire, thereby repelling the determined enemy. Reinforced by six men, he led his squad in

James L. Day

repelling three fierce night attacks but suffered five additional Marines killed and one wounded, whom he assisted to safety. Upon hearing nearby calls for corpsman assistance, Corporal Day braved heavy enemy fire to escort four seriously wounded Marines, one at a time, to safety. Corporal Day then manned a light machine gun, assisted by a wounded Marine, and halted another night attack. In the ferocious action, his machine gun was destroyed, and he suffered multiple white phosphorous and fragmentation wounds. He reorganized his defensive position in time to halt a fifth enemy attack with devastating small arms fire. On three separated occasions, Japanese soldiers closed to within a few feet of his foxhole, but were killed by Corporal Day. During the second day, the enemy conducted numerous unsuccessful swarming attacks against his exposed position. When the attacks momentarily subsided, over 70 enemy dead were counted around his position. On the third day, a wounded and exhausted Corporal Day repulsed the enemy's final attack, killing a dozen enemy soldiers at close range. Having yielded no ground and with more than 100 enemy dead around his position, Corporal Day preserved the lives of his fellow Marines and made a significant contribution to the success of the Okinawa campaign. By his extraordinary heroism, repeated acts of valor, and quintessential battlefield leadership, Corporal Day inspired the efforts of his outnumbered Marines to defeat a much larger enemy force, reflecting great credit upon himself and upholding the highest traditions of the Marine Corps and the United States Naval Service. [*Other Navy awards: Distinguished Service Medal, three Silver Stars, Bronze Star w/V. His Medal of Honor was a late WWII award to then, Major General Day, at White House on 20 January 1998.*]

DeBlanc, Jefferson Joseph. Captain, U.S. Marine Corps Reserve, Marine Fighting Squadron 112. *Place and date:* Off Kolombaiigara Island in the Solomons group, 31 January 1943. *Entered service at:* Louisiana. *Birth:* Lockport, LA. *Citation:* For conspicuous gallantry and intrepidity at the risk of his life above and beyond the call of duty as leader of a section of six fighter planes in Marine Fighting Squadron 112, during aerial operations against enemy Japanese forces off Kolombangara Island in the Solomons group, 31 January 1943. Taking off with his section as escort for a strike force of dive bombers and torpedo planes ordered to attack Japanese surface vessels, First Lieutenant DeBlanc led his flight directly to the target area where, at 14,000 feet, our strike force encountered a large number of Japanese Zeros protecting the enemy's surface craft. In company with the other

Jefferson Joseph DeBlanc

fighters, First Lieutenant DeBlanc instantly engaged the hostile planes and aggressively countered their repeated attempts to drive off our bombers, the diving planes and waging fierce combat until, picking up a call for assistance from the dive bombers under attack by enemy float planes at 1,000 feet, he broke off his engagement with the Zeros, plunged into the formation of float planes and disrupted the savage attack, enabling our dive bombers and torpedo planes to complete their runs on the Japanese surface disposition and withdraw without further incident. Although his escort mission was fulfilled upon the safe retirement of the bombers, First Lieutenant DeBlanc courageously remained on the scene despite a rapidly diminishing fuel supply and, boldly challenging the enemy's superior number of float planes, fought a valiant battle against terrific odds, seizing the tactical advantage and striking repeatedly to destroy three of the hostile aircraft and to disperse the remainder. Prepared to maneuver his damaged plane back to base, he had climbed aloft and set his course when he discovered two Zeros closing in behind. Undaunted, he opened fire and blasted both Zeros from the sky in a short, bitterly fought action which resulted in such hopeless damage to his own plane that he was forced to bail out at a perilously low altitude atop the trees on enemy-held Kolombangara. A gallant officer, a superb airman, and an indomitable fighter, First Lieutenant DeBlanc rendered decisive assistance during a critical stage of operations, and his unwavering fortitude in the face of overwhelming opposition reflects the highest credit upon himself and adds new luster to the traditions of the United States naval service. [*Other Navy awards: Distinguished Flying Cross, 4 Air Medals. He retired a colonel.*]

Dunlap, Robert Hugo. Captain, U.S. Marine Corps Reserve, Company C, 1st Battalion, 26th Marines, 5th Marine Division. *Place and date:* Iwo Jima, Volcano Islands, 20 and 21 February 1945. *Entered service at:* Illinois. *Birth:* Abingdon, IL. *Citation:* For conspicuous gallantry and intrepidity at the risk of his life above and beyond the call of duty as commanding officer of Company C, 1st Battalion, 26th Marines, 5th Marine Division, in action against enemy Japanese forces during the seizure of Iwo Jima in the Volcano Islands, on 20 and 21 February 1945. Defying uninterrupted blasts of Japanese artillery, mortar, rifle and machine gun fire, Captain Dunlap led his troops in a determined advance from low ground uphill toward the steep cliffs from which the enemy poured a devastating rain of shrapnel and bullets, steadily inching forward until the tremendous volume of enemy fire from the caves located high to his front temporarily halted his progress. Determined not to yield,

Robert Hugo Dunlap

he crawled alone approximately 200 yards forward of his front lines, took observation at the base of the cliff 50 yards from Japanese lines, located the enemy gun positions and returned to his own lines where he relayed the vital information to supporting artillery and naval gunfire units. Persistently disregarding his own personal safety, he then placed himself in an exposed vantage point to direct more accurately the supporting fire and, working without respite for 2 days and 2 nights under constant enemy fire, skillfully directed a smashing bombardment against the almost impregnable Japanese positions despite numerous obstacles and heavy Marine casualties. A brilliant leader, Captain Dunlap inspired his men to heroic efforts during this critical phase of the battle and by his cool decision, indomitable fighting spirit, and daring tactics in the face of fanatic opposition greatly accelerated the final decisive defeat of Japanese countermeasures in his sector and materially furthered the continued advance of his company. His great personal valor and gallant spirit of self-sacrifice throughout the bitter hostilities reflect the highest credit upon Captain Dunlap and the United States naval service. [*He retired a major on 1 December 1946.*]

Aquilla James Dyess

*Dyess, Aquilla James. Lieutenant Colonel, U.S. Marine Corps Reserve. *Born:* 11 January 1909, Augusta, GA. *Appointed from:* Georgia. *Citation:* For conspicuous gallantry and intrepidity at the risk of his life above and beyond the call of duty as Commanding Officer of the First Battalion, Twenty-fourth Marines, Reinforced, Fourth Marine Division, in action against enemy Japanese forces during the assault on Namur Island, Kwajalein Atoll, Marshall Islands, 1 and 2 February 1944. Undaunted by severe fire from automatic Japanese weapons, Lieutenant Colonel Dyess launched a powerful final attack on the second day of the assault, unhesitatingly posting himself between the opposing lines to point out. objectives and avenues of approach and personally leading the advancing troops. Alert, and determined to quicken the pace of the offensive against increased enemy fire, he was constantly at the head of advance units, inspiring his men to push forward until the Japanese had been driven back to a small center of resistance and victory assured. While standing on the parapet of an anti-tank trench directing a group of infantry in a. flanking attack against the last enemy position, Lieutenant Colonel Dyess was killed by a burst of enemy machine gun fire. His daring and forceful leadership and his valiant fighting spirit in the face of terrific opposition were in keeping with the highest traditions of the U.S. Naval Service. He gallantly gave his life for his country.

Edson, Merritt Austin. Colonel, U.S. Marine Corps. *Born:* 25 April 1897, Rutland, VT. *Appointed from:* VT. *Citation:* For extraordinary heroism and conspicuous intrepidity above and beyond the call of duty as Commanding Officer of the First Marine Raider Battalion, with Parachute Battalion attached, during action against enemy Japanese forces in the Solomon Islands on the night of 13–14 September 1942.

After the airfield on Guadalcanal had been seized from the enemy on 8 August, Colonel Edson, with a force of 800 men, was assigned to the occupation and defense of a ridge dominating the jungle on either side of the airport. Facing a formidable Japanese attack which, augmented by infiltration, had crashed through our front lines, he, by skillful handling of his troops, successfully withdrew his forward units to a reserve line with minimum casualties. When the enemy, in a subsequent series of violent assaults, engaged our force in desperate hand-to-hand combat with bayonets, rifles, pistols, grenades, and knives, Colonel Edson, although continuously exposed to hostile fire throughout the night, personally directed defense of the reserve position against a fanatical foe of greatly superior numbers. By his astute leadership and gallant devotion to duty, he enabled his men, despite severe losses, to cling tenaciously to their position on the vital ridge, thereby retaining command not only of the Guadalcanal airfield, but also of the First Division's entire offensive installations in the surrounding area. [*Other Navy awards: Navy Cross with Gold Star, Silver Star Medal, Legion of Merit with Gold Star. He retired a major general on 1 August 1947.*]

Merritt Austin Edson

*Elrod, Henry Talmage. Captain, U.S. Marine Corps. Born: 27 September 1905, Rebecca, GA. Appointed from: Georgia. Citation: For conspicuous gallantry and intrepidity at the risk of his life above and beyond the call of duty while attached to Marine Fighting Squadron Two Hundred Eleven, during action against enemy Japanese land, surface and aerial units at Wake Island, 8 to 23 December 1941. Engaging vastly superior forces of enemy bombers and warships on 9 and 12 December, Captain Elrod shot down 2 of a flight

Henry Talmage Elrod

of 22 hostile planes and, executing repeated bombing and strafing runs at extremely low altitude and close range, succeeded in inflicting deadly damage upon a large Japanese vessel, thereby sinking the first major warship to be destroyed by small-caliber bombs delivered from a fighter-type aircraft. When his plane was disabled by hostile fire and no other ships were operative, Captain Elrod assumed command of one flank of the line set up in defiance of the enemy landing and, conducting a brilliant defense, enabled his men to hold their positions and repulse intense hostile fusillades to provide covering fire for unarmed ammunition carriers. Capturing an automatic weapon during one enemy rush in force, he gave his own firearm to one of his men and fought on vigorously against the Japanese. Responsible in a large measure for the strength of his sector's gallant resistance, on 23 December, Captain Elrod led his men with bold aggressiveness until he fell, mortally wounded. His superb skill as a pilot, daring leadership and unswerving devotion to duty distinguished him among the defenders of Wake Island, and his valiant conduct reflects the highest credit upon himself and the United States Naval Service. He gallantly gave his life for his country.

*Epperson, Harold Glenn. Private First Class, U.S. Marine Corps Reserves. *Born:* 14 July 1923, Akron, OH. *Accredited to:* OH. *Citation:* For conspicuous gallantry and intrepidity at the risk of his life above and beyond the call of duty while serving with the First Battalion, Sixth Marines, Second Marine Division, in action against enemy Japanese forces on the Island of Saipan in the Marianas, on 25 June 1944. With his machine-gun emplacement bearing the full brunt of a fanatic assault initiate d by the Japanese under cover of predawn darkness, Private First Class Epperson manned his weapon with determined aggressiveness, fighting furiously in the defense of his battalion's position and maintaining a steady stream of devastating fire against rapidly infiltrating hostile troops to aid materially in annihilating several of the enemy and in breaking the abortive attack.

Harold Glenn Epperson

Suddenly a Japanese soldier, assumed to be dead, sprang up and hurled a powerful hand grenade into the emplacement. Determined to save his comrades, Private First Class Epperson unhesitatingly chose to sacrifice himself and, diving upon the deadly missile, absorbed the shattering violence of the exploding charge in his own body. Stout-hearted and indomitable in the face of certain death, Private First Class Epperson fearlessly yielded his own life that his able comrades might carry on the relentless battle against a ruthless enemy. His superb valor and unfaltering devotion to duty throughout reflect the highest credit upon himself and upon the United States Naval Service. He gallantly gave his life for his country.

John Peter Fardy

*Fardy, John Peter. Corporal, U.S. Marine Corps. *Born:* 8 August 1922, Chicago, IL. *Accredited to:* Illinois. *Gitation:* For conspicuous gallantry and intrepidity at the risk of his life above and beyond the call of duty as a Squad Leader, serving with Company C, First Battalion, First Marines, First Marine Division, in action against enemy Japanese forces on Okinawa Shima in the Ryukyu Islands, 7 May 1945. When his squad was suddenly assailed by extremely heavy small-arms fire from the front during a determined advance against strongly fortified, fiercely defended Japanese positions, Corporal Fardy temporarily deployed his men along a nearby drainage ditch. Shortly thereafter, an enemy grenade fell among the Marines in the ditch. Instantly throwing himself upon the deadly missile, Corporal Fardy absorbed the exploding blast in his own body, thereby protecting his comrades from certain and perhaps fatal injuries. Concerned solely for the welfare of his men, he willingly relinquished his own hope of survival that his fellow Marines might live to carry on the fight against a fanatic enemy. A stout-hearted leader and indomitable fighter, Corporal Fardy, by his prompt decision and resolute spirit of self-sacrifice in the face of certain death, had rendered valiant service, and his conduct throughout reflects the highest credit upon himself and the United States Naval Service. He gallantly gave his life for his country.

*Fleming, Richard E. Captain, U.S. Marine Corps Reserve. *Born:* 2 November 1917, St. Paul, MN. *Appointed from:* Minnesota. *Citation:* For extraordinary heroism and conspicuous intrepidity above and beyond the call of duty as Flight Officer, Marine Scout-Bombing Squadron 241, during action against enemy Japanese forces in the battle of Midway on 4 and 5 June 1942. When his Squadron Commander was shot down during the initial attack upon an enemy aircraft carrier, Captain Fleming led the remainder of the division with such fearless determination that he dived his own plane to the perilously low altitude of 400 feet before releasing his bomb. Although

Richard E. Fleming

his craft was riddled by 179 hits in the blistering hail of fire that burst upon him from Japanese fighter guns and antiaircraft batteries, he pulled out with only two minor wounds inflicted upon himself. On the night of 4 June, when the Squadron Commander lost his way and became separated from the others, Captain Fleming brought his own plane in for a safe landing at its base despite hazardous weather conditions and total darkness. The following day, after less than 4 hours' sleep, he led the second division of his squadron in a coordinated glide-bombing and dive-bombing assault upon a Japanese battleship. Undeterred by a fateful approach glide, during which his ship was struck and set afire, he grimly pressed home his attack to an altitude of 500 feet, released his bomb to score a near miss on the stern of his target, then crashed to the sea in flames. His dauntless perseverance and unyielding devotion to duty were in keeping with the highest traditions of the United States Naval Service.

Foss, Joseph Jacob. Captain, U.S. Marine Corps Marine Fighting Squadron 121, 1st Marine Aircraft Wing. *Place and date:* Over Guadalcanal, 9 October to 19 November 1942, January 1943. *Entered service at:* South Dakota. *Birth:* SD. *Citation:* For outstanding heroism and courage rid beyond the call of duty as executive officer of Marine Squadron 121, 1st Marine Aircraft Wing, at Guadalcanal. Engaging in almost daily combat with the enemy from 9 October to 19 November 1942, Captain Foss personally shot down 23 Japanese planes and damaged others so severely that their destruction was extremely probable. In addition, during this period, he successfully led a large number of

Joseph Jacob Foss

escort missions, skillfully covering reconnaissance, bombing, and photo graphic planes as well as surface craft. On 15 January 1943, he added three more enemy planes to his already brilliant successes for a record of aerial combat achievement unsurpassed in this war. Boldly searching out an approaching enemy force on 25 January,

Captain Foss led his eight F4F Marine planes and four Army P-38's into action and, undaunted by tremendously superior numbers, intercepted and struck with such force that four Japanese fighters were shot down and the bombers were turned back without releasing a single bomb. His remarkable flying skill, inspiring leadership, and indomitable fighting spirit were distinctive factors in the defense of strategic American positions on Guadalcanal. [*He retired a major in January 1947. He joined the South Dakota National Guad and retired a brigadier general.*]

*Foster, William Adelbert. Private First Class, U.S. Marine Corps Reserve. *Born:* 17 February 1915, Cleveland, OH. *Accredited to:* OH. *Citation:* For conspicuous gallantry and intrepidity at the risk of his life above and beyond the call of duty while serving as a Rifleman with the Third Battalion, First Marines, First Marine Division, in action against enemy Japanese forces on Okinawa Shima in the Ryukyu Chain, 2 May 1945. Dug in with another Marine on the point of the perimeter defense after waging a furious assault against a strongly fortified Japanese position, Private First Class Foster and his comrade engaged in a fierce hand-grenade duel with infiltrating enemy soldiers. Suddenly an enemy grenade landed beyond reach in the foxhole. Instantly diving on the deadly missile, Private First Class Foster absorbed the exploding charge in his own body, thereby protecting the other Marine from serious injury. Although mortally wounded as a result of his heroic action, he quickly rallied, handed his own remaining two grenades to his comrade and said, "Make them count." Stout-hearted and indomitable, he had unhesitatingly relinquished his own chance of survival that his fellow Marine might carry on the relentless fight against a fanatic enemy, and his dauntless determination, cool decision and valiant spirit of self-sacrifice in the face of certain death reflect the highest credit upon Private First Class Foster and upon the United States Naval Service. He gallantly gave his life in the service of his country.

William Adelbert Foster

Galer, Robert Edward. Major, U.S. Marine Corps, Marine Fighter Sqdn. 244. *Place:* Solomon Islands Area. *Entered service at:* Washington. *Birth:* Seattle, WA. *Citation:* For conspicuous heroism and courage above and beyond the call of duty as leader of a Marine fighter squadron in aerial combat with enemy Japanese forces in the Solomon Islands area. Leading his squadron repeatedly in daring and aggressive raids against Japanese aerial forces, vastly superior in numbers, Major Galer availed himself of every favorable attack opportunity, individually shooting down 11 enemy bomber and fighter aircraft over a period of 29 days. Though suffering the extreme physical strain attendant upon protracted fighter operations at an altitude above

25,000 feet, the squadron under his zealous and inspiring leadership, shot down a total of 27 Japanese planes. His superb airmanship, his outstanding skill and personal valor reflect great credit upon Major Galer's gallant fighting spirit and upon United States naval service. [*Other Navy awards: Distinguished Flying Cross, Legion of Merit, four Air Medals. He retired a brigadier general in July 1957.*]

*Gonsalves, Harold.** Private First Class, U.S. Marine Corps Reserve. *Born:* 28 January 1926, Alameda, CA. *Accredited to:* California. *Citation:* For conspicuous gallantry and intrepidity at the risk of his life above and beyond the call of duty while serving as Acting Scout Sergeant with the Fourth Battalion, Fifteenth Marines, Sixth Marine Division, during action against enemy Japanese forces on Okinawa Shima in the Ryukyu Chain, 15 April 1945. Undaunted by one powerfully organized opposition encountered on Motobu Peninsula during the fierce assault waged by his battalion against the Japanese stronghold at Mount Yaetake, Private First Class Gonsalves repeatedly braved the terrific enemy bombardment to aid his Forward Observation Team in directing well-placed artillery fire. When his commanding officer determined to move into the front lines in order to register a more effective bombardment in the enemy's defensive position, he unhesitatingly advanced uphill with the officer and another Marine despite a slashing barrage of enemy mortar and rifle fire. As they reached the front and a Japanese grenade fell close within the group, instantly Private First Class Gonsalves dived on the deadly missile, absorbing the exploding charge in his own body and thereby protecting the others from serious

Robert Edward Galer

Harold Gonsalves

ous and perhaps fatal wounds. Stout-hearted and indomitable, Private First Class Gonsalves readily yielded his own chances of survival that his fellow Marines might carry on the relentless battle against a fanatic enemy and his cool decision, prompt action and valiant spirit of self-sacrifice in the face of certain death reflect the highest credit upon himself and upon the United States Naval Service.

Gray, Ross Franklin. Sergeant, U.S. Marine Corps Reserve. *Born:* 1 August 1920, Marvel Valley, AL. *Accredited to:* Alabama. *Citation:* For conspicuous gallantry and intrepidity at the risk of his life above and beyond the call of duty as a Platoon Sergeant attached to Company A, First Battalion, Twenty-fifth Marines, Fourth Marine Division, in action against enemy Japanese forces on Iwo Jima, Volcano Islands, 21 February 1945. Shrewdly gaging the tactical situation when his platoon was held up by a sudden barrage of hostile grenades while advancing toward the high ground northeast of Airfield No. 1, Sergeant Gray promptly organized the withdrawal of his men from enemy grenade range, quickly moved forward alone to reconnoiter and discovered a heavily mined area extending along the front of a strong network of emplacements joined by covered trenches. Although assailed by furious gunfire, he cleared a path leading through the minefield to one of the fortifications, then returned to the platoon position and, informing his leader of the serious situation, volunteered to initiate an attack under cover of three fellow Marines. Alone and unarmed but carrying a huge satchel charge, he crept up on the Japanese emplacement, boldly hurled the short-fused explosive and sealed the entrance. Instantly taken under machine-gun fire from a second entrance to the same position, he unhesitatingly braved the increasingly vicious fusillades to crawl back for another charge, returned to his objective and blasted the second opening thereby demolishing the position. Repeatedly covering the ground between the savagely defended enemy fortifications and his platoon area, he systematically approached, attacked and withdrew under blanketing fire to destroy a total of six Japanese positions, more than 25 troops and a quantity of vital ordnance gear and ammunition. Stouthearted and indomitable, Sergeant Gray had singlehandedly overcome a strong enemy garrison and a completely disarmed a large minefield before finally rejoining his unit. By his great personal valor, daring tactics and tenacious perseverance in the face of extreme peril, he had contributed materially to the fulfillment of his company mission. His gallant conduct throughout enhanced and sustained the highest, traditions of the United States Naval Service. [*He was killed in action on 27 February 1945.*]

Ross Franklin Gray

*Gurke, Henry.** Private First Class. U.S. Marine Corps. *Born:* 6 November 1922, Neche, ND. *Accredited to:* North Dakota. *Citation:* For extraordinary heroism and courage above and beyond the call of duty while attached to the Third Marine Raider Battalion during action against enemy Japanese forces in the Solomon Islands area

Henry Gurke

on 9 November 1943. While his platoon was engaged in defense of a vital road block near Empress Augusta Bay on Bougainville Island. Private First Class Gurke, in company with another Marine, was delivering a fierce stream of fire against the main vanguard of the Japanese. Concluding from the increasing ferocity of grenade barrages that the enemy was determined to annihilate their small, two-man foxhole, he resorted to a bold and desperate measure for holding out despite the torrential hail of shells. When a Japanese grenade dropped squarely into the foxhole, Private Gurke, mindful that his companion manned an automatic weapon of superior power and therefore could provide more effective resistance, thrust him roughly aside and flung is own body over the missile to smother the explosion. With unswerving devotion to duty and superb valor Private Gurke sacrificed himself in order that his comrade might live to carry on the fight. He gallantly gave his life in the service of country.

*Halyburton, William David, Jr. Pharmacist's Mate Second Class, U.S. Navy. *Born:* 2 August 1924, Canton, NC. *Accredited to:* North Carolina. *Citation:* For conspicuous gallantry and intrepidity at the risk of his life above and beyond the call of duty while serving with a Marine Rifle Company in the Second Battalion, Fifth Marines, First Marine Division, during action against enemy Japanese forces on Okinawa Shima in the Ryukyu Chain, 19 May 1945. Undaunted by the deadly accuracy of Japanese counterfire as his unit pushed the attack through a strategically important draw, Halyburton unhesitatingly dashed across the draw and up the hill into an open, fire-swept field where the company advance squad was suddenly pinned down under a terrific concentration of mortar, machine-gun and sniper fire with resultant severe casualties. Moving steadily forward despite the enemy's merciless barrage, he reached the wounded Marine who lay farthest away and was rendering first aid when his patient was struck for the second time by a Japanese bullet. Instantly placing himself in the direct line of fire, he shielded the fallen fighter with his own body and staunchly continued his ministrations although constantly menaced by the slashing fury of shrapnel and bullets falling on all sides. Alert, determined and completely unselfish in his concern for the helpless Marine, he persevered in his efforts until he himself sustained mortal wounds and collapsed, heroically sacrificing himself that his comrade might live. By his outstanding valor and unwavering devotion to duty in the face of tremendous odds, Halyburton sustained and enhanced the highest traditions of the United States Naval Service. He gallantly gave his life in the service of his country.

Hansen, Dale Merlin. Private, U.S. Marine Corps. *Born:* 13 December 1922, Wisner, NE. *Accredited to:* Nebraska. *Citation:* For conspicuous gallantry and intrepidity at the risk of his life above beyond the call of duty while serving with Company E, Second Battalion, First Marines, First Marine Division, in action against Japanese forces on Okinawa Shima in the Ryukyu Chain, 7 May 1945. Cool and courageous in combat, Private Hansen unhesitatingly took the initiative during a critical stage of the action and, armed with a rocket launcher, crawled to an exposed position where he attacked and destroyed a strategically located hostile pillbox. With his weapon subsequently destroyed by enemy fire, he seized a rifle and continued his one-man assault. Reaching the crest of a ridge, he leaped across, opened fire on six Japanese and killed four before his rifle jammed. Attacked by the remaining two Japanese, he beat them off with the butt of his rifle and then climbed back to cover. Promptly returning with another weapon and supply of grenades, he fearlessly advanced, destroyed a strong mortar position and annihilated eight more of the enemy. In the forefront of battle throughout this bitterly waged engagement, Private Hansen, by his indomitable determination, bold tactics and complete disregard of all personal danger, contributed essentially to the

Dale Merlin Hansen

success of his company's mission and to the ultimate capture of this fiercely defended outpost of the Japanese Empire. His great personal valor in the face of extreme peril reflects the highest credit upon himself and the United States Naval Service. [*He was killed in action on 11 May 1945.*]

Robert Murray Hanson

Hanson, Robert Murray. First Lieutenant, U.S. Marine Corps Reserve. *Born:* 4 February 1920, Lucknow, India. *Accredited to:* Massachusetts. *Citation:* For conspicuous gallantry and intrepidity at the risk of his life and above and beyond the call of duty as Fighter Pilot attached to Marine Fighting Squadron 215 in action against enemy Japanese forces at Bougainville Island, 1 November 1943; and New Britain Island, 24 January 1944. Undeterred by fierce opposition, and fearless in the face of overwhelming odds, First Lieutenant Hanson fought the Japanese boldly and with daring aggressiveness. On 1 November, while flying cover for our landing operations at Empress Augusta Bay, he dauntlessly attacked six enemy torpedo bombers, forcing them to jettison their bombs and destroying one Japanese plane during the action. Cut off from his division while deep in enemy territory during a high cover flight over Simpson Harbor Oil 24 January, First Lieutenant Hanson waged a lone and gallant battle against hostile interceptors as they were orbiting to attack our bombers and, striking with devastating fury, brought down four Zeroes and probably a fifth. Handling his plane superbly in both pursuit and attack measures, lie was a master of individual air combat, accounting for a total of 25 Japanese aircraft in this theater of war. His great personal valor and invincible fighting spirit were in keeping with the highest traditions of the United States Naval Service. [*Other Navy awards: Navy Cross, Air Medal. He was killed in action on 3 February 1944.*]

Harrell, William George. Sergeant, U.S. Marine Corps, 1st Battalion, 28th Marines, 5th Marine Division. *Place and date:* Iwo Jima, Volcano Islands, 3 March 1945. *Entered service at:* Texas. *Birth:* Rio Grande City, TX. *Citation:* For conspicuous gallantry and intrepidity at the risk of his life above and beyond the call of duty as leader of an assault group attached to the 1st Battalion, 28th Marines, 5th Marine Division during hand-to-hand combat with enemy Japanese at Iwo Jima, Volcano Islands, on 3 March 1945. Standing watch alternately with another Marine in a terrain studded with caves and ravines, Sergeant Harrell was holding a position in a perimeter defense around the company command post when Japanese troops infiltrated our lines in the early hours of dawn. Awakened by a sudden attack, he quickly opened fire with his carbine and killed two of the

William George Harrell

enemy as they emerged from a ravine in the light of a star shell burst. Unmindful of his danger as hostile grenades fell closer, he waged a fierce lone battle until an exploding missile tore off his left hand and fractured his thigh. He was vainly attempting to reload the carbine when his companion returned from the command post with another weapon. Wounded again by a Japanese who rushed the foxhole wielding a saber in the darkness, Sergeant Harrell succeeded in drawing his pistol and killing his opponent and then ordered his wounded companion to a place of safety. Exhausted by profuse bleeding but still unbeaten, he fearlessly met the challenge of two more enemy troops who charged his position and placed a grenade near his head. Killing one man with his pistol, he grasped the sputtering grenade with his good right hand and, pushing it painfully toward the crouching soldier, saw his remaining assailant destroyed but his own hand severed in the explosion. At dawn Sergeant Harrell,was evacuated from a position hedged by the bodies of 12 dead Japanese, at least 5 of whom he had personally destroyed in his self-sacrificing defense of the command post. His grim fortitude, exceptional valor, and indomitable fighting spirit, against almost insurmountable odds, reflect the highest credit upon himself and enhance the finest traditions of the United States naval service.

*Hauge, Louis James, Jr.** Corporal, U.S. Marine Corps Reserve. *Born:* 12 December 1924, Ada, MN. *Accredited to:* Minnesota. *Citation:* For conspicuous gallantry and intrepidity at the risk of ha life above and beyond the call of duty as Leader of a Machine-gun Squad serving with Company C, First Battalion, First Marines, First Marine Division, in action against enemy Japanese Forces on Okinawa Shima in the Ryukyu Chain on 14 May 1945. Alert and aggressive during a determined assault against a strongly fortified Japanese hill position, Corporal Hauge boldly took the initiative when his company's left flank was pinned down under a heavy machine-gun and mortar barrage with resultant severe casualties and, quickly locating the two machine guns which were delivering the uninterrupted stream of enfilade fire, ordered his squad to maintain a covering barrage as he rushed across an exposed area toward the furiously blazing enemy weapons. Although painfully wounded as he charged the first machine gun, he launched a vigorous single-handed grenade attack, destroyed the entire hostile gun

Louis James Hauge, Jr.

position and moved relentlessly onward toward the other emplacement despite his wounds and the increasingly heavy Japanese fire. Undaunted by the savage opposition, he again hurled his deadly grenades with unerring aim and succeeded in demolishing the second enemy gun before he fell under the slashing fury of Japanese sniper fire. By his ready grasp of the critical situation and his heroic one-man assault tactics, Corporal Hauge had eliminated two strategically placed enemy weapons, thereby releasing the besieged troops from an overwhelming volume of hostile fire and enabling his company to advance. His indomitable fighting spirit and decisive valor in the face of almost certain death reflect the highest credit upon Corporal Hauge and the United States naval Service. He gallantly gave his life in the service of his country.

*Hawkins, William Dean.** First Lieutenant, U.S. Marine Corps. *Born:* 19 April 1914, Fort Scott, KS. *Appointed from:* Texas. *Citation:* For valorous and gallant conduct above and beyond the call of duty as Commanding Officer of a Scout Sniper Platoon attached to the Assault Regiment in action against Japanese-held Tarawa in the Gilbert Island, 20 and 21 November 1943. The first to disembark from the jeep lighter, First Lieutenant Hawkins unhesitatingly moved forward under heavy enemy fire at the end of the Betio Pier, neutralizing emplacements in coverage of troops assaulting the main beach positions. Fearlessly leading his men on to join the forces fighting desperately to gain a beachhead, he repeatedly risked his life throughout the day and night to direct and lead attacks on pillboxes and installations with grenades and demolitions. At dawn on the following day, First Lieutenant Hawkins resumed the dangerous mission of clearing the limited beachhead of Japanese resistance, personally initiating an assault on a hostile position fortified by five enemy machine guns, and, crawling forward in the face of withering fire, boldly fired point-blank into the loopholes and completed the destruction with grenades. Refusing to withdraw after being seriously wounded in the chest during this skirmish, First Lieutenant Hawkins steadfastly carried the fight to the enemy, destroying three more pillboxes before he was caught in a burst of Japanese shellfire and mortally

William Dean Hawkins

wounded. His relentless fighting spirit in the face of formidable opposition and his exceptionally daring tactics served as an inspiration to his comrades during the most crucial phase of the battle and reflect the highest credit upon the United States Naval Service. He gallantly gave his life for his country.

Jackson, Arthur J. Private First Class, U.S. Marine Corps, 3d Battalion, 7th Marines, 1st Marine Division. *Place and date:* Island of Peleliu in the Palau group, 18 September 1944. *Entered Service at:* Oregon. *Birth:* Cleveland, OH. *Citation:* For conspicuous gallantry and intrepidity at the risk of his life above and beyond the call of duty while serving with the 3d Battalion, 7th Marines, 1st Marine Division, in action against enemy Japanese forces on the Island of Peleliu in the Palau group, 18 September 1944. Boldly taking the initiative when his platoon's left flank advance was held up by the fire of Japanese troops concealed in strongly fortified positions, Private First Class Jackson unhesitatingly proceeded forward of our lines and, courageously defying the heavy barrages, charged a large pillbox housing approximately 35 enemy soldiers. Pouring his automatic fire in to the opening of the fixed

Arthur J. Jackson

installation to trap the occupying troops, he hurled white phosphorus grenades and explosive charges brought up by a fellow marine, demolishing the pillbox and killing all of the enemy. Advancing alone under the continuous fire from other hostile emplacements, he employed similar means to smash two smaller positions in the immediate vicinity. Determined to crush the entire pocket of resistance although harassed on all sides by the shattering blasts of Japanese weapons and covered only by small rifle parties, he stormed one gun position after another, dealing death and destruction to the savagely fighting enemy in his inexorable drive against the remaining defenses, and succeeded in wiping out a total of 12 pillboxes and 50 Japanese soldiers. Stout-hearted and indomitable despite the terrific odds, PFC Jackson resolutely maintained control of the platoon's left flank movement throughout his valiant one-man assault and, by his cool decision and relentless fighting spirit during a critical situation, contributed essentially to the complete annihilation of the enemy in the southern sector of the island. His gallant initiative and heroic conduct in the face of extreme peril reflect the highest credit upon PFC Jackson and the United States naval service.

Jacobson, Douglas Thomas. Private First Class, U.S. Marine Corps Reserve, 3d Battalion, 23d Marines, 4th Marine Division. *Place and date:* Iwo Jima, Volcano Islands, 26 February 1945. *Entered service at:* New York. *Birth:* Rochester, NY. *Citation:* For conspicuous gallantry and intrepidity at the risk of his life above and beyond the call of duty while serving with the 3d Battalion, 23d Marines, 4th Marine Division, in combat against enemy Japanese forces during the seizure of Iwo Jima in the Volcano Islands, 26 February 1945. Promptly destroying a stubborn 20-mm. antiaircraft gun and its crew after assuming the duties of a bazooka man who had been killed. Private First Class Jacobson waged a relentless battle as his unit fought desperately toward the summit of Hill 382 in an effort to penetrate the heart of .Japanese cross-island defense. Employing his weapon with ready accuracy when his platoon was

Douglas Thomas Jacobson

halted by overwhelming enemy fire on 26 February, he first destroyed two hostile machine gun positions, then attacked a large blockhouse, completely neutralizing the fortification before dispatching the five-man crew of a second pillbox and exploding the installation with a terrific demolitions blast. Moving steadily forward. he wiped out an earth-covered rifle emplacement, and, confronted by a cluster of similar emplacements which constituted the perimeter of enemy defenses in his assigned sector, fearlessly advanced, quickly reduced all 6 positions to a shambles, killed 10 of the enemy, and enabled our forces to occupy the strong point. Determined to widen the breach thus forced, he volunteered his services to an adjacent assault company, neutralized a pillbox holding up its advance, opened fire on a Japanese tank pouring a steady stream of bullets on one of our supporting tanks, and smashed the enemy tank's gun turret in a brief but furious action culminating in a singlehanded assault against still another blockhouse and the subsequent neutralization of its firepower. By his dauntless skill and valor, PFC Jacobson destroyed a total of 16 enemy positions and annihilated approximately 75 Japanese, thereby contributing essentially to the success of his division's operations against this fanatically defended outpost of the Japanese Empire. His gallant conduct in the face of tremendous odds enhanced and sustained the highest traditions of the United States naval service. [*He retired a major in 1967.*]

Joseph Rodolph Julian

***Julian, Joseph Rodolph.** Platoon Sergeant, U.S. Marine Corps Reserve. *Born:* 3 April 1918, Sturbridge, MA. *Accredited to:* Massachusetts. *Citation:* For conspicuous gallantry and intrepidity at the risk of his life above and beyond the call of duty as a Platoon Sergeant serving with the First Battalion, Twenty-seventh Marines, Fifth Marine Division, in action against enemy Japanese forces during the seizure of Iwo Jima in the Volcano Islands, 9 March 1945. Determined to force a break-through when Japanese troops occupying trenches and fortified positions on the left front laid down a terrific machine-gun and mortar barrage in a desperate effort to halt his company's advance, Platoon Sergeant Julian quickly established his platoon's guns in strategic supporting positions, and then, acting on his own initiative, fearlessly moved forward to execute a one-man assault on the nearest pillbox. Advancing alone, he hurled deadly demolitions and white phosphorus grenades into the emplacement, killing two of the enemy and driving the remaining five out into the adjoining trench system. Seizing a discarded rifle, he jumped into the trench and dispatched the five before they could make an escape. Intent on wiping out all resistance, he obtained more explosives and, accompanied by another Marine, again charged the hostile fortifications and knocked out two more cave positions. Immediately thereafter, he launched a bazooka attack unassisted, firing four rounds into the one remaining pillbox and completely destroying it before he fell, mortally wounded by a vicious burst of enemy fire. Stout-hearted and indomitable, Platoon Sergeant Julian consistently disregarded all personal danger and, by his bold decision, daring tactics, and relentless fighting spirit during a critical phase of time battle, contributed materially to the continued advance of his company and to the success of his division's operations in the sustained drive toward the conquest of this fiercely defended outpost of the Japanese Empire. His outstanding valor and unfaltering spirit of self-sacrifice throughout the bitter conflict sustained and enhanced the highest traditions of the United States Naval Service. He gallantly gave his life for his country.

Elbert Luther Kinser

*Kinser, Elbert Luther.** Sergeant, U.S. Marine Corps Reserve. *Born:* 21 October 1922, Greeneville, TN. *Accredited to:* Tennessee. *Citation:* For conspicuous gallantry and intrepidity at the risk of his life above and beyond the call of duty while acting as Leader of a Rifle Platoon, serving with Company I, Third Battalion, First Marines, First Marine Division, in action against Japanese forces on Okinawa Shima in the Ryukyu Chain, 4 May 1945. Taken under sudden, close attack by hostile troops entrenched on the reverse slope while moving up a strategic ridge along which his platoon was holding newly won positions, Sergeant Kinser engaged the enemy in a fierce hand-grenade battle. Quick to act when a Japanese grenade landed in the immediate vicinity, Sergeant Kinser unhesitatingly threw himself on the deadly missile absorbing the full charge of the shattering explosion in his own body and thereby protecting his men from serious injury and possible death. Stout-hearted and indomitable, he had yielded his own chance of survival that his comrades might live to carry on the relentless battle against a fanatic enemy. His courage, cool decision and valiant spirit of self-sacrifice in the face of certain death sustained and enhanced the highest traditions of the United States Naval Service. He gallantly gave his life for his country.

*Kraus, Richard Edward.** Private First Class, U.S. Marine Corps Reserve. *Born:* 24 November 1925, Chicago, IL. *Accredited to:* Minnesota. *Citation:* For conspicuous gallantry and intrepidity at the risk of his life above and beyond the call of duty while serving with the Eighth Amphibious Tractor Battalion, Fleet Marine Force, in action against enemy Japanese forces on Peleliu, Palau Islands, on 5 October 1944. Unhesitatingly volunteering for the extremely hazardous mission of evacuating a wounded comrade from the front lines, Private First Class Kraus and three companions courageously made their way forward and successfully penetrated the lines for some distance before the enemy opened with an intense, devastating barrage of hand grenades which forced the stretcher party to take cover and subsequently abandon the mission. While returning to the rear, they observed two men approaching who appeared to be Marines and immediately demanded the password. When, instead of answering, one of the two Japanese threw a hand grenade into the midst of the group, Private First Class Kraus heroically flung himself upon the grenade and, covering it with his body, absorbed the full impact of the explosion and was instantly killed. By his prompt action and great personal valor in the face of almost certain death, he saved the lives of his three companions, and his loyal spirit of self-sacrifice reflects the highest credit upon himself and the United States Naval Service. He gallantly gave his life for his comrades.

Richard Edward Kraus

*LaBelle, James Dennis. Private First Class, U.S. Marine Corps Reserve. *Born:* 22 November 1925, Columbia Heights, MN. *Accredited to:* Minnesota. *Citation:* For conspicuous gallantry and intrepidity at the risk of his life above and beyond the call of duty while attached to the Twenty-seventh Marines, Fifth Marine Division, in action against enemy Japanese forces during the seizure of Iwo Jima in the Volcano Islands, 8 March 1945. Filling a gap in the front lines during a critical phase of the battle, Private First Class LaBelle had dug into a foxhole with two other Marines and, grimly aware of the enemy's persistent attempts to blast a way through our lines with hand grenades, applied himself with steady concentration to maintaining a sharply vigilant watch during the hazardous night hours. Suddenly a hostile grenade landed beyond reach in his foxhole. Quickly estimating the situation, he determined to save the others if possible, shouted a warning, and instantly dived on the deadly missile, absorbing. the exploding charge in his own body and thereby protecting his com-

James Dennis LaBelle

rades from serious injury. Stouthearted and indomitable, he had unhesitatingly relinquished his own chance of survival that his fellow Marines might carry on the relentless fight against a fanatic enemy. His dauntless courage, cool decision and valiant spirit of self-sacrifice in the face of certain death reflect the highest credit upon Private First Class LaBelle and upon the United States Naval Service. He gallantly gave his life in the service of his country.

Leims, John Harold. Second Lieutenant, U.S. Marine Corps Reserve, Company B, 1st Battalion, 9th Marines, 3d Marine Division. *Place and date:* Iwo Jima, Volcano Islands, 7 March 1945. *Entered service at:* Illinois. *Birth:* Chicago, IL. *Citation:* For conspicuous gallantry and intrepidity at the risk of his life above and beyond the call of duty as commanding officer of Company B, 1st Battalion, 9th Marines, 3d Marine Division, in action against enemy Japanese forces on Iwo Jima in the Volcano Islands, 7 March 1945. Launching a surprise attack against the rock-imbedded fortifications of a dominating Japanese hill position, Second Lieutenant Leims spurred his company forward with indomitable determination and, skillfully directing his assault platoons against the cave-emplaced enemy troops and heavily fortified pillboxes, succeeded in capturing the objective in the late afternoon. When it became apparent that his assault platoons were cut off in this newly won position,

John Harold Leims

approximately 400 yards forward of adjacent units and lacked all communication with the command post, he personally advanced and laid telephone lines across the isolating expanse of open, fire-swept terrain. Ordered to withdraw his command after he had joined his forward platoons he immediately complied, adroitly effecting the withdrawal of his troops without incident. Upon arriving at the rear, he was informed that several casualties had been left at the abandoned ridge position beyond the front lines. Although suffering acutely from the strain and exhaustion of battle, he instantly went forward despite darkness and the slashing fury of hostile machine-gun fire, located and carried to safety one seriously wounded Marine and then, running the gauntlet of enemy fire for the third time that night, again made his tortuous way into the bullet-riddled deathtrap and rescued another of his wounded men. A dauntless leader, concerned at all times for the welfare of his men, Second Lieutenant Leims soundly maintained the coordinated strength of his battle-wearied company under extremely difficult conditions and, by his bold tactics, sustained aggressiveness, and heroic disregard of all personal danger, contributed essentially to the success of his division's operations against this vital Japanese base. His valiant conduct in the face of fanatic opposition sustains and enhances the highest traditions of the United States naval service.

***Lester, Fred Faulkner.** Hospital Apprentice First Class, U.S. Navy. *Born:* 29 April 1926, Downers Grove, IL. *Accredited to:* Illinois. *Citation:* For conspicuous gallantry and intrepidity at the risk of his life above and beyond the call of duty while serving as a Medical Corpsman with an Assault Rifle Platoon attached to the First Battalion, Twenty-second Marines, Sixth Marine Division, during action against enemy Japanese forces on Okinawa Shima in the Ryukyu Chain, 8 June 1945. Quick to spot a wounded Marine lying in an open field beyond the front lines following the relentless assault against a strategic Japanese hill position, Lester unhesitatingly crawled toward the casualty under a concentrated barrage from hostile machine guns, rifles, and grenades. Torn by enemy rifle bullets as he inched forward, he stoically disregarded the mounting fury of Japanese fire and his own pain to pull the wounded man toward a covered position. Struck by enemy fire a second time before he reached cover, he exerted tremendous effort and succeeded in pulling his comrade to safety where, too seriously wounded himself to administer aid, he instructed two of his squad in proper medical treatment of the rescued Marine. Realizing that his own wounds were fatal, he staunchly refused medical attention for himself and, gathering his fast-waning strength with calm determination coolly and expertly directed his men in the treatment of two other wounded Marines, succumbing shortly thereafter. Completely selfless in his concern for the welfare of his fighting comrades, Lester, by his indomitable spirit outstanding valor, and competent direction of others, had saved the life of one who otherwise must have perished and had contributed to the safety of countless others. Lester's fortitude in the face of certain death sustains and enhances the highest traditions of the United States naval service. He gallantly gave his life for his country.

Lucas, Jacklyn Harrell. Private First Class, U.S. Marine Corps Reserve, 1st Battalion, 26th Marines, 5th Marine Division. *Place and date:* Iwo Jima, Volcano Islands, 20 February 1945. *Entered service at:* North Carolina. *Birth:* Plymouth, NC. *Citation:* For conspicuous gallantry and intrepidity at the risk of his life above and beyond the call of duty while serving with the 1st Battalion, 26th Marines, 5th Marine Division, during action against enemy Japanese forces on Iwo Jima, Volcano Islands, 20 February 1945. While creeping through a treacherous, twisting ravine which ran in close proximity to a fluid and uncertain front line on D-plus-1 day, Private First Class Lucas

Jacklyn Harrell Lucas

and three other men were suddenly ambushed by a hostile patrol which savagely attacked with rifle fire and grenades. Quick to act when the lives of the small group were endangered by two grenades which landed directly in front of them, Private First Class Lucas unhesitatingly hurled himself over his comrades upon one grenade and pulled the other under him, absorbing the whole blasting forces of the explosions in his own body in order to shield his companions from the concussion and murderous flying fragments. By his inspiring action and valiant spirit of self-sacrifice, he not only protected his comrades from certain injury or possible death but also enabled them to rout the Japanese patrol and continue the advance. His exceptionally courageous initiative and loyalty reflect the highest credit upon Private First Class Lucas and the United States naval service.

Jack Lummus

*Lummus, Jack. First Lieutenant, U.S. Marine Corps Reserves. *Born:* 22 October 1915, Ennie, TX. *Appointed from:* Texas. *Citation:* For conspicuous gallantry and intrepidity at the risk of his life above and beyond the call of duty as Leader of a Rifle Platoon attached to the Second Battalion, Twenty-seventh Marines, Fifth Marine Division, in action against enemy Japanese forces on Iwo Jima in the Volcano Islands, 8 March 1945. Resuming his assault tactics with bold decision after fighting without respite for two days and nights, First Lieutenant Lummus slowly advanced his platoon against an enemy deeply entrenched in a network of mutually supporting positions. Suddenly halted by a terrific concentration of hostile fire, he unhesitatingly moved forward of his front lines in an effort to neutralize the Japanese position. Although knocked to the ground when an enemy grenade exploded close by, he immediately recovered himself and, again moving forward despite the intensified barrage, quickly located, attacked, and destroyed the occupied emplacement. Instantly taken under fire by the garrison of a supporting pillbox and further assailed by the slashing fury of hostile rifle fire, be fell under the impact of a second enemy grenade but, courageously disregarding painful shoulder wounds, staunchly continued his heroic one-man assault and charged the second pillbox, annihilating all the occupants. Subsequently returning to his platoon position, he fearlessly traversed his lines under fire, encouraging his men to advance and directing the fire of supporting tanks against other stubbornly holding Japanese emplacements. Held up again by a devastating barrage, he again moved into the open, rushed a third heavily fortified installation and killed the defending troops. Determined to crush all resistance, he led his men indomitably, personally attacking foxholes and spider traps with his carbine and systematically reducing the fanatic opposition, until, stepping on a land mine, he sustained fatal wounds. By his outstanding valor, skilled tactics, and tenacious perseverance in the face of overwhelming odds, First Lieutenant Lummus had inspired his stouthearted Marines to continue the relentless drive northward, thereby contributing materially to the success of his regimental mission. His dauntless leadership and unwavering devotion to duty throughout sustain and enhance the highest traditions of the United States Naval Service. He gallantly gave his life in the service of his country.

*Martin, Harry Linn. First Lieutenant, U.S. Marine Corps Reserve. *Born:* 4 January 1911, Bucyrus, OH. *Appointed from:* OH. *Citation:* For conspicuous gallantry and intrepidity at the risk of his life above and beyond the call of duty as Platoon Leader attached to Company C, Fifth Pioneer Battalion, Fifth Marine Division, in action against enemy Japanese forces on Iwo Jima, Volcano Islands, 26 March 1945. With his sector of the Fifth Pioneer Battalion bivouac area penetrated by a concentrated enemy attack launched a few minutes before dawn, First Lieutenant Martin instantly organized a firing line with the Marines nearest his foxhole and succeeded in checking momentarily the headlong rush of the Japanese. Determined to rescue several of his men trapped in positions overrun by the enemy, he defied intense hostile fire to work his way through the Japanese to the surrounded Marines. Although sustaining two severe wounds, he blasted the Japanese who attempted to intercept him, located his beleaguered men and directed them to their own lines. When four of the infiltrating enemy took possession of an abandoned machine-gun pit and subjected his sector to a barrage of hand grenades, First Lieutenant Martin, alone and armed only with a pistol, boldly charged the hostile position and killed all of its occupants. Realizing that his few remaining comrades could not repulse another organized attack, he called to his men to follow and then charged into the midst of the strong enemy force, firing his weapon and scattering them until he fell, mortally wounded by a grenade. By his outstanding valor, indomitable fighting spirit and tenacious determination in the face of overwhelming odds, First Lieutenant Martin permanently disrupted a coordinated Japanese attack and prevented a greater loss of life in his own and adjacent platoons. His inspiring leadership and unswerving devotion to duty reflect the highest credit upon

Harry Linn Martin

himself and the United States Naval Service. He gallantly gave his life in the service of his country.

Leonard Foster Mason

***Mason, Leonard Foster.** Private First Class, U.S. Marine Corps. *Born:* 2 February 1920, Middleborough, KY. *Accredited to:* Ohio. *Citation:* For conspicuous gallantry and intrepidity at the risk of his life above aud beyond the call of duty as an Automatic Rifleman serving with the Second Battalion, Third Marines, Third Marine Division, in action against enemy Japanese forces on the Asan-Adelup Beachhead, Guam, Marianas Islands on 22 July 1944. Suddenly taken under fire by two enemy machine guns not more than 15 yards away while clearing out hostile positions holding up the advance of his platoon through a narrow gully, Private First Class Mason, alone and entirely on his own initiative, climbed out of the gully and moved parallel to it toward the rear of the enemy position. Although fired upon immediately by hostile riflemen from a higher position and wounded repeatedly in the arm and shoulder, Private First Class Mason grimly pressed forward and had just reached his objective when hit again by a burst of enemy machine-gun fire, causing a critical wound to which he later succumbed. With valiant disregard for his own peril, he persevered, clearing out the hostile position, killing five Japanese, wounding another and then rejoining his platoon to report the results of his action before consenting to be evacuated. His exceptionally heroic act in the face of almost certain death enabled his platoon to accomplish its mission and reflects the highest credit upon Private First Class Mason and the United States Naval Service. He gallantly gave his life for his country.

***McCard, Robert Howard.** Gunnery Sergeant, U.S. Marine Corps. *Born:* 25 November 1918, Syracuse, NY. *Accredited to:* New York. *Citation:* For conspicuous gallantry and intrepidity at the risk of his life above and

Robert Howard McCard

beyond the call of duty while serving as Platoon Sergeant of Company A, Fourth Tank Battalion, Fourth Marine Division, during the battle for enemy Japanese-held Saipan, Marianas Islands, on 16 June 1944. Cut off from the other units of his platoon when his tank was put out of action by a battery of enemy 77-mm. guns, Gunnery Sergeant McCard carried on resolutely, bringing all the tank's weapons to bear on the enemy, until the severity of hostile fire caused him to order his crew out of the escape hatch while he courageously exposed himself to enemy guns by hurling hand grenades, in order to cover the evacuation of his men. Seriously wounded during this action and with his supply of grenades exhausted, Gunnery Sergeant McCard then dismantled one of the tank's machine guns and faced the Japanese for the second time to deliver vigorous fire into their positions, destroying 16 of the enemy but sacrificing himself to insure the safety of his crew. His valiant fighting spirit and supreme loyalty in the face of almost certain death reflect the highest credit upon Gunnery Sergeant McCard and the United States Naval Service. He gallantly gave his life for his country.

McCarthy, Joseph Jeremiah. Captain, U.S. Marine Corps Reserve, 2d Battalion, 24th Marines, 4th Marine Division. *Place and date:* Iwo Jima, Volcano Islands, 21 February 1945. *Entered service at:* Illinois. *Birth:* Chicago, IL. *Citation:* For conspicuous gallantry and intrepidity at the risk of his life above and beyond the call of duty as commanding officer of a rifle company attached to the 2d Battalion, 24th Marines, 4th Marine Division, in action against enemy Japanese forces during the seizure of Iwo Jima, Volcano Islands, on 21 February 1945. Determined to break through the enemy's cross-island defenses, Captain McCarthy acted on his own initiative when his company advance was held up by uninterrupted Japanese rifle, machine gun, and high-velocity 47mm. fire during the approach to Motoyama Airfield No. 2. Quickly organizing a demolitions and flamethrower team to

Joseph Jeremiah McCarthy

accompany his picked rifle squad, he fearlessly led the way across 75 yards of fire-swept ground, charged a heavily fortified pillbox on the ridge of the front and, personally hurling hand grenades into the emplacement as he directed the combined operations of his small assault group, completely destroyed the hostile installation. Spotting two Japanese soldiers attempting an escape from the shattered pillbox, he boldly stood upright in full view of the enemy and dispatched both troops before advancing to a second emplacement under greatly intensified fire and then blasted the strong fortifications with a well-planned demolitions attack. Subsequently entering the ruins, he found a Japanese taking aim at one of our men and, with alert presence of mind, jumped the enemy, disarmed and shot him with his own weapon. Then, intent on smashing through the narrow breach, he rallied the remainder of his company and pressed a full attack with furious aggressiveness until he had neutralized all resistance and captured the ridge. An inspiring leader and indomitable fighter, Captain McCarthy consistently disregarded all personal danger during the fierce conflict and, by his brilliant professional skill, daring tactics, and tenacious perseverance in the face of overwhelming odds, contributed materially to the success of his division's operations against this savagely defended outpost of the Japanese Empire. His cool decision and outstanding valor reflect the highest credit upon Captain McCarthy and enhance the finest traditions of the United States naval service. [*He retired a lieutenant colonel.*]

McTureous, Robert Miller, Jr. Private, U.S. Marine Corps. *Born:* 26 March 1924, Altoona, FL. *Accredited to:* Florida. *Citation:* For conspicuous gallantry and intrepidity at the risk of his life above and beyond the call of duty, while serving with the Third Battalion, Twenty-ninth Marines, Sixth Marine Division, during action against enemy Japanese forces on Okinawa in the Ryukyu Chain, 7 June 1945. Alert and ready for any hostile counteraction following his company's seizure of an important hill objective, Private McTureous was quick to observe the plight of company stretcher bearers who were suddenly assailed by slashing machine-gun fire as they attempted to evacuate wounded at the rear of the newly won position. Determined to prevent further casualties, he quickly filled his jacket with hand grenades and charged the enemy occupied caves from which the concentrated barrage was emanating. Coolly disregarding all personal danger as he waged his furi-

Robert Miller McTureous, Jr.

ous one-man assault, he smashed grenades into the cave entrances, thereby diverting the heaviest fire from the stretcher bearers to his own person and, resolutely returning to his own lines under a blanketing hail of rifle and machine-gun fire to replenish his supply of grenades, dauntlessly continued his systematic reduction of Japanese strength until he himself sustained serious wounds after silencing a large number of the hostile guns. Aware of his own critical condition and unwilling to further endanger the lives of his comrades, he stoically crawled a distance of 200 yards to a sheltered position within friendly lines before calling for aid. By his fearless initiative and bold tactics, Private McTureous had succeeded in neutralizing the enemy fire, killing six Japanese troops and effectively disorganizing the remainder of the savagely defending garrison. His outstanding valor and heroic spirit of self-sacrifice during a critical stage of operations reflect the highest credit upon himself and the United States Naval Service.

***Munro, Douglas Albert.** *Rank and organization:* Signalman first class, U.S. Coast Guard. *Born:* 11 October 1919, Vancouver, British Columbia. *Accredited to:* Washington. *Citation:* For extraordinary heroism and conspicuous gallantry in action above and beyond the call of duty as Petty Officer in Charge of a group of 24 Higgins boats, engaged in the evacuation of a battalion of Marines trapped by enemy Japanese forces at Point Cruz, Guadalcanal, on 27 September 1942. After making preliminary plans for the evacuation of nearly 500 beleaguered Marines, Munro, under constant strafing by enemy machine guns on the island, and at great risk of his life, daringly led five of his small craft toward the shore. As he closed the beach, he signalled the others to land, and then in order to draw the enemy's fire and protect the heavily loaded boats he valiantly placed his craft with its two small guns as a shield between the beachhead and the Japanese. When the perilous task of evacuation was nearly completed, Munro was instantly killed by enemy fire, but his crew, two of whom were wounded carried on until the last boat had loaded and cleared the beach. By his outstanding leadership, expert planning, and dauntless devotion to duty, he and his courageous comrades undoubtedly saved the lives of many who otherwise would have perished. He gallantly gave his life for his country.

***New, John Dury.** Private First Class, U.S. Marine Corps. *Born:* 12 August 1924, Mobile, AL. *Accredited to:* Alabama. *Citation:* For conspicuous gallantry and intrepidity at the risk of his life above and beyond the call of duty while serving with the Second Battalion, Seventh Marines, First Marine Division, in action against enemy Japanese forces on Peleliu Island, Palau Group, 25 September 1944. When a Japanese soldier emerged from a cave in a cliff directly below an observation post and suddenly hurled a grenade into the position from which two of our men were directing mortar tire against enemy emplacements, Private First Class New instantly perceived the dire peril to the other Marines and, with utter disregard for his own safety, unhesitatingly flung himself upon the grenade and absorbed the full impact of the explosion, thus saving the lives of the two observers.

John Dury New

Private First Class New's great personal valor and selfless conduct in the face of almost certain death reflect the highest credit upon himself and the United States Naval Service. He gallantly gave his life for his country.

Owens, Robert Allen. Sergeant, U.S. Marine Corps. *Born:* 13 September 1920, Greenville, SC. *Accredited to:* South Carolina. *Citation:* For conspicuous gallantry and intrepidity at the risk of his life above and beyond the call of duty while serving with a [*3d*] Marine Division, in action against enemy Japanese forces during extremely hazardous landing operations at Cape Torokina, Bougainville, Solomon Islands, on 1 November 1943. Forced to pass within disastrous range of a strongly protected, well-camouflaged Japanese 75-mm. regimental gun strategically located on the beach, our landing units were suffering heavy losses in casualties and boats while attempting to approach the beach, and the success of the operations was seriously threatened. Observing the ineffectiveness of Marine rifle and grenade attacks against the incessant, devastating fire of the enemy weapon and aware of the urgent need for prompt Sergeant Owens unhesitatingly determined to charge the gun bunker from the front and, calling on four of his comrade to assist him, carefully placed them to cover the fire of the two adjacent hostile bunkers. Choosing a moment that

Robert Allen Owens

provided a fair opportunity for passing these bunkers, he immediately charged into the mouth of the steadily firing cannon and entered the emplacement through the fire port driving the gun crew out of the rear door and insuring their destruction before he himself was wounded. Indomitable and aggressive In the face of almost certain death, Sergeant Owens silenced a powerful gun which was of inestimable value to the Japanese defense and, by his brilliant initiative and heroic spirit of self-sacrifice, contributed immeasurably to the success of the vital landing operations. His valiant conduct throughout reflects the highest credit upon himself and the United States Naval Service. [*Other Navy award: Navy Cross. He served with the 1st Bn., 3d Marines and was killed in action on 1 November 1943. A destroyer was named for him.*]

*Ozbourn, Joseph William. Private, U.S. Marine Corps. *Born:* 24 October 1919, Herrin, IL. *Accredited to:* Illinois. *Citation:* For conspicuous gallantry and intrepidity at the risk (his life above and beyond the call of duty as a Browning Automatic Rifleman serving with the First Battalion, Twenty-third Marines, Fourth Marine Division, during the battle for enemy Japanese-held Tinian Island, Marianas Islands, 30 July 1944. As a member of a platoon assigned the mission of clearing the remaining Japanese troops from dugouts and pillboxes along a tree line, Private Ozbourn, flanked by two men on either side, was moving forward to throw an armed hand grenade into a dugout when terrific blast from the entrance severely wounded the

Joseph William Ozbourn

Mitchell Paige

four men and himself. Unable to throw the grenade into the dugout and with no place to hurl it without endangering the other men, Private Ozbourn unhesitatingly grasped it close to his body and fell upon it, sacrificing his own life to absorb the full impact of the explosion, but saving his comrades. His great personal valor and unwavering loyalty reflect the highest credit upon Private Ozbourn and the United States Naval Service. He gallantly gave his life for country.

Paige, Mitchell. Platoon Sergeant, U.S. Marine Corps. *Born:* 31 August 1918, Charleroi, PA. *Accredited to:* Pennsylvania. For extraordinary heroism and conspicuous gallantry action above and beyond the call of duty while serving with a company of Marines in combat against enemy Japanese forces in the Solomon Islands on 26 October 1942. When the enemy broke through the line directly in front of position, Platoon Sergeant Paige, commanding a machine gun section with fearless determination, continued to direct the fire of his gunners until all his men were either killed or wounded. Alone, against the deadly hail of Japanese shell, he fought his gun and when it was destroyed, took over another, moving from gun to gun, never ceasing withering fire against the advancing hordes until reinforcements finally arrived. Then, forming a new line, he dauntlessly and aggressively led a bayonet charge, driving the enemy back and preventing a break-through in our lines. great personal valor and unyielding devotion to duty were in keeping with the highest traditions of the United Naval Service. [*He was in the 2d Bn, 7th Marines. He retired in November 1959 as a colonel.*]

*****Phelps, Wesley.** Private, U.S. Marine Corps Reserve. *Born:* 12 June 1923, Neafus, KY. *Accredited to:* Kentucky. *Citation:* For conspicuous gallantry and intrepidity at the risk his life above and beyond the call of duty while serving the Third Battalion, Seventh Marines, First Marine Division, in action against enemy Japanese forces on Peleliu, Palau Group, during a savage hostile counterattack the night of 4 October 1944. Stationed with another Marine in an advanced position when a Japanese hand grenade landed in his foxhole, Private First Class Phelps instantly shouted a warning to his comrade and rolled over on the deadly bomb, absorbing with his own body the full, shattering impact of the exploding charge. Courageous and indomitable, Private First Class Phelps fearlessly gave his life that another might be spared serious injury, and his great valor and heroic devotion to duty in the face of certain death reflect the highest credit upon himself and the United States Naval Service. He gallantly gave his life for his country.

***Phillips, George.** Private, U.S. Marine Corps Reserve. *Born:* 14 July 1926, Rich Hill, MO. *Accredited to:* Missouri. *Citation:* For conspicuous gallantry and intrepidity at the risk of his life above and beyond the call of duty while serving with the Second Battalion, Twenty-eighth Marines, Fifth Marine Division, in action against enemy Japanese forces during the seizure of Iwo Jima, in the Volcano Islands, on 14 March 1945. Standing the foxhole watch while other members of his squad rested after a night of bitter hand-grenade fighting against infiltrating Japanese troops, Private Phillips was the only member of his unit alerted when an enemy hand grenade was tossed into their midst. Instantly shouting a warning, he unhesitatingly threw himself on the deadly missile, absorbing the shattering violence of the exploding charge in his own body and protecting his comrades from serious injury. Stout-hearted and indomitable, Private Phillips willingly yielded his own life that his fellow Marines might carry on the relentless battle against a fanatic enemy. His superb valor and unfaltering spirit of self-sacrifice in the face of certain death reflect the highest credit upon himself and upon the United States Naval Service. He gallantly gave his life for his country.

Pierce, Francis Junior. Pharmacist's Mate Third Class. *Entered service at:* Iowa. *Birth:* Earlville, Iowa. Citation: For conspicuous gallantry and intrepidity at the risk of his life above and beyond the call of duty while attached to the 2d Battalion, 24th Marines, 4th Marine Division, during the Iwo Jima campaign, 15 and 16 March 1945. Almost continuously under fire while carrying out the most dangerous volunteer assignments Pierce gained valuable knowledge of the terrain and disposition of troops. Caught in heavy enemy rifle and machine-gun fire

Wesley Phelps

George Phillips

which wounded a corpsman and two of the eight stretcher bearers who were carrying two wounded Marines to a forward aid station on 15 March, Pierce quickly took charge of the party, carried the newly wounded men to a sheltered position, and rendered first aid. After directing the evacuation of three of the casualties he stood in the open to draw the enemy's fire and, with his weapon blasting, enabled the litter bearers to reach cover. Turning his attention to the other two casualties, he was attempting to stop the profuse bleeding of one man when a Japanese fired from a cave less than 20 yards away and wounded his patient again. Risking his own life to save his patient, Pierce deliberately exposed himself to draw the attacker from the cave and destroyed him with the last of his ammunition. Then lifting the wounded man to his back, he advanced unarmed through deadly rifle fire across 200 feet of open terrain. Despite exhaustion and in the face of warnings against such a suicidal mission, he again traversed the same fire-swept path to rescue the remaining Marine. On the following morning, he led a combat patrol to the sniper nest and, while aiding a stricken Marine, was seriously wounded. Refusing aid for himself, he directed treatment for the casualty, at the same time maintaining protective fire for his comrades. Completely fearless, completed devoted to the care of his patients, Pierce inspired the entire battalion. His valor in the face of extreme peril sustains and enhances the finest traditions of the United States naval service.

Pope, Everett Parker. Captain, U.S. Marine Corps. *Born:* 16 July 1919, Milton, MA. *Accredited to:* Massachusetts. For conspicuous gallantry and intrepidity at the risk of his life above and beyond the call of duty while serving as Commanding Officer of Company C, First Battalion, First Marines, First Marine Division, during action against enemy Japanese forces on Peleliu Island. Palau Group, on 19–20 September 1944. Subjected to point-blank cannon fire which caused heavy casualties and badly disorganized his company while assaulting a steep coral hill, Captain Pope rallied his men and gallantly led them to the summit in the face of machine-gun, mortar and sniper fire. Forced by widespread hostile attack to deploy the remnants of his company thinly in order to hold the ground won, and with his machine guns out of order and insufficient water and ammunition, he

Everett Parker Pope

remained on the exposed hill with 12 men and 1 wounded officer, determined to hold through the night. Attacked continuously with grenades, machine guns and rifles from three sides, he and his valiant men fiercely beat back or destroyed the enemy, resorting to hand-to-hand combat as the supply of ammunition dwindled, and still maintaining his lines with his eight remaining riflemen when daylight brought more deadly fire and he was ordered to withdraw. His valiant leadership against devastating odds while protecting the units below from heavy Japanese attack reflects the highest credit upon Captain Pope and the United States Naval Service. [*He resigned as a major in September 1951.*]

*Power, John Vincent. First Lieutenant, U.S. Marine Corps Reserve. *Born:* 20 November 1918, Worcester, MA. *Appointed from:* Massachusetts. For conspicuous gallantry and intrepidity at the risk of his life above and beyond the call of duty as Platoon Leader, attached to the Fourth Marine Division, during the landing and battle of Namur Island, Kwajalein Atoll, Marshall Islands, 1 February 1944. Severely wounded in the stomach while setting a demolition charge on a Japanese pillbox, First Lieutenant Power was steadfast in his determination to remain in action. Protecting his wound with his left hand and firing with his right, he courageously ad-

John Vincent Power

vanced as another hostile position was taken under attack, fiercely charging the opening made by the explosion and emptying his carbine into the pillbox. While attempting to reload and continue the attack, First Lieutenant Power was shot again in the stomach and head and collapsed in the doorway. His exceptional valor, fortitude and indomitable fighting spirit in the face of withering enemy fire were in keeping with the highest traditions of the United States Naval Service. He gallantly gave his life for his country.

*Roan, Charles Howard. Private First Class, U.S. Marine Corps Reserve. *Born:* 16 August 1923, Claude, TX. *Accredited to:* Texas. *Citation:* For conspicuous gallantry and intrepidity at the risk of his life above and beyond the call of duty while serving with the Second Battalion, Seventh Marines, First Marine Division, in action against enemy Japanese forces on Peleliu, Palau Islands, 18 September1944. Shortly after his leader ordered a withdrawal upon discovering that the squad was partly cut off from their company as a result of the rapid advance along an exposed ridge during an aggressive attack on the strongly entrenched enemy, Private First Class

Charles Howard Roan

Roan and his companions were suddenly engaged in a furious exchange of hand grenades by Japanese forces emplaced in a cave on higher ground and to the rear of the squad. Seeking protection with four other Marines in a depression in the rocky, broken terrain, Private First Class Roan was wounded by an enemy grenade which fell close to their position and, immediately realizing the imminent peril to his comrades when another grenade landed in the midst of the group, unhesitatingly flung himself upon it, covering it with his body and absorbing the full impact of the explosion. By his prompt action and selfless conduct in the face of almost certain death, he saved the lives of four men. His great personal valor reflects the highest credit upon himself and the United States Naval Service. He gallantly gave his life for his comrades.

Rouh, Carlton Robert. First Lieutenant, U.S. Marine Corps Reserve. *Born:* 11 May 1919, Lindenwold, NJ. *Accredited to:* New Jersey. *Citation:* For conspicuous gallantry and intrepidity at the risk of his life above and beyond the call of duty while attached to the First Battalion, Fifth Marines, First Marine Division, during action against enemy Japanese forces on Peleilu Island, Palau Group, 15 September 1944. Before permitting his men to use an enemy dugout as a position for an 81-mm. mortar observation post, First Lieutenant Rouh made a personal reconnaissance of the pillbox and, upon entering, was severely wounded by Japanese rifle fire from within, emerging from the dugout, he was immediately assisted by two Marines to a less exposed area but, while receiving first aid, was further endangered by an enemy grenade which was thrown into their midst. Quick to act in spite

Carlton Robert Rouh

of his weakened condition, he lurched to a crouching position and thrust both men aside, placing own body between them and the grenade and taking the blast of the explosion himself. His exceptional spirit loyalty and self-sacrifice in the face of almost certain death reflects the highest credit upon First Lieutenant Rouh and the United States Naval Service. [*He retired a captain.*]

Ruhl, Donald Jack. Private First Class, U.S. Marine Corps Reserve. *Born*: 2 July Columbus, MT. *Accredited to:* Montana. *Citation:* For conspicuous gallantry and intrepidity at the risk of his life above and beyond the call of duty while serving as a Rifleman in an Assault Platoon of Company E, Twenty-eighth Marines, Fifth Marine Division, in action against enemy Japanese forces on Iwo Jima, Volcano Islands, 19 to 21 February 1945. Quick to press the advantage after eight Japanese had been driven from a blockhouse D-day, Private First Class Ruhl single-handedly attacked the group, killing one of the enemy with his bayonet another by rifle fire In

his determined attempt to annihilate the escaping troops. Cool and un- daunted as the fury of hostile resistance steadily increased throughout the night he voluntarily left the shelter of his tank trap early in the morning of D-day plus 1 and moved out under a tremendous volume of mortar and machine-gun fire to rescue a wounded Marine lying in an exposed position approximately 40 yards forward of the Line. Half pulling and half carrying the wounded man, he removed him to a defiladed position, called for an assis- tant and a stretcher and, again running the gauntlet of hostile fire, carried the casualty to an station some 300 yards distant on the beach. Returning to his platoon, he continued his valiant efforts, volunteering to investigate an apparently abandoned Japanese gun placement 75 yards forward of the right flank during consolidation of the front lines, and subsequently occupy the position through the night to prevent

Donald Jack Ruhl

the enemy from repossessing the valuable weapon. Pushing forward in assault against the vast network of fortifications surrounding Mt. Suribachi the following morning, he crawled with his platoon guide to the top of a Japanese bunker to bring fire to bear on enemy troops located on the far side of bunker. Suddenly a hostile grenade landed between the Marines. Instantly Private First Class Ruhl called a warning to his fellow Marine and dived on the deadly missile absorbing the full impact of the shattering explosion in his own body and protecting all within range from the dan- ger of flying fragments although he might easily have dropped from his position on the edge of the bunker to the ground below. An indomitable fighter, Private First Class rendered heroic service toward the defeat of a ruthless enemy, and his valor, initiative and unfaltering spirit self-sacrifice in the face of almost certain death sus- tain and enhance the highest traditions of the United States Naval Service. He gal- lantly gave his life for his country.

Schwab, Albert Earnest. Private First Class, U.S. Marine Corps Reserve. *Born:* 17 July 1920, Washington, D. C. *Accredited to:* Oklahoma. *Citation:* For conspicu- ous gallantry and intrepidity at the risk of his life above and beyond the call of duty as a Flame Thrower Operator in action against enemy Japanese forces on Oki- nawa Shima in the Ryukyu Islands, 7 May 1945. Quick to take action when his company was pinned down in a valley and suffered resultant heavy casualties under blanketing machine-gun fire emanating from a high ridge to the front, Private First Class Schwab, unable to flank the enemy emplacement because of steep cliffs on either side, advanced up the face of the ridge in bold defiance of the intense barrage and, skillfully directing the fire of his flame-thrower, quickly demolished the hostile gun position, thereby enabling his company to occupy the ridge. Suddenly a second enemy machine-gun opened fire, killing and wounding several Marines with its initial bursts. Estimating with split-second decision the tactical difficulties confronting his comrades, Private First Class Schwab elected to continue his one-man assault despite a diminished supply of fuel for his flame-thrower. Cool and indomitable, he moved forward in the face of a direct concentration of hostile fire, relentlessly closed the enemy position and attacked. Although

Albert Earnest Schwab

severely wounded by a final vicious blast from the enemy weapon, Private First Class Schwab had succeeded in destroying two highly strategic Japanese gun positions during a critical stage of the operation and, by his dauntless single-handed efforts, had materially furthered the advance of his company. His aggressive initiative, outstanding valor and professional skill throughout the bitter conflict sustain and enhance the highest traditions of the United States Naval Service. [*He was a member of Headquarters Company, 1/5.*]

Shoup, David Monroe. Colonel, U.S. Marine Corps. *Born:* 30 December 1904, Covington, IN. *Accredited to:* Indiana. *Citation:* For conspicuous gallantry and intrepidity at the risk of his life above and beyond the call of duty as Commanding Officer of all Marine Corps troops in action against enemy Japanese forces on Betio Island, Tarawa Atoll, Gilbert Islands, from 20 to 22 November, 1943. Although severely shocked by an exploding enemy shell soon after landing at the pier, and suffering from a serious, painful leg wound which had become infected, Colonel Shoup fearlessly exposed himself to the terrific and relentless artillery,

David Monroe Shoup

machine-gun and rifle fire from hostile shore emplacements. Rallying his hesitant troops by his own inspiring heroism, he gallantly led them across the fringing reefs to charge the heavily fortified island and reinforce our hard-pressed, thinly held lines. Upon arrival on shore, he assumed command of all landed troops and, working without rest under constant, withering enemy fire during the next 2 days, conducted smashing attacks against unbelievably strong and fanatically defended Japanese positions despite innumerable obstacles and heavy casualties. By his brilliant leadership, daring tactics and selfless devotion to duty, Colonel Shoup was largely responsible for the final decisive defeat of the enemy, and his indomitable fighting spirit reflects great credit upon the United States Naval Service. [*Other Navy awards: Distinguished Service Medal, two Legions of Merit. As General Commandant, he retired in 1963.*]

Sigler, Franklin Earl. Private, U.S. Marine Corps Reserve. *Born:* 6 November 1924, Little Falls, NJ. *Accredited to:* New Jersey. For conspicuous gallantry and intrepidity at the risk of his life above and beyond the call of duty while serving with the Second Battalion, Twenty-sixth Marines, Fifth Marine Division, in action against enemy Japanese forces during the seizure of Iwo Jima in the Volcano Islands on 14 March, 1945. Voluntarily taking command of his rifle squad when the leader became a casualty, Private Sigler fearlessly led a bold charge against an enemy gun installation which had held up the advance of his company for several days and, reaching the position in advance of the others, assailed the emplacement with hand grenades and personally annihilated the entire crew. As additional Japanese troops

Franklin Earl Sigler

opened fire from concealed tunnels and caves above, he quickly scaled the rocks leading to the attacking guns, surprised the enemy with a furious one man assault and, although severely wounded in the encounter, deliberately crawled back to his squad position where he steadfastly refused evacuation, persistently directing heavy machine-gun and rocket barrages on the Japanese cave entrances. Undaunted by the merciless rain of hostile fire during the intensified action, he gallantly disregarded his own painful wounds to aid casualties, carrying three wounded squad members to safety behind the lines and returning to continue the battle with renewed determination until ordered to retire for medical treatment. Stout-hearted and indomitable in the face of extreme peril, Private Sigler, by his alert initiative, unfaltering leadership and daring tactics in a critical situation, effected the release of his besieged company from enemy fire and contributed essentially to its further advance against a savagely fighting enemy. His superb valor, resolute fortitude and heroic spirit of self-sacrifice throughout reflect the highest credit upon Private Sigler and the United States Naval Service.

Skaggs, Luther, Jr. Private First Class, U.S. Marine Corps. *Born:* 3 March 1923, Henderson, KY. *Accredited to:* Kentucky. For conspicuous gallantry and intrepidity at the risk of his life above and beyond the call of duty while serving as Squad Leader with a Mortar Section of a Rifle Company in the Third Battalion, Third Marines, Third Marine Division, during action against enemy Japanese forces on the Asan-Adelup Beachhead, Guam, Marianas Islands, 21–22 July 1944. When the section leader became a casualty under a heavy mortar barrage shortly after landing, Private First Class Skaggs promptly assumed command and led the section through intense fire for a distance of 200 yards to a position from which to deliver effective coverage of the assault on a strategic cliff. Valiantly defending this vital position against strong enemy counterattacks during the night, Private First Class Skaggs was critically wounded when a Japanese grenade lodged in his foxhole and exploded, shattering the lower part of one leg. Quick to act, he applied an improvised tourniquet and, while propped up in his foxhole, gallantly returned the enemy's fire with his rifle and hand grenades for a period of 8 hours, later crawling unassisted to the rear to continue the fight until the Japanese had been annihilated. Uncomplaining and calm throughout this critical period, Private First Class Skaggs served as a heroic example of courage and fortitude to other wounded men and, by his courageous leadership and inspiring devotion to duty, upheld the high traditions of the United States Naval Service.

Luther Skaggs, Jr.

Smith, John Lucian. Major, U.S. Marine Corps. *Born:* 26 December 1914, Lexington, OK. *Accredited to:* Oklahoma. *Citation:* For conspicuous gallantry and heroic achievement

John Lucian Smith

in aerial combat above and beyond the call of duty as Commanding Officer of Marine Fighting Squadron 223 during operations against enemy Japanese forces in the Solomon Islands Area, August-September 1942. Repeatedly risking his life in aggressive and daring attacks, Major Smith led his squadron against a determined force, greatly superior in numbers, personally shooting down 16 Japanese planes between 21 August and 15 September 1942. In spite of the limited combat experience of many of the pilots of this squadron, they achieved the notable record of a total of 83 enemy aircraft destroyed in this period, mainly attributable to the thorough training under Major Smith and to his intrepid and inspiring leadership. His bold tactics and indomitable fighting spirit, and the valiant and zealous fortitude of the men of his command not only rendered the enemy's attacks ineffective and costly to Japan, but contributed to the security of our advance base. His loyal and courageous devotion to duty sustains and enhances the finest traditions of the United States Naval Service. [*Other Navy award: Legion of Merit. He retired a colonel on 1 September 1960.*]

Richard Keith Sorenson

Tony Stein

Sorenson, Richard Keith. Private, U.S. Marine Corps Reserve. *Born:* 28 August 1924, Anoka, MN. *Accredited to:* Minnesota. *Citation:* For conspicuous gallantry and intrepidity at the risk of his life above and beyond the call of duty while serving with an Assault Battalion, attached to the Fourth Marine Division, during the battle of Namur Island, Kwajalein Atoll, Marshall Islands, on 1–2 February 1944. Putting up a brave defense against a particularly violent counterattack by the enemy during invasion operations, Private Sorenson and five other Marines occupying a shellhole were endangered by a Japanese grenade thrown into their midst. Unhesitatingly, and with complete disregard for his own safety, Private Sorenson hurled himself upon the deadly weapon, heroically taking the full impact of the explosion. As a result of his gallant action, he was severely wounded, but the lives of his comrades were saved. His great personal valor and exceptional spirit of self-sacrifice in the face of almost certain death were in keeping with the highest traditions of the United States Naval Service.

Stein, Tony. Corporal, U.S. Marine Corps Reserve. *Born:* 30 September 1921, Dayton, OH. *Accredited to:* Ohio. For conspicuous gallantry and intrepidity at the risk of his life above and beyond the call of duty while serving with Company A, First Battalion, Twenty-eighth Marines, Fifth Marine Division, in action against enemy Japanese forces on Iwo Jima, in the Volcano Islands, 19 February 1945. The first man of his unit to be on station after hitting the beach in the initial assault, Corporal Stein, armed with a personally improvised aircraft-type weapon, provided rapid covering fire as the remainder of his platoon attempted to move into position. When his comrades were stalled by a concentrated machine-gun and mortar barrage, he gallantly stood upright and exposed himself to the enemy's view, thereby drawing the hostile fire to his own person and enabling him to observe the location of the furiously blazing hostile guns. Determined to neutralize the strategically placed weapons, he boldly charged the enemy pill-boxes one by one and succeeded in killing 20 of the enemy during the furious single-handed assault. Cool and courageous under the merciless hail of exploding shells and bullets which fell on all sides, he continued to deliver the fire of his skillfully improvised weapon at a extreme rate of speed which rapidly exhausted his ammunition. Undaunted, he removed his helmet and shoes to his movements and ran back to the beach for a ammunition, making a total of eight trips under intense fire and carrying or assisting a wounded man back time. Despite the unrelenting savagery and confusing battle, he rendered prompt assistance to his platoon whenever the unit was in position, directing the fire of a half-track against a stubborn pillbox until he had effected the ultimate destruction of the Japanese fortification. Later in the day, although his weapon was twice shot from his hand, he personally covered the withdrawal of his platoon to the company position. Stout-hearted and indomitable, Corporal Stein, by his aggressive initiative, sound judgment and unwavering devotion to duty In the face of terrific odds, attributed materially to the fulfillment of his mission, his outstanding valor throughout the bitter hours of conflict sustains and enhances the highest traditions of the United States Naval Service.

Swett, James Elms. First Lieutenant, U.S. Marine Corps Reserve. *Born:* 15 June 1920. Seattle, WA. *Accredited to:* California. *Citation:* For extraordinary heroism and personal valor and beyond the call of duty, as Division Leader of Marine Fighting Squadron 220, Marine Aircraft Group Twelve, First Marine Air, in action against enemy Japanese aerial forces in Solomon Islands Area, 7 April 1943. In a daring flight to intercept a wave of 150 Japanese planes, First Lieutenant Swett unhesitatingly hurled his four-plane division into action against a formation of 15 enemy bombers and personally exploded 3 hostile planes in midair with accurate deadly fire during his dive. Although separated from his division while clearing the heavy concentration of antiaircraft fire, he boldly attacked six enemy bombers, engaged the first four in turn and, unaided, shot down all in flames.

James Elms Swett

Exhausting his ammunition as he closed the fifth Japanese bomber, he relentlessly drove his attack against terrific opposition which partially disabled his engine, shattered the windscreen and slashed his face. In spite of this, he brought his battered plane down with skillful precision in the waters off Tulagi without further injury. The superb airman and tenacious fighting spirit which enabled First Lieutenant Swett to destroy seven enemy bombers in a single flight were in keeping with the highest traditions of the United States Naval Service.

Herbert Joseph Thomas

*Thomas, Herbert Joseph.** Sergeant, U.S. Marine Corps Reserve. *Born:* 8 February 1918, Columbus, OH. *Accredited to:* West Virginia. *Citation:* For extraordinary heroism and conspicuous gallantry above and beyond the call of duty while serving with Third Marines, Third Marine Division, in action against enemy forces during the battle at the Koromokina River, Bougainville Island, Solomon Islands, on 7 November 1943. Although several of his men were struck by enemy bullets as he led his squad through dense jungle undergrow the face of severe hostile machine-gun fire, Sergeant Thomas and his group fearlessly pressed forward into the center of the Japanese position and destroyed the crews of two machine guns by accurate rifle fire and grenades. Discovering a third gun, more difficult to approach, he carefully placed his men closely around him in strategic positions from which they were to have charge after he had thrown a grenade into the emplacement. When the grenade struck vines and fell back into the midst of the group, Sergeant Thomas deliberately flung himself upon it to smother the explosion, valiantly sacrificing himself for his comrades. Inspired by his selfless action, his men unhesitatingly charged the enemy machine-gun and, with fierce determination, killed the crew and several other nearby defenders. The splendid initiative and extremely heroic conduct of Sergeant Thomas in carrying out his prompt decision with full knowledge of his fate reflect great credit upon himself and the United States Naval Service. He gallantly gave his life for his country.

*Thomason, Clyde.** Sergeant, U.S. Marine Corps Reserve. *Born:* 23 May 1914, Atlanta, GA. *Accredited to:* Georgia. *Citation:* For conspicuous heroism and intrepidity above and beyond the call of duty during the Marine Raider Expedition against the Japanese-held island of Makin on 17–18 August 1942. Leading the advance element of the assault echelon, Sergeant Thomason disposed his men with keen judgment and discrimination and, by his exemplary leadership and great personal valor, exhorted them to like fearless efforts. On one occasion, he dauntlessly walked up to a house which concealed an enemy Japanese sniper, forced in the door and shot the

man before he could resist. Later in the action, while leading an assault on an enemy position, he gallantly gave his life in the service of his country. His courage and loyal devotion to duty in the face of grave peril were in keeping with the finest traditions of the United States Naval Service. [*His was the first Medal of Honor awarded to an enlisted Marine in WWII.*]

Clyde Thomason

Grant Frederick Timmerman

*Timmerman, Grant Frederick. Sergeant, U.S. Marine Corps. *Born:* 14 February 1919, Americus, KS. *Accredited to:* Kansas. *Citation:* For conspicuous gallantry and intrepidity at the risk of his life above and beyond the call of duty as Tank Commander serving with the Second Battalion, Sixth Marine, Second Marine Division, during action against enemy Japanese forces on Saipan, Marianas Islands, on 8 July 1944. Advancing with his tank a few yards ahead of the infantry In support of a vigorous attack on hostile positions, Sergeant Timmerman maintained steady fire from his antiaircraft sky mount machine gun until progress was impeded by a series of enemy trenches and pillboxes. Observing a target of opportunity, he immediately ordered the tank stopped and, mindful of the danger from the muzzle blast as he prepared to open fire with the 75-mm., fearlessly stood up in the exposed turret and ordered the infantry to hit the deck. Quick to act as a grenade, hurled by the

Japanese, was about to drop into the open turret hatch, Sergeant Timmerman unhesitatingly blocked the opening with his body holding the grenade against his chest and taking the brunt of the explosion. His exceptional valor and loyalty In saving his men at the cost of his own life reflect the highest credit upon Sergeant Timmerman and the United States Naval Service. He gallantly gave his life in the service of his country.

Vandegrift, Alexander Archer. Major General, U.S. Marine Corps. *Born:* 13 March 1887, Charlottesville, VA. *Appointed from:* Virginia. *Citation:* For outstanding and heroic accomplishment above and beyond the call of duty as Commanding Officer of the First Marine Division in operations against enemy Japanese forces in the Solomon Islands during the period, 7 August to 9 December 1942. With the adverse factors of weather, terrain and disease making his task a difficult and hazardous undertaking, and with his command eventually including sea, land and air forces of Army, Navy and Marine Corps, Major General Vandegrift achieved marked success in commanding the initial landings of the United States forces in the Solomon Islands and In their subsequent occupation. His tenacity, courage and resourcefulness prevailed against a strong, determined and experienced enemy, and the gallant fighting spirit of the men under his inspiring leadership enabled them to withstand aerial, land and sea bombardment, to surmount all obstacles and leave a disorganized and ravaged enemy. This dangerous but vital mission, accomplished at the constant risk of his life, resulted in securing a valuable base for further operations of our forces against the enemy, and its successful completion reflects great credit upon Major General Vandegrift, his command and the United States Naval Service. [*Other Navy awards: Navy Cross, Distinguished Service Medal. He retired as Lieutenant General Commandant on 1 April 1949.*]

Alexander Archer Vandegrift

Wahlen, George Edward. Pharmacist's Mate Second Class, USN. *Born:* 8 August 1924, Ogden, Utah. *Accredited to:* Utah. *Citation:* For conspicuous gallantry and intrepidity at the risk of his life above and beyond the call of duty while serving with the Second Battalion, Twenty-sixth Marines, Fifth Marine Division, during action against enemy Japanese forces on Iwo Jima in the Volcano Group on 3 March 1945. Painfully wounded in the bitter action on 26 February, Wahlen remained on the battlefield, advancing well forward of the front lines to aid a wounded Marine and carrying him back to safety despite a terrific concentration of fire. Tireless in his ministrations, he consistently disregarded all danger to attend his fighting comrades as they fell under the devastating rain of shrapnel and bullets, and rendered prompt assistance to various elements of his combat group as required. When an adjacent platoon suffered heavy casualties, he defied the continuous pounding of heavy mortars and deadly fire of enemy rifles to care for the wounded, working rapidly in an area swept by constant fire and treating fourteen casualties before returning to his own platoon. Wounded again on 2 March, he gallantly refused evacuation, moving out with his company the following day in a furious assault across 600 yards of open terrain and repeatedly rendering medical aid while exposed to the blasting fury of powerful Japanese guns. Stout-hearted and indomitable, he persevered in his determined efforts as his unit waged fierce battle and, unable to walk after sustaining a third agonizing wound, resolutely crawled 50 yards to administer first aid to still another fallen fighter. By his dauntless fortitude and valor, Wahlen served as a constant inspiration and contributed vitally to the high morale of his company during critical phases of this strategically important engagement. His heroic spirit of self-sacrifice in the face of overwhelming enemy fire upheld the highest traditions of the United States Naval Service.

Walsh, Kenneth Ambrose. First Lieutenant, U.S. Marine Corps. *Born:* 24 November 1916 Brooklyn, NY. *Accredited to:* New York. *Citation:* For extraordinary heroism and intrepidity above and beyond the call of duty as a Pilot in Marine Fighting Squadron 124 in aerial combat against enemy Japanese forces in the Solomon Islands Area. Determined to thwart the enemy's attempt to bomb Allied ground forces and shipping at Vella Lavella on 15 August 1943, First Lieutenant Walsh repeatedly dived his plane into an enemy formation outnumbering his own division 6 to 1 and, although his plane was hit numerous times, shot down two Japanese dive bombers and one fighter. After developing engine trouble on 30 August during a vital escort mission, First Lieutenant Walsh landed his mechanically disabled plane at Munda, quickly replaced it with another, and proceeded to rejoin his flight over

Kenneth Ambrose Walsh

Kuhili. Separated from his escort group when he encountered approximately 50 Japanese Zeros, he unhesitatingly attacked, striking with relentless fury in his lone battle against a powerful force. He destroyed four hostile fighters before cannon shellfire forced him to make a dead-stick landing off Vella Lavella where he was later picked up. His valiant leadership and his daring skill as a flier served as a source of confidence and inspiration to his fellow pilots and reflect the highest credit upon the United States Naval Service. [*He retired as a colonel in 1962.*]

*****Walsh, William Gary.** Gunnery Sergeant, U.S. Marine Corps Reserve. *Born:* 7 April 1922, Roxbury, MA. *Accredited to:* Massachusetts. *Citation:* For extraordinary gallantry and intrepidity at the risk of his life above and beyond the call of duty as Leader of an Assault Platoon, attached to Company G, Third Battalion, Twenty-seventh Marines, Fifth Marine Division, in action against enemy Japanese forces at Iwo Jima, Volcano Islands, on 27 February 1945. With the advance of his company toward Hill 362 disrupted by vicious machine-gun fire from a forward position which guarded the approaches to this key enemy stronghold, Gunnery Sergeant Walsh fearlessly charged at the head of his platoon against the Japanese entrenched on the ridge above him, utterly oblivious to the unrelenting fury of hostile automatic weapons fire and hand grenades employed with fanatic desperation to smash his daring assault. Thrown back by the enemy's savage resistance, he once again led his men in a seemingly impossible attack up the steep, rocky slope, boldly defiant of the annihilating streams of bullets which saturated the area. Despite his own casualty losses and the overwhelming advantage held by the Japanese in superior numbers and dominant position, he gained the ridge's top only to be subjected to an intense barrage of hand grenades thrown by the remaining Japanese staging a suicidal last stand on the reverse slope. When one of the grenades fell in the midst of his surviving, men, huddled together in a small trench, Gunnery Sergeant Walsh, in a final valiant act of complete self-sacrifice, instantly threw himself upon the deadly bomb, absorbing with his own body the full and terrific force of the explosion. Through his extraordinary initiative and inspiring valor In the face of almost certain death, he saved his comrades from injury and possible loss of life and enabled his company to seize and hold this vital enemy position. He gallantly gave his life for his country.

William Gary Walsh

Watson, Wilson Douglas. Private U.S. Marine Corps Reserve. *Born:* 18 February 1921, Tuscumbia, AL. *Accredited to:* Arkansas. *Citation:* For conspicuous gallantry and

Wilson Douglas Watson

intrepidity at the risk of his life above and beyond the call of duty as Automatic Rifleman serving with the Second Battalion, Ninth Marines, Third Marine Division, during action against enemy Japanese forces on Iwo Jima, Volcano Islands, 26 and 27 February 1945. With his squad abruptly halted by intense fire from enemy fortifications in the high rocky ridges and crags commanding the line of advance, Private Watson boldly rushed one pillbox and fired into the embrasure with his weapon, keeping the enemy pinned down singlehandedly until he was in a position to hurl in a grenade, and then running to the rear of the emplacement to destroy the retreating Japanese and enable his platoon to take its objective. Again pinned down at the foot of a small hill, he dauntlessly scaled the jagged incline under fierce mortar and machine-gun barrages and, with his assistant BAR man, charged the crest of the hill, firing from his hip. Fighting furiously against Japanese troops attacking with grenades and knee mortars from the reverse slope, he stood fearlessly erect in his exposed position to cover the hostile entrenchments and held the hill under savage fire for 15 minutes, killing 60 Japanese before his ammunition was exhausted and his platoon was able to join him. His courageous initiative and valiant fighting spirit against devastating odds were directly responsible for the continued advance of his platoon, and his inspiring leadership throughout this bitterly fought action reflects the highest credit upon Private Watson and the United States Naval Service.

Williams, Hershel Woodrow. Corporal, U.S. Marine Corps Reserve. *Born:* 2 October 1923, Quiet Dell, WV. *Accredited to:* West Virginia. *Citation:* For conspicuous gallantry and intrepidity at the risk of his life above and beyond the call of duty as Demolition Sergeant serving with the Twenty-first Marines, Third Marine Division, in action against enemy Japanese forces on Iwo Jima, Volcano Islands, 23 February 1945. Quick to volunteer his services when our tanks were maneuvering vainly to open a lane for the infantry through the network of reinforced concrete pillboxes, buried mines and black volcanic sands, Corporal Williams daringly went forward alone to attempt the reduction of devastating machine gun fire from the unyielding positions. Covered only by riflemen, he fought desperately for 4 hours under terrific enemy small-arms fire and repeatedly returned to own lines to prepare

Hershel Woodrow Williams

demolition charges and obtain serviced flame throwers, struggling back, frequently to rear of hostile emplacements, to wipe out one position after another. On one occasion, he daringly mounted a pillbox to insert the nozzle of his flame-thrower through the air vent, killing the occupants and silencing the gun; on another he grimly charged enemy riflemen who attempted to stop him with bayonets and destroyed them with a burst of flame from his weapon. His unyielding determination and extraordinary heroism in the face of ruthless enemy resistance were directly instrumental in neutralizing one of the most fanatically defended Japanese strong points encountered by his regiment and aided vitally enabling his company to reach its objective. Corporal Williams's aggressive fighting spirit and valiant devotion to duty throughout this fiercely contested action sustain and enhance the highest traditions of the United States Naval Service.

***Williams, Jack.** Pharmacist's Mate Third Class, U.S. Navy Reserve. *Born:* 18 October 1924, Harrison, AR. *Accredited to:* Arkansas. *Citation:* For conspicuous gallantry and intrepidity at the risk of his life above and beyond the call of duty while serving with the Third Battalion, Twenty-eighth Marines, Fifth Marine Division, during the occupation of Iwo Jima, Volcano Islands, 3 March 1945. Gallantly going forward of the front lines under intense enemy small-arms fire to assist a Marine wounded in a fierce grenade battle, Williams dragged the man to a shallow depression and was kneeling, using his own body as a screen from the sustained fire as he administered first aid, when struck in the abdomen and groin three times by hostile rifle fire. Momentarily stunned, he quickly recovered and completed his ministration before applying battle dressings to his own multiple wounds. Unmindful of his own urgent need for medical attention, he remained in the perilous fire-swept area to care for another Marine casualty. Heroically completing his task despite pain and profuse bleeding, he then endeavored to make his way to the rear in search of adequate aid for himself when struck down by a Japanese sniper bullet which caused his collapse. Succumbing later as a result of his self-sacrificing service to others, Williams, by his courageous determination, unwavering fortitude and valiant performance of duty, served as an inspiring example of heroism, in keeping with the highest traditions of the United States Naval Service. He gallantly gave his life for his country.

***Willis, John Harlan.** Pharmacist's Mate First Class, U.S. Navy. *Born:* 10 June 1921, Columbia, TN. *Accredited to:* Tennessee. *Citation:* For conspicuous gallantry and intrepidity at the risk of his life above and beyond the call of duty as Platoon Corpsman serving with the Third Battalion, Twenty-seventh Marines, Fifth Marine Division, during operations against enemy Japanese forces on Iwo Jima, Volcano Islands, 28 February 1945. Constantly imperiled by artillery and mortar fire from strong and mutually supporting pillboxes and caves studding Hill 362 in the enemy's cross-island defenses, Willis resolutely administered first aid to the many Marines wounded during the furious close-infighting until he himself was struck by shrapnel and was ordered back to the battle-aid station. Without waiting for official medical release, he quickly returned to his company and, during a savage hand-to-hand enemy counterattack, daringly advanced to the extreme front lines under mortar and sniper fire to aid a Marine lying wounded in a shell-hole. Completely unmindful of his own danger as the Japanese intensified their attack, Willis calmly continued to administer blood plasma to his patient, promptly returning the first hostile grenade which landed in the shell-hole while he was working and hurling back seven more in quick succession before the ninth one exploded in his hand and instantly killed him. By his great personal valor in saving others at the sacrifice of his own life, he inspired his companions, although terrifically outnumbered, to launch a fiercely determined attack and repulse the enemy force. His exceptional fortitude and courage in the performance of duty reflect the highest credit upon Willis and the United States Naval Service. He gallantly gave his life for his country.

Wilson, Louis Hugh, Jr. Captain, U.S. Marine Corps. *Born:* 11 February 1920, Brandon, MS. *Appointed from:* Mississippi. *Citation:* For conspicuous gallantry and intrepidity at the risk of his life above and beyond the call of duty as Commanding Officer of a Rifle Company, attached to the Second Battalion, Ninth Marines, Third Marine Division, In action against enemy Japanese forces at Fonte Hill, Guam, 26 July 1944. Ordered to take that portion of the hill within his zone of action, Major Wilson initiated his attack in mid-afternoon, pushed up the rugged, open terrain, against terrific machine-gun and rifle fire for 300 yards, and successfully captured the objective. Promptly assuming command of other disorganized units and motorized equipment in addition to his own company and one reinforced platoon, he organized his night defenses. In the face of continuous hostile fire and, although wounded three times during this 5-hour period, completed his disposition of men and guns before retiring to the company command for medical attention. Shortly thereafter, when the enemy launched the first of a series of savage counterattacks lasting all night, he voluntarily rejoined his besieged men and repeatedly exposed himself to the merciless hail of shrapnel and bullets, dashing 50 yards into the open on one occasion to rescue a wounded Marine lying helpless beyond the front lines. Fighting fiercely in hand-to-hand encounters, he led his men in furiously waged battle for approximately 10 hours, tenaciously holding his line and repelling the fanatically renewed counter thrusts until he succeeded in crushing the last efforts of the hard-pressed Japanese early the following morning. Then organizing 17-man patrol, he immediately advanced upon a strategic slope essential to the security of his position and, boldly defying intense mortar, machine-gun and rifle fire which struck down 13 of his men, drove relentlessly forward with the remnants of his patrol to seize the vital ground. By indomitable leadership, daring combat tactics and valor in the face of over-whelming odds, Major Wilson succeeded in capturing and holding the strategic high ground in his regimental sector, thereby contributing essentially to the success of his regimental mission and to the annihilation of 350 Japanese troops. His inspiring conduct throughout the critical periods of this decisive action sustains and enhances the highest traditions of the United States Naval Service. [*Other Navy awards: two Distinguished Service Medals, three Legions of Merit. He retired as General Commandant on 30 June 1979.*]

*****Wilson, Robert Lee.** Private First Class, U.S. Marine Corps. *Born:* 24 May 1921, Centralia, IL. *Accredited to:* Illinois. *Citation:* For conspicuous gallantry and intrepidity at the risk of his life above and beyond the call of duty while serving with the Second Battalion, Sixth Marines, Second Marine Division, during action against enemy Japanese forces at Tinian Island, Marianas Group, on 4 August 1944. As one of a group of Marines advancing through heavy underbrush to neutralize isolated points of resistance, Private First Class Wilson daringly preceded his companions

Robert Lee Wilson

Frank Peter Witek

toward a pile of rocks where Japanese troops were supposed to be hiding. Fully aware of the danger involved, he was moving forward while the remainder of the squad, armed with automatic rifles, closed together in the rear when an enemy grenade landed in the midst of the group. Quick to act, Private First Class Wilson cried a warning to the men and unhesitatingly threw himself on the grenade, heroically sacrificing his own life that the others might live and fulfill their mission. His exceptional valor, his courageous loyalty and unwavering devotion to duty in the face of grave peril reflect the highest credit upon Private First Class Wilson and the United States Naval Service. He gallantly gave his life for his country.

*Witek, Frank Peter. Private First Class, U.S. Marine Corps Reserve. *Born:* 10 December 1921, Derby, CT. *Accredited to:* Illinois. *Citation:* For conspicuous gallantry and intrepidity at the risk of his life above and beyond the call of duty while serving with the First Battalion, Ninth Marines, Third Marine Division, during the battle of Finegayen at Guam, Marianas, on 3 August 1944. When his rifle platoon was halted by heavy surprise fire from well-camouflaged enemy positions, Private First Class Witek daringly remained standing to fire a full magazine from his automatic at point-blank range into a depression housing Japanese troops, killing eight of the enemy and enabling the greater part of his platoon to take cover. During his platoon's withdrawal for consolidation of lines, he remained to safeguard a severely wounded comrade, courageously returning the enemy's fire until the arrival of stretcher bearers, and then covering the evacuation by sustained fire as he moved backward toward his own lines. With his platoon again pinned down by a hostile machine gun, Private First Class Witek, on his own initiative, moved forward boldly to the reinforcing tanks and infantry, alternately throwing hand grenades and firing as he advanced to within 5 to 10 yards of the enemy position, and destroying the hostile machine-gun emplacement and an additional eight Japanese before he himself was struck down by an enemy rifleman. His valiant and inspiring action effectively reduced the enemy's fire power, thereby enabling his platoon to attain its objective, and reflects the highest credit upon Private First Class Witek and the United States Naval Service. He gallantly gave his life for his country.

Korea • 1950–1953

*Abrell, Charles Gene.** Corporal, U.S. Marine Corps, 1082642. *Born:* 12 August 1931, Terre Haute, IN. *Accredited to:* Indiana. *Citation:* For conspicuous gallantry and intrepidity at the risk of his life above and beyond the call of duty while serving as a Fire Team Leader in Company E, Second Battalion, First Marines, First Marine Division (Reinforced), in action against enemy aggressor forces in Korea on 10 June 1951. While advancing with his platoon in an attack against well-concealed and heavily-fortified enemy hill positions, Corporal Abrell voluntarily rushed forward through the assaulting squad which was pinned down by a hail of intense and accurate automatic-weapons fire from a hostile bunker situated on commanding ground. Although previously wounded by enemy hand-grenade fragments, he proceeded to carry out a bold, singlehanded attack against the bunker, exhorting his comrades to follow him. Sustaining two additional wounds as he stormed toward the emplacement, he resolutely pulled the pin from a grenade clutched in his hand and hurled himself bodily into the bunker with the live missile still in his grasp. Fatally wounded in the resulting explosion which killed the entire

Charles Gene Abrell

enemy gun crew within the stronghold, Corporal Abrell, by his valiant spirit of self-sacrifice in the face of certain death, served to inspire all his comrades and contributed directly to the success of his platoon in attaining its objective. His superb courage and heroic initiative sustain and enhance the highest traditions of the United States Naval Service. He gallantly gave his life for his country.

Barber, William Earl. Captain, U.S. Marine Corps, 028331. *Born:* 30 November 1919, Dehart, KY. *Entered service at:* Middletown, OH. *Citation:* For conspicuous gallantry and intrepidity at the risk of his life above and beyond the call of duty as Commanding Officer of Company F, Second Battalion, Seventh Marines, First Marine Division (Reinforced), in action against enemy aggressor forces in Korea from 28 November to 2 December 1950. Assigned to defend a three-mile mountain pass along the division's main supply line and commanding the only route of approach in the march from Yudam-ni to Hagaru-ri, Captain Barber took position with his battle weary troops and, before nightfall, had dug in and set up a defense along the frozen, snow-covered hillside. When a force of estimated regimental strength savagely attacked during the night, inflicting heavy casualties and finally surrounding his position following a bitterly fought seven-hour conflict, Captain Barber, after repulsing the enemy, gave assurance that he could hold if supplied by air drops and requested permis-

William Earl Barber

sion to stand fast when orders were received by radio to fight his way back to a relieving force after two reinforcing units had been driven back under fierce resistance in their attempts to reach the isolated troops. Aware that leaving the position would sever contact with the 8,000 Marines trapped at Yudam-ni and jeopardize their chances of joining the 3,000 more awaiting their arrival in Hagaru-ri for the continued drive to the sea, he chose to risk loss of his command rather than sacrifice more men if the enemy seized control and forced a renewed battle to regain the position, or abandon his many wounded who were unable to walk. Although severely wounded in the leg the early morning of the 29th, Captain Barber continued to maintain personal control, often moving up and down the lines on a stretcher to direct the defense and consistently encouraging and inspiring his men to supreme efforts despite the staggering opposition. Waging desperate battle throughout five days and six nights of repeated onslaughts launched by the fanatical aggressors, he and his heroic command accounted for approximately 1,000 enemy dead in this epic stand in bitter sub-zero weather, and when the company was relieved, only 82 of his original 220 men were able to walk away from the position so valiantly defended against insuperable odds. His profound faith and courage, great personal valor and unwavering fortitude were decisive factors in the successful withdrawal of the division from the deathtrap in the Chosin Reservoir sector and reflect the highest credit upon Captain Barber, his intrepid officers and men and the United States Naval Service. [*Other Navy awards: Silver Star, Legion of Merit. He retired a colonel on 1 May 1970.*]

*Baugh, William Bernard. Private First Class, U.S. Marine Corps, 655899. *Born:* 7 July 1930 at McKinney, KY. *Entered service at:* Harrison, OH. *Citation:* For conspicuous gallantry and intrepidity at the risk of his life above and beyond the call of duty while serving as a member of an Anti-Tank Assault Squad attached to Company G, Third Battalion, First Marines, First Marine Division (Reinforced), during a nighttime enemy attack against a motorized column enroute from Koto-ri to Hagaru-ri, Korea, on 29 November 1950. Acting instantly when a hostile hand grenade landed in his truck as he and his squad prepared to alight and assist In the repulse of an enemy force delivering Intense automatic-weapons and grenade fire from deeply entrenched and well-concealed roadside positions, Private First Class Baugh

William Bernard Baugh

quickly shouted a warning to the other men in the vehicle and, unmindful of his own personal safety, hurled himself upon the deadly missile, thereby saving his comrades from serious injury or possible death. Sustaining severe wounds from which he died a short time afterward, Private First Class Baugh, by his superb courage and valiant spirit of self-sacrifice, upheld the highest traditions of the United States Naval Service. He gallantly gave his life for his country.

*Benfold, Edward C. Hospital Corpsman Third Class, USN, 4168234. *Born:* Staten Island, New York. *Entered service at:* New York. *Citation:* For gallantry and intrepidity at the risk of his life above and beyond the call of duty while serving as a Hospital Corpsman attached to a Company in the First Marine Division during operations against enemy aggressor forces in Korea on 5 September 1952. When his company was subjected to heavy artillery and mortar barrages, followed by a determined assault during the hours of darkness by an enemy force estimated at battalion strength, Benfold resolutely moved from position to position in the face of intense hostile fire, treating the wounded and lending words of encouragement. Leaving the protection of his sheltered position to treat the wounded when the platoon area in which he was working was attacked from both the front and rear, he moved forward to an exposed ridge line where he observed two Marines in a large crater. As he approached the two men to determine their condition, an enemy soldier threw two grenades into the crater while two other enemy charged the position. Picking up a grenade in each hand, Benfold leaped out of the crater and hurled himself against the onrushing hostile soldiers, pushing the grenades against their chests and killing both the attackers. Mortally wounded while carrying out this heroic act, Benfold, by his great personal valor and resolute spirit of self- sacrifice in the face of almost certain death, was directly responsible for saving the lives of his two comrades. His exceptional courage reflects the highest credit upon himself and enhances the finest traditions of the United States Naval Service. He gallantly gave his life for others.

Cafferata, Hector Albert, Jr. Private, U.S. Marine Corps Reserve, 1069789, Born 4 November 1929, New York, NY. *Entered service at:* Montville, NJ. *Citation:* For

Hector Albert Cafferata, Jr.

conspicuous gallantry and intrepidity at the risk of his life above and beyond the call of duty while serving as a Rifleman with Company F, Second Battalion, Seventh Marines, First Marine Division (Reinforced), in action against enemy aggressor forces in Korea on 28 November 1950. When all the other members of his fire team became casualties, creating a gap In the lines, during the initial phase of a vicious attack launched by a fanatical enemy of regimental strength against his company's hill position, Private Cafferata waged a lone battle with grenades and rifle fire as the attack gained momentum and the enemy threatened penetration through the gap and endangered the integrity of the entire defensive perimeter. Making a target of himself under the devastating fire from automatic weapons, rifles, grenades and mortars, he maneuvered up and down the line and delivered accurate and effective fire against the onrushing force, killing fifteen, wounding many more and forcing the others to withdraw so that reinforcements could move up and consolidate the position. Again fighting desperately against a renewed onslaught later that same morning when a hostile grenade landed in a shallow entrenchment occupied by wounded Marines, Private Cafferata rushed into the gully under heavy fire, seized the deadly missile in his right hand and hurled it free of his comrades before it detonated, severing part of one finger and seriously wounding him in the right hand and arm. Courageously ignoring the intense pain, he staunchly fought on until he was struck by a sniper's bullet and forced to submit to evacuation for medical treatment. Stouthearted and indomitable, Private Cafferata, by his fortitude, great personal valor and dauntless perseverance in the face of almost certain death, saved the lives of several of his fellow Marines and contributed essentially to the success achieved by his company In maintaining its defensive position against tremendous odds. His extraordinary heroism throughout was in keeping with the highest traditions of the United States Naval Service.

*Champagne, David Bernard.** Corporal, U.S. Marine Corps, 1187155. *Born:* 13 November 1932 at Waterville, ME. *Entered service at:* Wakefield, RI. *Citation:* For conspicuous gallantry and intrepidity at the risk of his life above and beyond the call of duty while serving as a Fire Team Leader of Company A, First Battalion, Seventh Marines, First Marine Division (Reinforced), in action against enemy aggressor forces In Korea on 28 May 1952. Advancing with his platoon in the initial assault of the company against a strongly fortified and heavily defended hill position, Corporal Champagne skillfully led his fire team through a veritable hail of intense enemy machine-gun, small-arms and grenade fire, overrunning trenches and a series of almost impregnable bunker positions before reaching the crest of the hill and placing his men in defensive positions. Suffering a painful leg wound while assisting in repelling the ensuing hostile counterattack, which was launched under cover of a murderous hail of mortar and artillery fire, he steadfastly refused evacuation and fearlessly continued to control his fire team. When the enemy counterattack increased in intensity, and a hostile grenade landed in the midst of the fire team, Corporal Champagne unhesitatingly seized the deadly missile and hurled it in the direction of the approaching enemy. As the grenade left his hand, it exploded, blowing off his hand and throwing him out of the trench. Mortally wounded by enemy mortar fire while in this exposed position, Corporal Champagne, by his valiant leadership, fortitude and gallant spirit of self-sacrifice in the face of almost certain death, undoubtedly saved the lives of several of his fellow Marines. His heroic actions served to inspire all who observed him and reflect the highest credit upon himself and the United States Naval Service. He gallantly gave his life for his country.

David Bernard Champagne

Charette, William R. Hospital Corpsman Third Class, USN, 3039272. *Born:* Ludington, MI. *Entered service at:* Michigan. *Citation:* For conspicuous gallantry and intrepidity at the risk of his life above and beyond the call of duty as a Medical Corpsman, serving with a Marine Rifle Company, in action against enemy aggressor forces in Korea during the early morning hours of 27 March 1953. Participating in a fierce encounter with a cleverly concealed and well-entrenched enemy force occupying positions on a vital and bitterly contested outpost far in advance of the main line resistance, Charette repeatedly and unhesitatingly moved about through a murderous barrage of hostile small-arms and mortar fire to render assistance to his wounded comrades. When an enemy grenade landed within a few feet of a Marine he was attending, he immediately threw himself upon the stricken man and absorbed the entire concussion of the deadly missile with his own body. Although sustaining painful facial wounds, and undergoing shock from the intensity of the blast which ripped the helmet and medical aid kit from his person, Charette resourcefully improvised emergency bandages by tearing off part of his clothing, and gallantly continued to administer medical aid to the wounded in his own unit and to those in adjacent platoon areas as well. Observing a seriously wounded comrade whose armored vest had been torn from his body by the blast from an exploding shell, he selflessly removed his own battle vest and placed it upon the helpless man although fully aware of the added jeopardy to himself. Moving to the side of another casualty who was suffering excruciating pain from a serious leg wound, Charette stood upright in the trench line and exposed himself to a deadly hail of enemy fire in order to lend more effective aid to the victim and to alleviate his anguish while being removed to a position of safety. By his indomitable courage and inspiring efforts in behalf of his wounded comrades, Charette was directly responsible for saving many lives. His great personal valor reflects the highest credit upon himself and enhances the finest traditions of the United States Naval Service.

Stanley Reuben Christianson

*Christianson, Stanley Reuben. Private First Class, U.S. Marine Corps, 474713. *Born:* 24 January 1925 at Mindoro, WI. *Entered service at:* Mindoro, Wisconsin. *Citation:* For conspicuous gallantry and intrepidity at the risk of his life above and beyond the call of duty while serving with Company E, Second Battalion, First Marines, First Marine Division (Reinforced), In action against enemy aggressor forces at Hill 132, Seoul, Korea, In the early morning hours of 29 September 1950. Manning one of the several listening posts covering approaches to the platoon area when the enemy commenced the attack, Private First Class Christanson quickly sent another Marine to alert the rest of the platoon. Without orders, he remained in his position and, with full knowledge that he would have slight chance of escape, fired relentlessly at oncoming hostile troops attacking furiously with rifles, automatic weapons and incendiary grenades. Accounting for seven enemy dead in the immediate vicinity before his position was overrun and he himself fatally struck down, Private First Class Christianson, by his superb courage, valiant fighting spirit and devotion to duty, was responsible for allowing the rest of the platoon time to man positions, build up a stronger defense on that flank and repel the attack with 41 of the enemy destroyed, many more wounded and three taken prisoner. His self-sacrificing actions in the face of overwhelming odds sustain and enhance the finest traditions of the United States Naval Service. Private First Class Christianson gallantly gave his life for his country.

Henry Alfred Commiskey

Commiskey, Henry Alfred. First Lieutenant, U.S. Marine Corps, 050382. *Born:* 10 January 1927 Hattiesburg, MS.

Entered service at: Hattiesburg, MS. *Citation:* For conspicuous gallantry and intrepidity at the risk his life above and beyond the call of duty while serving a Platoon Leader in Company C, First Battalion, First Marines, First Marine Division (Reinforced), in action against enemy aggressor forces near Yongdungp'o, Korea, 20 September 1950. Directed to attack hostile forces well dug in on Hill 85, First Lieutenant Commiskey, then Second Lieutenant, spearheaded the assault, charging up steep slopes on the run. Coolly disregarding the heavy enemy machine-gun and small-arms fire, he plunged on forward of the rest of his platoon and was the first to reach the crest of the objective. Armed only with a pistol, he jumped into a hostile machine-gun emplacement occupied by five enemy troops and quickly disposed of four of the soldiers with his automatic pistol. Grappling with the fifth, First Lieutenant Commiskey knocked him to the ground and held him until he could obtain a weapon from another member of his platoon and kill the last of the enemy crew. Continuing his bold assault, he moved to the next emplacement, killed two more of the enemy and then led platoon toward the rear nose of the hill to rout the remainder of the hostile troops and destroy them as they fled from their positions. His valiant leadership and courageous fighting spirit served to inspire the men of his company to heroic endeavor in seizing the objective and reflected the highest credit upon First Lieutenant Commiskey and the United States Naval Service. [*He retired a major in 1966.*]

*Davenport, Jack Arden. Corporal, U.S. Marine Corps, 1126686. *Born:* 7 September 1931 at Kansas City, MO. *Entered service at:* Mission, KS. *Citation:* For conspicuous gallantry and intrepidity at the risk life above and beyond the call of duty while serving as a Squad Leader in Company G, Third Battalion, Fifth Marines, First Marine Division (Reinforced), in action enemy aggressor forces in the vicinity of Songnae Dong, Korea, early on the morning of 21 September 1951. While expertly directing the defense of his position during a probing attack by hostile forces attempting to infiltrate area, Corporal Davenport, acting quickly when an grenade fell into the foxhole which he was occupying with another Marine, skillfully located the deadly projectile in the dark and, undeterred by the personal risk involved, heroically threw himself over the live missile, thereby saving his com-

Jack Arden Davenport

panion from serious injury or possible death. His cool and resourceful leadership were contributing factors in the successful repulse of the enemy attack and his superb courage and admirable spirit of self-sacrifice in the face of almost certain death enhance and sustain the highest traditions of the United States Naval Service. Corporal Davenport gallantly gave his life for his country.

Davis, Raymond Gilbert. Lieutenant Colonel, U.S. Marine Corps, 05831. *Born:* 13 January 1915 at Fitzgerald, GA. *Entered service at:* Atlanta, GA. *Citation:* For conspicuous gallantry and intrepidity at the risk of his life above and beyond the call of duty as Commanding Officer of the First Battalion, Seventh Marines, First Marine Division (Reinforced), in action against enemy aggressor forces in Korea from 1 through 4 December 1950. Although keenly aware that the operation involved breaking through a surrounding enemy and advancing eight miles along primitive icy trails in the bitter cold with every passage disputed by a savage and determined foe, Lieutenant Colonel Davis boldly led his battalion into the attack in a daring attempt to relieve a beleaguered rifle company and to seize, hold and defend a vital mountain pass controlling the only route available for two Marine regiments in danger of being cut off by numerically superior hostile forces during their redeployment to the port of Hungnam. When the battalion immediately encountered strong opposition from entrenched enemy forces command-

Raymond Gilbert Davis

ing high ground in the path of the advance, he promptly spearheaded his unit In a fierce attack up the steep, ice-covered slopes in the face of withering fire and, personally leading the assault groups In a hand-to-hand encounter, drove the hostile troops from their positions, rested his men and reconnoitered the area under enemy fire to determine the best route for continuing the mission. Always in the thick of the fighting, Lieutenant Colonel Davis led his battalion over three successive ridges in the deep snow in continuous attacks against the enemy and, constantly inspiring and encouraging his men throughout the night, brought his unit to a point within 1500 yards of the surrounded rifle company by daybreak. Although knocked to the ground when a shell fragment struck his helmet and two bullets pierced his clothing, he arose and fought his way forward at the head of his men until he reached the isolated Marines. On the following morning, he bravely led his battalion in securing the vital mountain pass from a strongly entrenched and numerically superior hostile force, carrying all his wounded with him, including 22 litter cases and numerous ambulatory patients. Despite repeated savage and heavy assaults by the enemy, he stubbornly held the vital terrain until the two regiments of the division had deployed through the pass and, on the morning of 4 December, led his battalion into Hagaru-ri intact. By his superb leadership, outstanding courage and brilliant tactical ability, Lieutenant Colonel Davis was directly instrumental in saving the beleaguered rifle company from complete annihilation and enabled the two Marine regiments to escape possible destruction. His valiant devotion to duty and unyielding fighting spirit in the face of almost insurmountable odds enhance and sustain the highest traditions of the United States Naval Service. [*Other Navy awards: Navy Cross, two Distinguished Service Medals, two Legions of Merit, two Silver Stars, Bronze Sta w/V. General Davis retired on 31 March 1972.*]

***Dewert, Richard David.** Hospitalman, United States Navy. Medical Corpsman attached to Marine infantry company, 1st Marine Division. *Entered service at:* Massachusetts. *Birth:* Massachusetts. *Citation:* For conspicuous gallantry and intrepidity at the risk of his life above and beyond the call of duty while serving as a Medical Corpsman, attached to a Marine infantry company, First Marine Division, in action against enemy aggressor forces on 5 April 1951. When a fire team from the point platoon of his company was pinned down by a deadly barrage of hostile automatic weapons fire and suffered many casualties, Dewert rushed to the assistance of one of the more seriously wounded and, despite a painful leg wound sustained while dragging the stricken marine to safety, steadfastly refused medical treatment for himself and immediately dashed back through the fire-swept area to carry a second wounded man out of the line of fire. Undaunted by the mounting hail of devastating enemy fire, he bravely moved forward a third time and received another serious wound in the shoulder after discovering that a wounded marine had already died. Still persistent in his refusal to submit to first aid, he resolutely answered the call of a fourth stricken comrade and, while rendering medical assistance, was himself mortally wounded by a burst of enemy fire. His courageous initiative, great personal valor, and heroic spirit of self-sacrifice in the face of overwhelming odds reflect the highest credit upon Dewert and enhance the finest traditions of the United States naval service. He gallantly gave his life for his country.

Dewey, Duane Edgar. Corporal, U.S. Marine Corps Reserve, 1189960. *Born:* 16 November 1931 at Grand Rapids, MI. *Entered service at:* Muskegon, MI. *Citation:* For conspicuous gallantry and intrepidity at the risk of his life above and beyond the call of duty while serving as a Gunner in a Machine-Gun Platoon of Company E, Second Battalion, Fifth Marines, First Marine Division (Reinforced), in action against enemy aggressor forces near Panmunjom, Korea, on 16 April 1952. When an enemy grenade landed close to his position while he and his assistant gunner were receiving medical attention for their wounds during a fierce night attack by numerically superior hostile forces, Corporal Dewey, although suffering intense pain, immediately pulled the corpsman to the ground and, shouting a warning to the other Marines around him, bravely smothered the deadly missile with his body, person-

Duane Edgar Dewey

ally absorbing the full force of the explosion to save his comrades from possible injury or death. His indomitable courage, outstanding initiative and valiant efforts in behalf of others in the face of almost certain death reflect the highest credit upon Corporal Dewey and enhance the finest traditions of the United States Naval Service.

*Garcia, Fernando Luis. Private First Class, U.S. Marine Corps, 1225452. *Born:* 14 October 1929 at Puerto Rico. *Entered service at:* San Juan, PR. *Citation:* For conspicuous gallantry and intrepidity at the risk of his life above and beyond the call of duty while serving as a member of Company I, Third Battalion, Fifth Marines, First Marine Division (Reinforced), in action against enemy aggressor forces in Korea on 5 September 1952. While participating in the defense of a combat outpost located more than one mile forward of the main line of resistance during a savage night attack by a fanatical enemy force employing grenades, mortars and artillery, Private First Class Garcia, although suffering painful wounds, moved through the intense hail of hostile fire to a supply point to secure more hand grenades. Quick to act when a hostile grenade landed nearby, endangering the life of another Marine,

Fernando Luis Garcia

as well as his own, he unhesitatingly chose to sacrifice himself and immediately threw his body upon the deadly missile, receiving the full impact of the explosion. His great personal valor and cool decision in the face of almost certain death sustain and enhance the finest traditions of the United States Naval Service. He gallantly gave his life for his country.

*Gomez, Edward. Private First Class, U.S. Marine Corps Reserve, 1102547 *Born:* 10 August 1932 at Omaha, NE. *Entered service at:* Omaha, NE. *Citation:* For conspicuous gallantry and intrepidity at the risk of his life above and beyond the call of duty while serving as an Ammunition Bearer in Company E, Second Battalion, First Marines, First Marine Division (Reinforced), in action against enemy aggressor forces in Korea on 14 September 1951. Boldly advancing with his squad in support of a group of riflemen assaulting a series of strongly fortified and bitterly defended hostile positions on Hill 749, Private First Class Gomez consistently exposed himself to the withering barrage to keep his machine gun supplied with ammunition during the drive forward to seize the objective. As his squad deployed to meet an imminent counterattack, he voluntarily moved down an abandoned trench to search for a new location for the gun and, when a hos-

Edward Gomez

tile grenade landed between himself and his weapon, shouted a warning to those around him as he grasped the activated charge in his hand. Determined to save his comrades, he unhesitatingly chose to sacrificed himself and, diving into the ditch with the deadly missile absorbed the shattering violence of the explosion in his own body.

By his stouthearted courage, incomparable valor and decisive spirit of self-sacrifice, Private First Class Gomez inspired the others to heroic efforts in subsequently repelling the outnumbered [outnumbering] foe, and his valiant conduct throughout sustained and enhanced the finest traditions the United States Naval Service. He gallantly gave his life for his country.

*Guillen, Ambrosio. Staff Sergeant, U.S. Marine Corps, 661099 *Born:* 7 December 1929 at La Junta, CO. *Entered service at:* El Paso, TX. *Citation:* For conspicuous gallantry and intrepidity at the risk of his life above and beyond the call of duty while serving as a Platoon Sergeant of Company F, Second Battalion Seventh Marines, First Marine Division (Reinforced), action against enemy aggressor forces in Korea on 25 July 1953. Participating in the defense of an outpost forward of the main line of resistance, Staff Sergeant maneuvered his platoon over unfamiliar terrain in the face of hostile fire and placed his men in fighting position. With his unit pinned down when the outpost was attacked under cover of darkness by an estimated force of two enemy battalions supported by mortar and artillery fire, he deliberately exposed himself to the heavy barrage and attacks

Ambrosio Guillen

to direct his men in defending their positions and personally supervise the treatment and evacuation of the wounded. inspired by his leadership, the platoon quickly rallied and engaged the enemy in fierce hand-to-hand combat. Although critically wounded during the course of the battle, Staff Sergeant Guillen refused medical aid and continued to direct his men throughout the remainder of the engagement until the enemy was defeated and thrown into disorderly retreat. Succumbing to his wounds within a few hours, Staff Sergeant Guillen, by his outstanding courage and indomitable spirit, was directly responsible for the success of his platoon in repelling a numerically superior enemy. His personal valor reflects the highest credit upon him. and enhances the finest traditions of th United States Naval Service. He gallantly gave his life for his country.

*Hammond, Francis C. Hospitalman, United States Navy, attached as a medical corpsman to 1st Marine Division. *Entered service at:* Virginia. *Birth:* Virginia. *Citation:* For conspicuous gallantry and intrepidity at the risk of his life above and beyond the call of duty as a medical corpsman serving with the 1st Marine Division in action against enemy aggressor forces in Korea on the night of 26–27 March 1953.

After reaching an intermediate objective during a counterattack against a heavily entrenched and numerically superior hostile force occupying ground on a bitterly contested outpost far in advance of the main line of resistance, Hammond's platoon was subjected to a murderous barrage of hostile mortar and artillery fire, followed by a vicious assault by onrushing enemy troops. Resolutely advancing through the veritable curtain of fire to aid his stricken comrades, Hammond moved among the stalwart garrison of Marines and, although critically wounded himself, valiantly continued to administer aid to the other wounded throughout an exhausting 4-hour period. When the unit was ordered to withdraw, he skillfully directed the evacuation of casualties and remained in the fire-swept area to assist the corpsmen of the relieving unit until he was struck by a round of enemy mortar fire and fell, mortally wounded. B\y his exceptional fortitude, inspiring initiative and self-sacrificing efforts, Hammond undoubtedly saved the lives of many Marines. His great personal valor in the face of overwhelming odds enhances and sustains the finest traditions of the United States naval service. He gallantly gave his life for his country.

James Edmund Johnson

*Johnson, James Edmund. Sergeant, U.S. Marine Corps, 548072. *Born:* 1 January 1926 at Pocatello, ID. *Entered service at:* Pocatello, ID. *Citation:* For conspicuous gallantry and intrepidity at the risk of his life above and beyond the call of duty while serving as a Squad Leader in a Provisional Rifle Platoon composed of Artillerymen and attached to Company J, Third Battalion, Seventh Marines, First Marine Division (Reinforced), in action against enemy aggressor forces at Yudam-ni, Korea, on 2 December 1950. Vastly outnumbered by a well-entrenched and cleverly concealed enemy force wearing uniforms of friendly troops and attacking his platoon's open and unconcealed positions, Sergeant Johnson unhesitatingly took charge of his platoon in the absence of the leader exhibiting great personal valor in the face of a heavy barrage of hostile fire, coolly proceeded to move about among his men, shouting words of encouragement and inspiration and skillfully directing their fire. Ordered to displace his platoon during the fire fight, he immediately placed himself in an extremely hazardous position from which he could provide covering fire for his men. Fully aware that his voluntary action meant either certain death or capture to himself, he courageously continued to provide effective cover for his men and was last observed in a wounded condition single-handedly engaging enemy troops in close hand grenade and hand-to-hand fighting. By his valiant and inspiring leadership, Sergeant Johnson was directly responsible for the successful completion of the platoon's displacement and the saving of many lives. His dauntless fighting spirit and unfaltering devotion to duty in the face of terrific odds reflect the highest credit upon himself and the United States Naval Service.

*Kelly, John Doran. Private First Class, U.S. Marine Corps, 1198164. *Born:* 8 July 1928 at Youngstown, OH. *Entered service at:* Homestead, PA. *Citation:* For conspicuous gallantry and intrepidity at the risk of his life above and beyond the call of duty while serving as a Radio Operator of Company C, First Battalion, Seventh Marines, First Marine Division (Reinforced), in action against enemy aggressor forces in Korea on 28 May 1952. With his platoon pinned down by a numerically superior enemy force employing intense mortar, artillery, small-arms and grenade fire, Private First Class Kelly requested permission to leave his radio in the care of another man and to participate in an assault on enemy key positions. Fearlessly charging forward in the face of a murderous hail of machine-gun fire and hand grenades, he initiated a daring attack against a hostile strong-point and personally neutralized the position, killing two of the enemy. Unyielding in the face of heavy odds, he continued forward and singlehandedly assaulted a machine-gun bunker. Although painfully wounded, he bravely charged the bunker destroyed it, killing three of the enemy. Courageously continuing his one-man assault, he again stormed forward a valiant attempt to wipe out a third bunker and boldly delivered point-blank fire into the aperture of the hostile emplacement. Mortally wounded by enemy fire while carrying out this heroic action, Private First Class Kelly, his great personal valor and aggressive fighting spirit, inspired his comrades to sweep on, overrun and secure objective. His extraordinary heroism in the face of almost certain death reflects the highest credit upon himself and enhances the finest traditions of the United States Naval Service. He gallantly gave his life for his country.

John Doran Kelly

*Kelso, Jack William. Private, U.S. Marine Corps, 1100839. *Born:* 23 January 1934 at Madera, CA. *Entered service at:* Caruthers, CA. *Citation:* For conspicuous gallantry and intrepidity at the risk of his life above and beyond the call of duty while serving as a Rifleman of Company I, Third Battalion, Seventh Marines, First Marine Division (Reinforced), in action against enemy aggressor forces in Korea on 2 October 1952. When both the platoon commander and the platoon sergeant became casualties during the defense of a vital outpost against a numerically superior enemy force attacking at night under cover of intense small-arms, grenade and mortar fire, Private Kelso bravely exposed himself to the hail of enemy fire in a determined effort to reorganize the unit and to repel the onrushing attackers. Forced to seek cover, along with four other Marines, in a nearby bunker which immediately came under attack, he unhesitatingly picked up an enemy grenade which landed in the shelter, rushed out into the open and hurled it back enemy. Although painfully wounded when the grenade exploded as it left his hand, and again forced to seek the protection of the bunker when the hostile fire became more intensified, Private Kelso refused to remain

Jack William Kelso

in his position in comparative safety and moved out into the fire-swept area to return the enemy fire, thereby permitting the pinned-down Marines in the bunker to escape. Mortally wounded while providing covering fire for his comrades, Private Kelso, by his valiant fighting spirit, aggressive determination and self-sacrificing efforts in behalf of others, served to inspire all who observed him. His heroic actions sustain and enhance the highest traditions of the United States Naval Service. He gallantly gave his life for his country. [*Other Navy award: Silver Star.*]

Kennemore, Robert Sidney. Staff Sergeant, U.S. Marine Corps, 285921. *Born:* 21 June 1920 at Greenville, SC. *Entered service at:* Greenville, SC. *Citation:* For conspicuous gallantry and intrepidity at the risk of his life above and beyond the call of duty as Leader of a Machine-Gun Section in Company E, Second Battalion, Seventh Marines, First Marine Division (Reinforced), in action against enemy aggressor forces in Korea on 27 and 28 November 1950. With the company's defensive perimeter overrun by a numerically superior hostile force during a savage night attack north of Yudam-ni and his platoon commander seriously wounded, Staff Sergeant Kennemore unhesitatingly assumed command, quickly reorganized the unit and directed the men in consolidating the position. When an enemy grenade landed in the midst of a machine-gun squad, he

Robert Sidney Kennemore

bravely placed his foot on the missile and, in the face of almost certain death, personally absorbed the full force of the explosion to prevent injury to his fellow Marines. By his indomitable courage, outstanding leadership and selfless efforts in behalf of his comrades, Staff Sergeant Kennemore was greatly instrumental in driving the enemy from the area and upheld the highest traditions of the United States Naval Service.

Kilmer, John E. Hospitalman, United States Navy, attached to duty as a medical corpsman with a Marine rifle company in the 1st Marine Division. *Entered service at:* Texas. *Birth:* Illinois. *Citation:* For conspicuous gallantry and intrepidity at the risk of his life above and beyond the call of duty as a medical corpsman while serving with a Marine rifle company in the 1st Marine Division in action against enemy aggressor forces in Korea on 13 August 1952. With his company engaged in defending a vitally important hill position well forward of the main line of resistance during an assault by large concentrations of hostile troops, Kilmer repeatedly braved intense enemy mortar, artillery, and sniper fire to move from one position to another, administering aid to the wounded and expediting their evacuation. Painfully wounded himself when struck by mortar fragments while moving to the aid of a casualty, he persisted in his efforts and inched his way to the side of the stricken Marine through a hail of enemy shells falling around him. Undaunted by the devastating hostile fire, he skillfully administered first aid to his comrade and, as another mounting barrage of enemy fire shattered the immediate area, unhesitatingly shielded the wounded man with his own body. Mortally wounded by flying shrapnel while

carrying out this heroic action, Kilmer, by his great personal valor and gallant spirit of self-sacrifice in saving the life of a comrade, served to inspire all who observed him. His unyielding devotion to duty in the face of heavy odds reflects the highest credit upon himself and enhances the finest traditions of the United States naval service. He gallantly gave his life for another.

*Littleton, Herbert A. Private First Class, U.S. Marine Corps Reserve, 1084704. *Born:* 1 July 1930 at Mena, AR. *Entered service at:* Blackhawk, SD. *Citation:* For conspicuous gallantry and intrepidity at the risk of his life above and beyond the call of duty while serving as a Radio Operator with an Artillery Forward Observation Team of Company C, First Battalion, Seventh Marines, First Marine Division (Reinforced), in action against enemy aggressor forces in Korea on 22 April 1951. Standing watch when a well-concealed and numerically superior enemy force launched a violent night attack from near-by positions against his company, Private First Class Littleton quickly alerted the forward observation team and immediately moved into an advantageous position to assist in calling down artillery fire on the hostile force. When an enemy hand grenade was thrown into his vantage point shortly

Herbert A. Littleton

after the arrival of the remainder of the team, he unhesitatingly hurled himself on the deadly missile, absorbing its full, shattering impact in his own body. By his prompt action and heroic spirit of self-sacrifice, he saved the other members of his team from serious injury or death and enabled them to carry on the vital mission which culminated in the repulse of the hostile attack. His indomitable valor in the face of almost certain death reflects the highest credit upon Private First Class Littleton and the United States Naval Service. He gallantly gave his life for his country.

*Lopez, Baldomero. First Lieutenant, U.S. Marine Corps, 049344 *Born:* 23 August 1925 at Tampa, FL. *Entered service at:* Tampa, FL. *Citation:* For conspicuous gallantry and intrepidity at the risk of his life above and beyond the call of duty as a Rifle Platoon Commander of Company A, First Battalion, Fifth Marines, First Marine Division (Reinforced), in action against enemy aggressor forces during the Inchon invasion in Korea on 15 September 1950. With his platoon, First Lieutenant Lopez was engaged in the reduction of immediate enemy beach defenses after landing with the assault waves.

Baldomero Lopez

Exposing himself to hostile fire, he moved forward alongside a bunker and prepared to throw a hand grenade into the next pillbox whose fire was pinning down that sector of the beach. Taken under fire by an enemy automatic weapon and hit in the right shoulder and chest as he lifted his arm to throw, he fell backward and dropped the deadly missile. After a moment, he turned and dragged his body forward in an effort to retrieve the grenade and throw it. In critical condition from pain and loss of blood, and unable to grasp the hand grenade firmly enough to hurl it, he chose to sacrifice himself rather than endanger the lives of his men and, with a sweeping motion of his wounded right arm, cradled the grenade under him and absorbed the full impact of the explosion. His exceptional courage, fortitude and devotion to duty reflect the highest credit upon First Lieutenant Lopez and the United States Naval Service. He gallantly gave his life for his country.

*Matthews, Daniel Paul.** Sergeant, U.S. Marine Corps, 1185342. *Born:* 31 December 1931 at Van Nuys, CA. *Entered service at:* Van Nuys, CA. *Citation:* For conspicuous gallantry and intrepidity at the risk of his life above and beyond the call of duty while serving as a Squad Leader of Company F, Second Battalion, Seventh Marines, First Marine Division (Reinforced), in action against enemy aggressor forces in Korea on 28 March 1953. Participating in a counterattack against a firmly entrenched and well-concealed hostile force which had re-pelled six previous assaults on a vital enemy-held outpost far forward of the main line of resistance, Sergeant Matthews fearlessly advanced in the attack until his squad was pinned down by a murderous sweep of fire from an enemy machine gun located on the peak of the outpost. Observing that the deadly

Daniel Paul Matthews

fire prevented a corpsman from removing a wounded man lying in an open area fully exposed to the brunt of the devastating gunfire, he worked his way to the base of the hostile machine-gun emplacement, leaped onto the rock fortification surrounding the gun and, taking the enemy by complete surprise, singlehandedly charged the hostile emplacement with his rifle. Although severely wounded when the enemy brought a withering hail of fire to bear upon him, he gallantly continued his valiant one-man assault and, firing his rifle with deadly effectiveness, succeeded in killing two of the enemy, routing a third and completely silencing the enemy weapon, thereby enabling his comrades to evacuate the stricken Marine to a safe position. Succumbing to his wounds before aid could reach him, Sergeant Matthews, by his indomitable fighting spirit, courageous initiative and resolute determination in the face of almost certain death, served to inspire all who observed him and was directly instrumental in saving the life of his wounded comrade. His great personal valor reflects the highest credit upon himself and enhances the finest traditions of the United States Naval Service. He gallantly gave his life for his country.

*Mausert, Frederick William, III.** Sergeant, U.S. Marine Corps, 1071166. *Born:* 2 May 1930 at Cambridge, NY. *Entered service at:* Dresher, PA. *Citation:* For conspicuous gallantry and intrepidity at the risk of his life above and beyond the call of duty while serving as a Squad Leader In Company B, First Battalion, Seventh Marines, First Marine Division (Reinforced), in action against enemy aggressor forces in Korea on 12 September 1951. With his company pinned down and suffering heavy casualties under murderous machine-gun, rifle, artillery and mortar fire laid down from heavily fortified, deeply entrenched hostile strongholds on Hill 673, Sergeant Mausert unhesitatingly left his covered position and ran through a heavily mined and fire-swept area to bring back two critically wounded men to the comparative safety of the lines. Staunchly refusing evacuation despite a

Frederick William Mausert III

painful head wound sustained during his voluntary act, he insisted on remaining with his squad and, with his platoon ordered into the assault moments later, took the point position and led his men in a furious bayonet charge against the first of a literally impregnable series of bunkers. Stunned and knocked to the ground when another bullet struck his helmet, he regained his feet and resumed his drive, personally silencing the machine gun and leading his men in eliminating several other emplacements in the area. Promptly reorganizing his unit for a renewed fight to the final objective on top of the ridge, Sergeant Mausert boldly left his position when the enemy's fire gained momentum and, making a target of himself, boldly advanced alone into the face of the machine gun, drawing the fire away from his men and enabling them to move into position to assault. Again severely wounded when the enemy's fire found its mark, he still refused aid and continued spearheading the assault to the topmost machine-gun nest and bunkers, the last bulwark of the fanatic aggressors. Leaping into the wall of fire, he destroyed another machine gun with grenades before he was mortally wounded by bursting grenades and machine-gun fire. Stouthearted and indomitable, Sergeant Mausert, by his fortitude, great personal valor and extraordinary heroism In the face of almost certain death, had inspired his men to sweep on, overrun and finally secure the objective. His unyielding courage throughout reflects the highest credit upon himself and the United States Naval Service. He gallantly gave his life for his country.

McLaughlin, Alford Lee. Private First Class, U.S. Marine Corps, 570048. *Born:* 18 March 1928 at Leeds, AL. *Entered service at:* Leeds, AL. *Citation:* For conspicuous gallantry and intrepidity at the risk of his life above and beyond the call of duty while serving as a Machine Gunner of Company I, Third Battalion, Fifth Marines, First Marine Division (Reinforced), in action against enemy aggressor forces in Korea on the night of 4–5 September 1952. Volunteering for his second continuous tour of duty on a strategic combat outpost far in advance of the main line of resistance, Private First Class McLaughlin, although operating under a barrage of enemy artillery and mortar fire, set up plans for the defense of his position which proved decisive in the successful defense of the outpost. When hostile forces attacked in battalion strength during the night, he maintained a constant flow of devastating fire upon the enemy, alternately employing two machine guns, a carbine and hand grenades. Although painfully wounded,

Alford Lee McLaughlin

he bravely fired the machine guns from the hip until his hands became blistered by the extreme heat from the weapons and, placing the guns on the ground to allow them to cool, continued to defend the position with his carbine and grenades. Standing up in view, he shouted words of encouragement to his comrades above the din of battle and, throughout a series of fanatical enemy attacks, sprayed the surrounding area with deadly fire, accounting for an estimated one hundred and fifty enemy dead and wounded. By his indomitable courage, superb leadership, and valiant fighting spirit in the face of overwhelming odds, Private First Class McLaughlin served to inspire his fellow Marines in their gallant stand against the enemy and was directly instrumental in preventing the vital outpost from falling into the hands of a determined and numerically superior hostile force. His outstanding and unwavering devotion to duty reflect the highest credit upon himself and enhance the finest traditions of the United States Naval Service. [*He retired a master sergeant in 1972.*]

Mitchell, Frank Nicias. First Lieutenant, U.S. Marine Corps, 048132. *Born:* 18 August 1921 at Indian Gap, TX. *Entered service at:* Roaring Springs, TX. *Citation:* For conspicuous gallantry and intrepidity at the risk of his life above and beyond the call of duty as Leader of a Rifle Platoon of Company A, First Battalion, Seventh Marines, First Marine Division (Reinforced), in action against enemy aggressor forces in Korea on 26 November 1950. Leading his platoon in point position during a patrol by his company through a thickly wooded and snow-covered area in the vicinity of Hansan-ni, First Lieutenant Mitchell acted immediately when the enemy suddenly opened fire at point-blank range, pinning down his forward elements and inflicting numerous casualties in his ranks. Boldly dashing to the front under blistering fire from automatic weapons and small arms, he seized an automatic rifle from one of the wounded men and effectively trained it against the attackers and, when his ammunition was expended, picked up and hurled grenades with deadly accuracy, at the same time directing and encouraging his men in driving the outnumbering enemy from his position. Maneuvering to setup a defense when the enemy furiously counterattacked to the front and left flank, First Lieutenant Mitchell, despite wounds sustained early in the action, reorganized his platoon under the devastating fire and spearheaded a fierce hand-to-hand struggle to repulse the onslaught. Asking for volunteers to assist in searching for and evacuating the wounded, he personally led a party of litter bearers through hostile lines in growing darkness and, although suffering intense pain from multiple wounds, stormed ahead and waged a singlehanded battle against the enemy, successfully covering the withdrawal of his men before he was fatally truck down by a burst of small-arms fire. Stouthearted

Frank Nicias Mitchell

and indomitable in the face of tremendous odds, First Lieutenant Mitchell, by his fortitude, great personal valor and extraordinary heroism, saved the lives of several Marines and inflicted heavy casualties among the aggressors. His unyielding courage throughout reflects the highest credit upon himself and the United States Naval Service. He gallantly gave his life for his country.

*Monegan, Walter Carleton, Jr. Private First Class, U.S. Marine Corps, 658171. *Born:* 25 December 1930 at Melrose, MA. *Entered service at:* Reading, MA. *Citation:* For conspicuous gallantry and intrepidity at the risk of his life above and beyond the call of duty while serving a Rocket Gunner attached to Company F, Second Battalion, First Marines, First Marine Division (Reinforced), in action against enemy aggressor forces near Sosa-ri, Korea, on 17 and 20 September 1950. Dug in on a hill overlooking the main Seoul highway when six enemy tanks threatened to break through the Battalion position during a pre-dawn attack on 17 September, Private First Class Monegan promptly moved froward with his bazooka under heavy hostile automatic weapons fire and engaged the lead tank at a range of less than 50 yards. After scoring a direct hit and killing the sole surviving tank man with his carbine as

Walter Carleton Monegan, Jr.

he came through the escape hatch, he boldly fired two more rounds of ammunition at the oncoming tanks, disorganizing the attack and enabling our tank crews to continue blasting with their 90-mm. guns. With his own and an adjacent company's position threatened by annihilation when an overwhelming enemy tank-infantry force by-passed the area and proceeded toward the Battalion Command Post during the early morning of September 20, he seized his rocket launcher and, in total darkness, charged down the slope of the hill where the tanks had broken through. Quick to act when an illuminating shell lit the area, he scored a direct hit on one of the tanks as hostile rifle and automatic weapons fire raked the area at close range. Again exposing himself, he fired another round to destroy a second tank and, as the rear tank turned to retreat, stood upright to fire and was fatally struck down by hostile machine-gun fire when another illuminating shell silhouetted him against the sky. Private First Class Monegan's daring initiative, gallant fighting spirit and courageous devotion to duty were contributing factors in the success of his company in repelling the enemy, and his self-sacrificing efforts throughout sustain and enhance the highest traditions of the United States Naval Service. He gallantly gave his life for his country.

***Moreland, Whitt Lloyd.** Private First Class, U.S. Marine Corps Reserve, 1083876. *Born:* 7 March 1930 at Waco, TX. *Entered service at:* Austin, TX. *Citation:* For conspicuous gallantry and intrepidity at the risk of his life above and beyond the call of duty while serving as an Intelligence Scout attached to Company C, First Battalion, Fifth Marines, First Marine Division (Reinforced), in action against enemy aggressor forces in Korea on 29 May 1951. Voluntarily accompanying a rifle platoon in a daring assault against a strongly defended enemy hill position. Private First Class Moreland delivered accurate rifle fire on the hostile emplacement and thereby aided materially in seizing the objective. After the position had been secured, he unhesitatingly led a party forward to neutralize an enemy bunker which he had observed some 400 meters beyond and, moving

Whitt Lloyd Moreland

boldly through a fire-swept area, almost reached the hostile emplacement when the enemy launched a volley of hand grenades on his group. Quick to act despite the personal danger involved, he kicked several of the grenades off the ridge line where they exploded harmlessly and, while attempting to kick away another, slipped and fell near the deadly missile. Aware that the sputtering grenade would explode before he could regain his feet and dispose of it, he shouted a warning to his comrades, covered the missile with his body and absorbed the full blast of the explosion, but in saving his companions from possible injury or death, was mortally wounded. His heroic initiative and valiant spirit of self-sacrifice in the face of certain death reflect the highest credit upon Private First Class Moreland and the United States Naval Service. He gallantly gave his life for his country.

Murphy, Raymond Gerald. Second Lieutenant, U.S. Marine Corps Reserve, 054837. *Born:* 14 January 1930 at Pueblo, CO. *Entered service at:* Pueblo, CO. *Cita-*

tion: For conspicuous gallantry and intrepidity at the risk of his life above and beyond the call of duty as a Platoon Commander of Company A, First Battalion, Fifth Marines, First Marine Division (Reinforced), in action against enemy aggressor forces in Korea on 3 February 1953. Although painfully wounded by fragments from an enemy mortar shell while leading his evacuation platoon in support of assault units attacking a cleverly concealed and well-entrenched hostile force occupying commanding ground, Second Lieutenant Murphy steadfastly refused medical aid and continued to lead his men up a hill through a withering barrage of hostile mortar and small-arms fire, skillfully maneuvering his force from on position to the next and shouting words of encouragement. Undeterred by the increasing intense enemy fire, he immediately located casualties as they fell and made several trips up and down the fire-swept hill to direct evacuation

Raymond Gerald Murphy

teams to the wounded, personally carrying many of the stricken Marines to safety. When reinforcements were needed by the assaulting elements, Second Lieutenant Murphy employed part of his unit as support and, during the ensuing battle, personally killed two of the enemy with his pistol. With all the wounded evacuated and the assaulting units beginning to disengage, he remained behind with a carbine to cover the movement of friendly forces off the hill and, though suffering intense pain from his previous wounds, seized an automatic rifle to provide more firepower when the enemy reappeared in the trenches. After reaching the base of the hill, he organized a search party and again ascended the slope for a final check on missing Marines, locating and carrying the bodies of a machine-gun crew back down the hill. Wounded a second time while conducting the entire force to the line of departure through a continuing barrage of enemy small-arms, artillery and mortar fire, he again refused medical assistance until assured that every one of his men, including all casualties, had preceded him to the main lines. His resolute and inspiring leadership, exceptional fortitude and great personal valor reflect the highest credit upon Second Lieutenant Murphy and enhance the finest traditions of the United States Naval Service.

Myers, Reginald Rodney. Major, U.S. Marine Corps, 08160. Born 26 November 1919 at Boise, ID. *Entered service at:* Twin Falls, ID. *Citation:* For conspicuous gallantry and intrepidity at the risk of his life above and beyond the call of duty as Executive Officer of the Third Battalion, First Marines, First Marine Division (Reinforced), in action against enemy aggressor forces in Korea on 29 November 1950. Assuming command of a composite unit of Army and Marine service and headquarters elements totaling approximately 250 men, during a critical stage in the vital defense of the strategically important military base at Hagaru-ri, Major

Myers immediately initiated a determined and aggressive counterattack against a well-entrenched and cleverly concealed enemy force numbering an estimated 4,000. Severely handicapped by a lack of trained personnel and experienced leaders in his valiant efforts to regain maximum ground prior to daylight, he persisted in constantly exposing himself to intense, accurate and sustained hostile fire in order to direct and supervise the employment of his men and to encourage and spur them on in pressing the attack. Inexorably moving forward up the steep, snow-covered slope with his depleted group in the face of apparently insurmountable odds, he concurrently directed artillery and mortar fire with superb skill and, although losing 170 of his men during fourteen hours of raging combat in sub-zero temperatures, continued to reorganize his unit and spearhead the attack which

Reginald Rodney Myers

resulted in 600 enemy killed and 500 wounded. By his exceptional and valorous leadership throughout, Major Myers contributed directly to the success of his unit in restoring the perimeter. His resolute spirit of self-sacrifice and unfaltering devotion to duty enhance and sustain the highest traditions of the United States Naval Service. [*Other Navy awards: two Bronze Stars w/V. He retired a colonel.*]

*Obregon, Eugene Arnold.** Private First Class, U.S. Marine Corps, 667824. Born 12 November 1930 at Los Angeles, CA. *Entered service at:* Los Angeles, CA. Citation: For conspicuous gallantry and intrepidity at the risk of his life above and beyond the call of duty while serving with Company G, Third Battalion, Fifth Marines, First Marine Division (Reinforced), in action against enemy aggressor forces at Seoul, Korea, on 26 September 1950. While serving as an ammunition carrier of a machine-gun squad in a Marine Rifle Company which was temporarily pinned down by hostile fire, Private First Class Obregon observed a fellow Marine fall wounded in the line of fire. Armed only with a pistol, he unhesitatingly dashed from his covered position to the side of the casualty. Firing his pistol with one hand as he ran, he grasped his

Eugene Arnold Obregon

comrade by the arm with his other hand and, despite and great peril to himself, dragged him to the side of the road. Still under enemy fire, he was bandaging the man's wounds when hostile troops of approximately platoon strength began advancing toward his position. Quickly seizing the wounded Marine's carbine, he placed his own body as a shield in front of him and lay there firing accurately and effectively into the hostile group until he himself was fatally wounded by enemy machine-gun fire. By his courageous fighting spirit, fortitude and loyal devotion to duty, Private First Class Obregon enabled his fellow Marines to rescue the wounded man and aided essentially in repelling the attack, thereby sustaining and enhancing the highest traditions of the United States Naval Service. He gallantly gave his life for his country.

George Herman O'Brien, Jr.

O'Brien, George Herman, Jr. Second Lieutenant, U.S. Marine Corps Reserve, 055937. *Born:* 10 September 1926 at Fort Worth, TX. *Entered service at:* Big Springs, TX. *Citation:* For conspicuous gallantry and intrepidity at the risk of his life above and beyond the call of duty as a Rifle Platoon Commander of Company H, Third Battalion, Seventh Marines, First Marine Division (Reinforced), in action against enemy aggressor forces in Korea on 27 October 1952. With his platoon subjected to an intense mortar and artillery bombardment while preparing to assault a vitally important hill position on the main line of resistance which had been over run by a numerically superior enemy force on the preceding night, Second Lieutenant O'Brien leaped from his trench when the attack signal was given and, shouting for his men to follow, raced across an exposed saddle and up the enemy-held hill through a virtual hail of deadly small-arms, artillery and mortar fire. Although shot through the arm and thrown to the ground by hostile automatic-weapons fire as he neared the well-entrenched enemy position, he bravely regained his feet, waved his men onward and continued to spearhead the assault, pausing only long enough to go to the aid of a wounded Marine. Encountering the enemy at close range, he proceeded to hurl hand grenades into the bunkers and, utilizing his carbine to best advantage in savage hand-to-hand combat, succeeded in killing at least three of the enemy. Struck down by the concussion of grenades on three occasions during the subsequent action, he steadfastly refused to be evacuated for medical treatment and continued to lead his platoon in the assault for a period of nearly four hours, repeatedly encouraging his men and maintaining superb direction of the unit. With the attack halted, he set up a defense with his remaining forces to prepare for a counterattack, personally checking each position, attending to the wounded and expediting their evacuation. When a relief of the position was effected by another unit, he remained to cover the withdrawal and to assure that no wounded were left behind. By his exceptionally daring and forceful leadership in the face of overwhelming odds, Second Lieutenant O'Brien served as a constant source of inspiration to all who observed him and was greatly Instrumental in the recapture of a strategic position on the main line of resistance. His indomitable determination and valiant fighting spirit reflect the highest credit upon himself and enhance the finest traditions of the United States Naval Service. [*He retired a major.*]

Phillips, Lee Hugh. Corporal, U.S. Marine Corps, 654797. *Born:* 3 February 1930 at Stockbridge, GA. *Entered service at:* Ben Hill, GA. *Citation:* For conspicuous gallantry and intrepidity at the risk of his life above and beyond the call of duty while serving as a Squad Leader of Company E, Second Battalion, Seventh Marines, First Marine Division (Reinforced), in action at enemy aggressor forces in Korea on 4 November 1950. Assuming the point position in the attack against a strongly defended and well-entrenched numerically superior enemy force occupying a vital hill position which had been unsuccessfully assaulted on five separate occasions by units of the Marine Corps and other friendly forces, Corporal Phillips fearlessly led his men in a bayonet charge up a precipitous slope under a deadly hail of hostile mortar, small-arms and machine-gun fire. Quickly rallying his squad when it was pinned down by a heavy and accurate mortar barrage, he continued to lead his men through the bombarded area and, although only five members were left the casualty ridden unit, gained the military crest of the where he was immediately subjected to an enemy counter-attack. Although greatly outnumbered by an estimated enemy squad, Corporal Phillips boldly engaged the hostile force with hand grenades and rifle fire and, exhorting his valiant group of Marines to follow him, stormed forward to completely overwhelm the enemy. With only three men now in his squad, he proceeded to spearhead an assault on the last remaining strong point which was defended by four the enemy on a rocky and almost inaccessible portion of hill position. Using one hand to climb up the extremely hazardous precipice, he hurled grenades with the other and, with two remaining comrades, succeeded in annihilating the pocket of resistance and in consolidating the position. Immediately subjected to a sharp counterattack by an estimated enemy squad, he skillfully directed the fire of his men and employed his own weapon with deadly effectiveness repulse the numerically superior hostile force. By his brilliant leadership, indomitable fighting spirit and resolute determination In the face of heavy odds, Corporal Phillips to inspire all who observed him and was directly responsible for the destruction of the enemy stronghold. His great personal valor reflects the highest credit upon himself and enhances and sustains the finest traditions of the United States Naval Service.

*Poynter, James Irsley. Sergeant, U.S. Marine Corps Reserve, 369715. *Born:* 1 December 1916 at Bloomington, IL. *Entered service at:* Bloomington, IL. *Citation:* For conspicuous gallantry and intrepidity at the risk of his life above and beyond the call of duty while serving as a Squad Leader in a Rifle Platoon of Company A, First Battalion, Seventh Marines, First Marine Division (Reinforced), in action against enemy

James Irsley Poynter

aggressor forces during the defense of Hill 532, south of Sudong, Korea, on 4 November 1950. When a vastly outnumbering, well-concealed hostile force launched a sudden, vicious counterattack against his platoon's hasty defensive position, Sergeant Poynter displayed superb skill and courage in leading his squad and directing its fire against the onrushing enemy. With his ranks critically depleted by casualties and he himself critically wounded as the onslaught gained momentum and the hostile force surrounded his position, he seized his bayonet and engaged in bitter hand-to-hand combat as the break-through continued. Observing three machine guns closing in at a distance of twenty-five yards, he dashed from his position and, grasping hand grenades from fallen Marines as he ran, charged the emplacements in rapid succession, killing the crews of two and putting the other out of action before he fell, mortally wounded. By his self-sacrificing and valiant conduct, Sergeant Poynter inspired the remaining members of his squad to heroic endeavor in bearing down upon and repelling the disorganized enemy, thereby enabling the platoon to move out of the trap to a more favorable tactical position. His indomitable fighting spirit, fortitude and great personal valor maintained in the face of overwhelming odds sustain and enhance the finest traditions of the United States Naval Service. He gallantly gave his life for his country.

*Ramer, George Henry. Second Lieutenant, U.S. Marine Corps Reserve, 051575. *Born:* 27 March 1927 at Meyersdale, PA. *Entered service at:* Lewisburg, PA. *Citation:* For conspicuous gallantry and intrepidity at the risk of his life above and beyond the call of duty as Leader of the Third Platoon in Company I, Third Battalion, Seventh Marines, First Marine Division (Reinforced), in action against enemy aggressor forces in Korea on 12 September 1951. Ordered to attack and seize hostile positions atop a hill, vigorously defended by well-entrenched enemy forces delivering massed small-arms, mortar and machine-gun fire, Second Lieutenant Ramer fearlessly led his men up the steep slopes and, although he and the majority of his unit were wounded during the ascent, boldly continued to spearhead the assault. With the terrain becoming more precipitous near the summit and the climb more perilous as the

George Henry Ramer

hostile forces added grenades to the devastating hail of fire, he staunchly carried the attack to the top, personally annihilated one enemy bunker with grenade and carbine fire and captured the objective with his remaining eight men. Unable to hold the position against an immediate, overwhelming hostile counter-attack, he ordered his group to withdraw and singlehandedly fought the enemy to furnish cover for his men and for the evacuation of three fatally wounded Marines. Severely wounded a second time, Second Lieutenant Ramer refused aid when his men returned to help him and, after ordering them to seek shelter, courageously manned his post until the hostile troops overran his position and he fell mortally wounded. His indomitable fighting spirit, inspiring leadership and unselfish concern for others in the face of death reflect the highest credit upon Second Lieutenant Ramer and the United States Naval Service. He gallantly gave his life for his country.

*Reem, Robert Dale. Second Lieutenant, U.S. Marine Corps, 049636. *Born:* 4 June 1928 at Lancaster, PA. *Entered service at:* Elizabethtown, PA. *Citation:* For conspicuous gallantry and intrepidity at the risk of his life above and beyond the call of duty as a Platoon Commander in Company H, Third Battalion, Seventh Marines, First Marine Division (Reinforced), in action against enemy aggressor forces in the vicinity of Chinhung-ni, Korea, on 6 November 1950. Grimly determined to dislodge a group of heavy enemy infantry units occupying well-concealed and strongly fortified positions on commanding ground overlooking unprotected terrain, Second Lieutenant Reem moved slowly forward up the side of the ridge with his platoon in the face of a veritable hail of shattering hostile machine-gun, grenade and rifle fire. Three times repulsed by a resolute enemy force in

Robert Dale Reem

achieving his objective, and pinned down by the continuing fury of hostile fire, he rallied and regrouped the heroic men in his depleted and disorganized platoon in preparation for a fourth attack. Issuing last-minute orders to his non-commissioned officers when an enemy grenade landed in a depression of the rocky ground in which the group was standing, Second Lieutenant Reem unhesitatingly chose to sacrifice himself and, springing upon the deadly missile, absorbed the full impact of the explosion in his own body, thus protecting others from serious injury and possible death. Stout-hearted and indomitable, he readily yielded his own chance of survival that his subordinate leaders might live to carry on the fight against a fanatic enemy. His superb courage, cool decisiveness and valiant spirit of self-sacrifice in the face of certain death reflect the highest credit upon Second Lieutenant Reem and the United States Naval Service. He gallantly gave his life for his country.

*Shuck, William Edward, Jr. Staff Sergeant, U.S. Marine Corps, 658047. *Born:* 16 August 1926 in Maryland. *Entered service at:* Ridgeley, WV. *Citation:* For conspicuous gallantry and intrepidity at the risk of his life above and beyond the call of duty while serving as a Squad Leader of Company G, Third Battalion, Seventh Marines, First Marine Division (Reinforced), in action against enemy aggressor forces in Korea on 3 July 1952. When his platoon was subjected to a devastating barrage of enemy small-arms, grenade, artillery and mortar fire during an assault against strongly fortified hill positions well forward of the main line of resistance, Staff Sergeant Shuck, although painfully wounded, refused medical attention and continued to lead his machine-gun squad in the attack. Unhesitatingly assuming command of a rifle squad when the leader became a casualty, he skillfully organized the two squads into an attacking force and led two more daring assaults upon the hostile positions. Wounded a second time, he steadfastly refused evacuation and remained in the foremost position under heavy fire until assured that all dead and wounded were evacuated. Mortally wounded by an enemy sniper bullet while voluntarily assisting in the removal of the last casualty, Staff Sergeant Shuck, by his fortitude and great personal valor in the face of overwhelming odds, served to inspire all who observed him. His unyielding courage throughout reflects the highest credit upon himself and the United States Naval Service. He gallantly gave his life for his Country.

William Edward Shuck, Jr.

Simanek, Robert Ernest. Private First Class, U.S. Marine Corps, 1207049. *Born:* 26 April 1930 at Detroit, MI. *Entered service at:* Detroit, MI. *Citation:* For conspicuous gallantry and intrepidity at the risk of his life above and beyond the call

Robert Ernest Simanek

of duty while serving with Company F, Second Battalion, Fifth Marines, First Marine Division (Reinforced), in action against enemy aggressor forces in Korea on 17 August 1952. While accompanying a patrol en route to occupy a combat outpost forward of friendly lines, Private First Class Simanek exhibited a high degree of courage and a resolute spirit of self-sacrifice in protecting the lives of his fellow Marines. With his unit ambushed by an intense concentration of enemy mortar and small-arms fire, and suffering heavy casualties, he was forced to seek cover with the remaining members of the patrol in a near-by trench line. Determined to save his comrades when a hostile grenade was hurled into their midst, he unhesitatingly threw himself on the deadly missile, absorbing the shattering violence of the exploding charge in his own body and shielding his fellow Marines from serious injury or death. Gravely wounded as a result of his heroic action, Private First Class Simanek, by his daring initiative and great personal valor in the face of almost certain death, served to inspire all who observed him and upheld the highest traditions of the United States Naval Service.

Carl Leonard Sitter

Sitter, Carl Leonard. Captain, U.S. Marine Corps, 016377. *Born:* 2 December 1921 at Syracuse, MO. *Entered service at:* Pueblo, CO. *Citation:* For conspicuous gallantry and intrepidity at the risk of his life above and beyond the call of duty as Commanding Officer of Company G, Third Battalion, First Marines, First Marine Division (Reinforced), in action against enemy aggressor forces at Hagaru-ri, Korea, on 29 and 30 November 1950. Ordered to break through enemy-infested territory to reinforce his Battalion the early morning of 29 November, Captain Sitter continuously exposed himself to enemy fire as he led his company forward and, despite twenty-five percent casualties suffered in the furious action, succeeded in driving through to his objective. Assuming the responsibility of attempting to seize and occupy a strategic area occupied by a hostile force of regiment strength deeply entrenched on a snow-covered hill commanding the entire valley southeast of the town, as well as the line of march of friendly troops withdrawing to the south, he reorganized his depleted units the following morning and boldly led them up the steep, frozen hillside under blistering fire, encouraging and redeploying his troops as casualties occurred and directing forward platoons as they continued the drive to the top of the ridge. During the night when a vastly outnumbering enemy launched a sudden, vicious counterattack, setting the hill ablaze with mortar, machine-gun and automatic weapons fire and taking a heavy toll in troops, Captain Sitter visited each foxhole and gun position, coolly deploying and integrating reinforcing units consisting of service personnel unfamiliar with infantry tactics into a coordinated combat team and instilling in every man the will and determination to hold his position at all costs. With the enemy penetrating his lines in repeated counterattacks which often required hand-to-hand combat and, on one occasion infiltrating to the command post with hand grenades, he fought gallantly with his men in repulsing and killing the fanatic attackers in each encounter. Painfully wounded in the face, arms and chest by bursting grenades, he staunchly refused to be evacuated and continued to fight on until a successful defense of the area was assured with a loss to the enemy of more than fifty percent dead, wounded and captured. His valiant leadership, superb tactics and great personal valor throughout thirty-six hours of bitter combat reflect the highest credit upon Captain Sitter, and the United States Naval Service. [*Other Navy awards: Silver Star, Legion of Merit. He retired a colonel on 30 June 1970.*]

Sherrod Emerson Skinner, Jr.

*Skinner, Sherrod Emerson, Jr.** Second Lieutenant, U.S. Marine Corps Reserve, 054537. *Born:* 29 October 1929 at Hartford, CT. *Entered service at:* East Lansing, MI. *Citation:* For conspicuous gallantry and intrepidity at the risk of his life above and beyond the call of duty as an Artillery Forward Observer of Battery F, Second Battalion, Eleventh Marines, First Marine Division (Reinforced), in action against enemy aggressor forces in Korea on the night of 26 October 1952. When his observation post in an extremely critical and vital sector of the main line of resistance was subjected to a sudden and fanatical attack by hostile forces, supported by a devastating barrage of artillery and mortar fire which completely severed communication lines connecting the outpost with friendly firing batteries, Second Lieutenant Skinner, in a determined effort to hold his position, immediately organized and directed the surviving personnel in the defense of the outpost, continuing to call down fire on the enemy by means of radio alone until this equipment became damaged beyond repair. Undaunted by the intense hostile barrage and the rapidly closing attackers, he twice left the protection of his bunker in order to direct accurate machine-gun fire and to replenish the depleted supply of ammunition and grenades. Although painfully wounded on each occasion, he steadfastly refused medical aid until the rest of the men received treatment. As the ground attack reached its climax, he gallantly directed the final defense until the meager supply of ammunition was exhausted and the position overrun. During the three hours that the outpost was occupied by the enemy, several grenades were thrown into the bunker which served as protection for Second Lieutenant Skinner and his remaining comrades. Realizing that there was no chance for other than passive resistance, he directed his men to feign death even though the hostile troops entered the bunker and searched their persons. Later, when an enemy grenade was thrown between him and two other survivors, he immediately threw himself on the deadly missile in an effort to protect the others, absorbing the full force of the explosion and sacrificing his life for his comrades. By his indomitable fighting spirit, superb leadership and great personal valor in the face of tremendous odds, Second Lieutenant Skinner served to inspire his fellow Marines in their heroic stand against the enemy and upheld the highest traditions of the United States Naval Service. He gallantly gave his life for his country.

Van Winkle, Archie. Staff Sergeant, U.S. Marine Corps Reserve, 506441 Born 17 March 1925 at Juneau, AK. *Entered service at:* Arlington, WA. *Citation:* For conspicuous gallantry and intrepidity at the risk of his life above and beyond the call of duty while serving as a Platoon Sergeant in Company B, First Battalion, Seventh Marines, First Marine Division (Reinforced), In action against enemy aggressor forces in the vicinity of Sudong, Korea, on 2 November 1950. Immediately rallying the men in his area after a fanatical and numerically superior enemy force penetrated the center of the line under cover of darkness and pinned down the platoon with a devastating barrage of deadly automatic weapons and grenade fire, Staff Sergeant Van Winkle boldly spearheaded a determined attack through withering fire against hostile frontal positions and, though he and all the others who charged

Archie Van Winkle

with him were wounded, succeeded in enabling his platoon to gain the fire superiority and the opportunity to reorganize. Realizing that the left-flank squad was isolated from the rest of the unit, he rushed through forty yards of fierce enemy fire to reunite his troops despite an elbow wound which rendered one of his arms totally useless. Severely wounded a second time when a direct hit in the chest from a hostile hand grenade caused serious and painful wounds, he staunchly refused evacuation and continued to shout orders and words of encouragement to his depleted and battered platoon. Finally carried from his position unconscious from shock and loss of blood, Staff Sergeant Van Winkle served to inspire all who observed him to heroic efforts in successfully repulsing the enemy attack. His superb leadership, valiant fighting spirit and unfaltering devotion to duty in the face of heavy odds reflect the highest credit upon himself and the United States Naval Service.

*****Vittori, Joseph.** Corporal, U.S. Marine Corps Reserve, 645720. *Born:* 1 August 1929 at Beverly, MA. *Entered service at:* Beverly, MA. *Citation:* For conspicuous gallantry and intrepidity at the risk of his life above and beyond the call of duty while serving as an Automatic Rifleman in Company F, Second Battalion, First Marines, First Marine Division (Reinforced), in action against enemy aggressor forces in Korea on 15 and 16 September 1951. With a forward platoon suffering heavy casualties and forced to withdraw under a vicious enemy counterattack as his company assaulted strong hostile forces entrenched on Hill 749, Corporal Vittori boldly rushed through the withdrawing troops with two other volunteers from his reserve platoon and plunged directly into the midst of the enemy. Overwhelming them in a fierce hand-to-hand struggle, he enabled his company to consolidate its positions to meet further imminent onslaughts. Quick to respond to an urgent call for a rifleman to defend a heavy machine gun positioned on the extreme point of the northern flank and virtually isolated from the remainder of the unit when the enemy again struck in force during the night, he assumed position under the devastating barrage and, fighting a singlehanded battle, leaped from one flank to the other, covering each foxhole in turn as casualties continued to mount, manning a machine gun when the gunner was struck down and making repeated trips through the heaviest shell fire to replenish ammunition. With the situation becoming extremely critical, reinforcing units to the rear pinned

Joseph Vittori

down under the blistering attack and foxholes left practically void by dead and wounded for a distance of 100 yards, Corporal Vittori continued his valiant stand, refusing to give ground as the enemy penetrated to within feet of his position, simulating strength in the line and denying the foe physical occupation of the ground. Mortally wounded by enemy machine-gun and rifle bullets while persisting in his magnificent defense of the sector where approximately 200 enemy dead were found the following morning, Corporal Vittori, by his fortitude, stouthearted courage and great personal valor, had kept the point position intact despite the tremendous odds and undoubtedly prevented the entire battalion position from collapsing. His extraordinary heroism throughout the furious night-long battle reflects the highest credit upon himself and the United States Naval Service. He gallantly gave his life for his country.

*Watkins, Lewis George. Staff Sergeant, U.S. Marine Corps, 1152688. *Born:* 7 June 1925 at Waldo, AR. *Entered service at:* Texas. *Citation:* For conspicuous gallantry and intrepidity at the risk of his life above and beyond the call of duty while serving as a Guide of a Rifle Platoon of Company I, Third Battalion, Seventh Marines, First Marine Division (Reinforced), in action against enemy aggressor forces in Korea during the hours of darkness on the morning of 7 October 1952. With his platoon assigned the mission of retaking an outpost which had been overrun by the enemy earlier in the night, Staff Sergeant Watkins skillfully led his unit in the assault up the

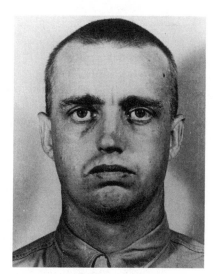

Lewis George Watkins

designated hill. Although painfully wounded when a well-entrenched hostile force at the crest of the hill engaged the platoon with intense small-arms and grenade fire, he gallantly continued to lead his men. Obtaining an automatic rifle from one of the wounded men, he assisted in pinning down an enemy machine gun holding up the assault. When an enemy grenade landed among Staff Sergeant Watkins and several other Marines while they were moving forward through a trench on the hill crest, he immediately pushed his companions aside, placed himself in a position to shield them and picked up the deadly missile in an attempt to throw it outside the trench. Mortally wounded when the grenade exploded in his hand, Staff Sergeant Watkins, by his great personal valor in the face of almost certain death, saved the lives of several of his comrades and contributed materially to the success of the mission. His extraordinary heroism, inspiring leadership and resolute spirit of self-sacrifice reflect the highest credit upon himself and enhance the finest traditions of the United States Naval Service. He gallantly gave his life for his country.

Wilson, Harold Edward. Technical Sergeant, U.S. Marine Corps Reserve, 376827. *Born:* 5 December 1921 at Birmingham, AL. *Entered service at:* Birmingham, AL. *Citation:* For gallantry and intrepidity at the risk of his life above and beyond the call of duty while serving as Platoon Sergeant of a Rifle Platoon attached to Company G, Third Battalion, First Marines, First Marine Division (Reinforced), in action against enemy aggressor forces in Korea on the night of 23–24 April 1951. When the company outpost was overrun by the enemy while his platoon, firing from hastily-constructed foxholes, was engaged in resisting the brunt of a fierce mortar, machine-gun, grenade and small-arms attack launched by hostile forces from high ground under cover of darkness, Technical Sergeant Wilson braved intense fire to assist the survivors back into the line and to direct

Harold Edward Wilson

the treatment of casualties. Although twice wounded by gunfire, in the right arm and the left leg, he refused medical aid for himself and continued to move about among his men, shouting words of encouragement. After receiving further wounds in the head and shoulder as the attack increased in intensity, he again insisted upon remaining with his unit. Unable to use either arm to fire, and with mounting casualties among our forces, he re-supplied his men with rifles and ammunition taken from the wounded. Personally reporting to his company commander on several occasions, he requested and received additional assistance when the enemy attack became even more fierce and, after placing the reinforcements in strategic positions in the line, directed effective fire until blown off his feet by the bursting of a hostile mortar round in his face. Dazed and suffering from concussion, he still refused medical aid and, despite weakness from loss of blood, moved from foxhole to foxhole, directing fire, re-supplying ammunition, rendering first aid and encouraging his men. By his heroic actions in the face of almost certain death, when the unit's ability to hold the disadvantageous position was doubtful, he instilled confidence in his troops, inspiring them to rally repeatedly and turn back the furious assaults. At dawn, after the final attack had been repulsed, he personally accounted for each man in his platoon before walking unassisted one-half mile to the aid station where he submitted to treatment. His outstanding courage, initiative and skilled leadership in the face of overwhelming odds were contributing factors in the success of his company's mission and reflect the highest credit upon Technical Sergeant Wilson and the United States Naval Service.

*Windrich, William Gordon.** Staff Sergeant, U.S. Marine Corps, 266468. *Born:* 14 May 1921 at Chicago, IL. *Entered service at:* Hammond, IN. *Citation:* For conspicuous gallantry and intrepidity at the risk of his life above and beyond the call of duty as a Platoon Sergeant of Company I, Third Battalion, Fifth Marines, First Marine Division (Reinforced), in action against enemy aggressor forces in the vicinity of Yudam-ni, Korea, the night of 1 December 1950. Promptly organizing a squad of men when the enemy launched a sudden, vicious counterattack against the forward elements of his company's position, rendering it untenable, Staff Sergeant Windrich, armed with a Carbine, spearheaded the assault to the top of the knoll immediately confronting the overwhelming force and, under shattering hostile automatic weapons, mortar and grenade fire, directed

William Gordon Windrich

effective fire to hold back the attackers and cover the withdrawal of our troops to commanding ground. With seven of his men struck down during the furious action and he, himself, wounded in the head by a bursting grenade, he made his way to his company's position and, organizing a small group of volunteers, returned with them to evacuate the wounded and dying from the frozen hillside, staunchly refusing medical attention himself. Immediately redeploying the remainder of his troops, Staff Sergeant Windrich placed them on the left flank of the defensive sector before the enemy again attacked in force. Wounded in the leg during the bitter fight that followed, he bravely fought on with his men, shouting words of encouragement and directing their fire until the attack was repelled. Refusing evacuation although unable to stand, he still continued to direct his platoon in setting up defensive positions until, weakened by the bitter cold, excessive loss of blood and severe pain, he lapsed into unconsciousness and died. His valiant leadership, fortitude and courageous fighting spirit against tremendous odds served to inspire others to heroic endeavor in holding the objective and reflect the highest credit upon Staff Sergeant Windrich and the United States Naval Service. He gallantly gave his life for his country.

Vietnam • 1964–1973

***Anderson, James, Jr.** Private First Class, U.S. Marine Corps, 2nd Platoon, Company F, 2nd Battalion, 3rd Marines, 3rd Marine Division. *Place and date:* Republic of Vietnam, 28 February 1967. *Entered service at:* Los Angeles, CA. *Date and place of birth:* January 22, 1947, Los Angeles, CA. *Citation:* For conspicuous gallantry and intrepidity at the risk of his life above and beyond the call of duty. Company F was advancing in dense jungle northwest of Cam Lo in an effort to extract a heavily besieged reconnaissance patrol. Private First Class Anderson's platoon was the lead element and had advanced only about 200 meters when they were brought under extremely intense enemy small arms and automatic weapons fire. The platoon reacted swiftly, getting on line as best they could in the thick terrain, and began returning fire. Private First Class Anderson found himself tightly bunched together with the other members of the platoon only 20 meters from the enemy positions. As the fire fight continued several of the men were wounded by the deadly enemy assault. Suddenly, an enemy grenade landed in the midst of the Marines and rolled along side Private First Class Anderson's head. Unhesitatingly and with complete disregard for his own personal safety, he reached out, grasped the grenade, pulled it to his chest and curled around it as it went off. Although several Marines received shrapnel from the grenade, his body absorbed the major force of the explosion. In this singularly heroic act, Private First Class Anderson saved his comrades from serious injury and possible death. His personal heroism, extraordinary valor, and inspirational supreme self-sacrifice reflected great credit upon himself and the Marine Corps and upheld the highest traditions of the United States Naval Service. He gallantly gave his life for his country.

***Anderson, Richard Allen.** Lance Corporal, U.S. Marine Corps, Company E, 3rd Reconnaissance Battalion, 3rd Marine Division. *Place and date:* Quang Tri Province, Republic of Vietnam, 24 August 1969. *Entered service at:* Houston, TX. *Date and place of birth:* 16 April 1948, Washington, D.C. *Citation:* For conspicuous gallantry and intrepidity at the risk of his life above and beyond the call of duty while serving as an Assistant Team Leader with Company E, 3rd Reconnaissance Battalion, 3rd Marine Division, in connection with combat operations against an armed enemy in the Republic of Vietnam. While conducting a patrol during the early hours of 24 August 1969, Lance Corporal Anderson's reconnaissance team came under a heavy volume of automatic weapons and machine gun fire from a numerically superior and well concealed enemy force. Although painfully wounded in both legs and knocked

Richard Allen Anderson

to the ground during the initial moments of the fierce fire fight, Lance Corporal Anderson assumed a prone position and continued to deliver intensive suppressive fire in an attempt to repulse the attackers. Moments later he was wounded a second time by an enemy soldier who had approached to within eight feet of the team's position. Undaunted, he continued to pour a relentless stream of fire at the assaulting unit, while a companion was treating his leg wounds. Observing an grenade land between himself and the other Marine, Lance Corporal Anderson immediately rolled over and covered the lethal weapon with his body, absorbing the full effects of the detonation. By his indomitable courage, inspiring initiative, and selfless devotion to duty, Lance Corporal Anderson was instrumental in saving several Marines from serious injury or possible death. His actions were in keeping with the highest traditions of the Marine Corps and of the United States Naval Service. He gallantly gave his life in the service of his country.

*Austin, Oscar P. Private First Class, U.S. Marine Corps, Company E, 2nd Battalion, 7th Marines, 1st Marine Division (Rein), FMF. *Place and date:* West of Da Nang, Republic of Vietnam, 23 February 1969. *Entered service at:* Phoenix, AZ. *Date and place of Birth:* 15 January 1948, Nacogdoches, TX. *Citation:* For conspicuous gallantry and intrepidity at the risk of his life above and beyond the call of duty while serving as an Assistant Machine Gunner with Company E, 2nd Battalion, 7th Marines, 1st Marine Division, in connection with operations against enemy forces in the Republic of Vietnam. During the early morning hours of 23 February 1969, Private First Class Austin's observation post was subjected to a fierce ground attack by a large North Vietnamese Army force supported by a heavy volume of hand grenades, satchel charges, and small arms fire. Observing that

Oscar P. Austin

one of his wounded companions had fallen unconscious in a position dangerously exposed to the hostile fire, Private First Class Austin unhesitatingly left the relative security of his fighting hole and, with complete disregard for his own safety, raced across the fire-swept terrain to assist the Marine to a covered location. As he neared the casualty he observed an enemy grenade land nearby and, reacting instantly, leaped between the injured Marine and the lethal object, absorbing the effects of its detonation. As he ignored his painful injuries and turned to examine the wounded man, he saw a North Vietnamese Army soldier aiming a weapon at his unconscious companion. With full knowledge of the probable consequences and thinking only to protect the Marine, Private First Class Austin resolutely threw himself between the casualty and the hostile soldier, and, in doing, was mortally wounded. Private First Class Austin's indomitable courage, inspiring initiative and selfless devotion to duty upheld the highest traditions of the Marine Corps and the United States Naval Service. He gallantly gave his life for his country.

Ballard, Donald E. Hospital Corpsman Third Class, United States Navy, Company M, 3rd Battalion, 4th Marines, 3rd Marine Division. *Place and date:* Quang Tri Province, Republic of Vietnam, 16 May 1968. *Entered service at:* Kansas City, MO. *Date and place of birth:* 5 December 1945, Kansas City, MO. *Citation:* For conspicuous intrepidity at the risk of his life and beyond the call of duty on 16 May 1968 while serving as a Corpsman with Company M, 3rd Battalion, 4th Marines, 3rd Marine Division in connection with operations against enemy aggressor forces in the Republic of Vietnam. During the afternoon hours, Company M was moving to join the remainder of the 3rd Battalion in Quang Tri Province. After treating and evacuating two heat casualties, Petty Officer Ballard was returning to his platoon from the evacuation landing zone when the company was ambushed by a North Vietnamese Army unit employing automatic weapons and mortars, and sustained numerous casualties. Observing a wounded Marine, Petty Officer Ballard unhesitatingly moved across the fire-swept terrain to the injured man and swiftly rendered medical assistance to his comrade. Petty Officer Ballard then directed four Marines to carry the casualty to a position of relative safety. As the four men prepared to move the wounded Marine, an enemy soldier suddenly left his concealed position and, after hurling a hand grenade which landed near the casualty, commenced firing upon the small group of men. Instantly shouting a warning to the Marines, Petty Officer Ballard fearlessly threw himself upon the lethal explosive device to protect his comrades from the deadly blast. When the grenade failed to detonate, he calmly arose from his dangerous position and resolutely continued his determined efforts in treating other Marine casualties. Petty Officer Ballard's heroic actions and selfless concern for the welfare of his companions served to inspire all who observed him and prevented possible injury or death to his fellow Marines. His courage, daring initiative, and unwavering devotion to duty in the face of extreme personal danger, sustain and enhance the finest traditions of the United States Naval Service.

*Barker, Jedh Colby. Lance Corporal, U.S. Marine Corps, Company F, 2nd Battalion, 4th Marines, 3rd Marine Division (Rein), FMF. *Place and date:* Near Con Thein, Republic of Vietnam, 21 September 1967. *Entered service at:* New York, NY. *Date and place of birth:* 20 June 1945, Franklin, NH. *Citation:* For conspicuous gallantry and intrepidity at the risk of his life above and beyond the call of duty while serving as a machine gunner with Company F, 2nd Battalion, 4th Marines, 3rd Marine Division, in the Republic of Vietnam on 21 September 1967. During a reconnaissance operation near Con Thien, Corporal Barker's squad was suddenly hit by enemy sniper fire. The squad immediately deployed to a combat formation and advanced to a strongly fortified enemy position, when it was again struck by small arms and automatic weapons fire, sustaining numerous casualties. Although wounded by the initial burst of fire, Corporal Barker boldly remained in the open, delivering a devastating volume of accurate fire on the numerically superior force. The enemy was intent upon annihilating the small Marine force and, realizing that Corporal Barker was a

Jedh Colby Barker

threat to their position, directed the preponderance of their fire on his position. He was again wounded, this time in the right hand, which prevented him from operating his vitally needed machine-gun. Suddenly, and without warning, an enemy grenade landed in the midst of the few surviving Marines. Unhesitatingly and with complete disregard for his own personal safety, Corporal Barker threw himself upon the deadly grenade, absorbing with his own body the full and tremendous force of the explosion. In a final act of bravery, he crawled to the side of a wounded comrade and administered first aid before succumbing to his grievous wounds. His bold initiative, intrepid fighting spirit and unwavering devotion to duty in the face of almost certain death undoubtedly saved his comrades from further injury or possible death and reflected great credit upon himself, the Marine Corps, and the United States Naval Service. He gallantly gave his life for his country.

Barnum, Harvey Curtiss, Jr. Captain, U.S. Marine Corps, Company H, 2nd Battalion, 9th Marines, 3d Marine Division, (Reinforced). *Place and date:* Ky Phu in Quang Tri Province, Republic of Vietnam, 18 December 1965. *Place and place of birth:* 21 July 1940, Waterbury, CT. *Entered service at:* Cheshire, CT. *Citation:* For conspicuous gallantry and intrepidity at the risk of his life above and beyond the call of duty When the company was suddenly pinned down by a hail of extremely accurate enemy fire and was quickly separated from the remainder of the battalion by over 500 meters of open and fire-swept ground, and casualties mounted rapidly. Lieutenant Barnum quickly made a hazardous reconnaissance of the area seeking targets for his artillery. Finding the rifle company commander mortally wounded and the radio operator killed, he, with complete disregard for his own safety, gave aid to the dying commander, then removed the radio from

Harvey Curtiss Barnum, Jr.

the dead operator then strapped it to himself. He immediately assumed command of the rifle company, and moving at once into the midst of the heavy fire, rallying and giving encouragement to all units, reorganized them and led their attack on enemy positions from which deadly fire continued to come. His sound and swift decisions and his obvious calm served to stabilize the badly decimated units and his gallant example as he stood exposed repeatedly to point out targets served as an inspiration to all. Provided with two armed helicopters, he moved fearlessly through enemy fire to control the air attack against the firmly entrenched enemy while skillfully directing one platoon in a successful counterattack on the key enemy positions.

Having thus cleared a small area, he requested and directed the landing of two transport helicopters for the evacuation of the dead and wounded. He then assisted in the mopping up and final seizure of the battalion's objective. His gallant initiative and heroic conduct reflected great credit upon himself and were in keeping with the highest traditions of the Marine Corps and the United States Naval Service. [*Other Navy awards: two Bronze Stars w/V. He retired a colonel.*]

John Paul Bobo

***Bobo, John Paul.** Second Lieutenant U.S. Marine Corps, 3rd Battalion, 9th Marines, 3rd Marine Division (Rein) FMF. *Place and date:* Quang Tri Province, Republic of Vietnam, 30 March 1967. *Entered service at:* Buffalo, NY. *Date and place of birth:* 14 February 1943, Niagara Falls, NY. *Citation:* For conspicuous gallantry and intrepidity at the risk of his life above and beyond the call of duty. Company I was establishing night ambush sites when the command group was attacked by a reinforced North Vietnamese company supported by heavy automatic weapons and mortar fire. Lieutenant Bobo immediately organized a hasty defense and moved from position to position encouraging the outnumbered Marines despite the murderous enemy fire. Recovering a rocket launcher from among the friendly casualties, he organized a new launcher team and directed its fire into the enemy machine-gun positions. When an exploding enemy mortar round severed Lieutenant Bobo's right leg below the knee, he refused to be evacuated and insisted upon being placed in a firing' position to cover the movement of the command group to a better location. With a web belt around his leg serving as a tourniquet and with his leg jammed into the dirt to curtain the bleeding, he remained in this position and delivered devastating fire into the ranks of the enemy attempting to overrun the Marines, Lieutenant Bobo was mortally wounded while firing his weapon into the main-point of the enemy attack but his valiant spirit inspired his men to heroic efforts, and his tenacious stand enabled the command group to gain a protective position where it repulsed the enemy onslaught. Lieutenant Bobo's superb leadership, dauntless courage, and bold initiative reflected great credit upon himself and upheld the highest traditions of the Marine Corps and the United States Naval Service. He gallantly gave his life for his country.

***Bruce, Daniel D.** Private First Class, U.S. Marine Corps, Headquarters and Service Company, 3rd Battalion, 5th Marines, 1st Marine Division. *Place and date:* Quang Nam Province, Republic of Vietnam, 1 March 1969. *Entered service at:* Chicago, IL. *Date and place of birth:* 18 May 1950, Michigan City, IN. *Citation:* For conspicu-

Daniel D. Bruce

ous gallantry and intrepidity at the risk of his life above and beyond the call of duty while serving as a Mortar Man with Headquarters and Service Company, 3rd Battalion, 5th Marines, 1st Marine Division, against the enemy in the Republic of Vietnam. Early on the morning of 1 March 1969, Private First Class Bruce was on watch in his night defensive position at Fire Support Base Tomahawk in Quang Nam Province when he heard movements ahead of him. An enemy explosive charge was thrown toward his position and he reacted instantly, catching the device and shouting to alert his companions. Realizing the danger to the adjacent position with its two occupants, Private First Class Bruce held the device to his body and attempted to carry it from the vicinity of the entrenched Marines. As he moved away, the charge detonated and he absorbed the full force of the explosion. Private First Class Bruce's indomitable courage, inspiring valor and selfless devotion to duty saved the lives of three of his fellow Marines and upheld the highest traditions of the Marine Corps and the United States Naval Service. He gallantry gave his life for his country.

*Burke, Robert C. Private First Class, U.S. Marine Corps, Company I, 3rd Battalion, 27th Marines, 1st Marine Division (Rein), FMF. *Place and date:* Southern Quang Nam Province, Republic of Vietnam, 17 May 1968. *Entered service* at: Chicago, IL. *Date and place of birth:* 7 November 1949, Monticello, IL. *Citation:* For conspicuous gallantry and intrepidity at the risk of his life above and beyond the call of duty for service as a Machine Gunner with Company I, 3rd Battalion, 27th Marines, 1st Marine Division in the Republic of Vietnam on 17 May 1968. While on Operation ALLEN BROOK, Company I was approaching a dry river bed with a heavily wooded tree-line that borders the hamlet of Le Nam (1), when they suddenly came under intense mortar, rocket propelled grenade, automatic weapons and small arms fire from a large, well concealed enemy force which halted the company's advance and

Robert C. Burke

wounded several Marines. Realizing that key points of resistance had to be eliminated to allow the units to advance and casualties to be evacuated, Private Burke, without hesitation, seized his machine-gun and launched a series of one-man assaults against the fortified emplacements. As he aggressively maneuvered to the edge of the steep river bank, he delivered accurate suppressive fire upon several enemy bunkers, which enabled his comrades to advance and move the wounded Marines to positions of relative safety. As he continued his combative actions, he located an opposing automatic weapons emplacement and poured intense fire into the position, killing three North Vietnamese soldiers as they attempted to flee. Private Burke then fearlessly moved from one position to another, quelling the hostile fire until his weapon malfunctioned. Obtaining a casualty's rifle and hand grenades, he advanced further into the midst of the enemy fire in an assault against another pocket of resistance, killing two more of the enemy. Observing that a fellow Marine had cleared his malfunctioning machine-gun he grasped his weapon and moved into a dangerously exposed area and saturated the hostile tree-line until he fell mortally wounded. Private Burke's gallant actions upheld the highest traditions of the Marine Corps and the United States Naval Service. He gallantly gave his life for his country.

*Capodanno, Vincent R. Lieutenant, Chaplain Corps, United States Navy, 3rd Battalion, 5th Marines, 1st Marine Division (Rein) FMF. *Place and date:* Quang Tin Province, Republic of Vietnam, 4 September1967. *Entered service* at: Staten Island, NY. *Date and place of:* 13 February 13, 1929, Richmond County, NY. *Citation:* For conspicuous gallantry and intrepidity at the risk of his life above and beyond the call of duty as Chaplain of the 3rd Battalion, 5th Marines, Marine Division (Rein), FMF, in connection with operations against enemy forces in Quang Tin Province, Republic of Vietnam 4 September 1967. In response to reports that the 2nd Platoon of M Company was in danger of being overrun by a massed enemy assaulting force, Lieutenant Capodanno left the relative safety of the Company Command Post and ran through an open area raked fire, directly to the beleaguered platoon. Disregarding the intense enemy small arms, automatic weapons, and mortar fire, he moved about the battlefield administering last rites to the dying and giving medical aid to the wounded. When an exploding mortar inflicted painful multiple wounds to his arms and legs, and severed a portion of his right hand, he steadfastly refused all medical aid. Instead, he directed the corpsmen to help their wounded comrades and, with calm vigor, continued to move about the battle as he provided encouragement by voice and example to the valiant Marines. Upon encountering a wounded corpsman in the direct of fire of an enemy machine gunner positioned approximately fifteen yards away, Lieutenant Capodanno rushed forward in a daring attempt to aid and assist the mortally wounded corpsman. At that instant, only inches from his goal, he was struck down by a burst of machine-gun fire. By his heroic conduct on the battlefield, and his inspiring example, Lieutenant Capodanno upheld the finest traditions of the United States Naval Service. He gallantly gave his life in the cause of freedom.

*Caron, Wayne Maurice. Hospital Corpsman Third Class, United States Navy, Headquarters and Service Company, 3rd Battalion, 7th Marines, 1st Marine Division (Rein), FMF. *Place and date:* Quang Nam Province, Republic of Vietnam, 28 July 1968.

Entered service: Boston, MA. *Date and place of birth:* 2 November 1946 Middleboro, MA. *Citation:* For conspicuous gallantry and intrepidity at the risk of his life above and beyond the call of duty on 28 July 1968 while serving as Platoon Corpsman with Company K, 3rd Battalion, 7th Marines, 1st Marine Division, during combat operations against forces in the Republic of Vietnam. While on a sweep through a rice field in Quang Nam Province, Petty Officer Caron's unit receiving enemy small-arms fire. Upon seeing two Marines fall, he immediately ran forward to render first aid, but found that they were dead. At this time, the platoon was taken under small-arms and automatic-weapons fire, sustaining additional casualties. As he moved to the aid of his wounded comrades, Petty Officer Caron was hit in the arm by enemy fire. Although knocked down he regained his feet and continued to the injured rendered medical assistance to the first Marine he reached, who was grievously wounded, and undoubtedly was instrumental in saving the man's life. Petty Officer Caron then ran toward the second wounded Marine, but was again hit by enemy fire, this time in the leg. Nonetheless, he crawled the remaining distance and provided medical aid for this severely wounded man. Petty Officer Caron started to make his way to yet another injured comrade, when he was again struck by enemy small-arms fire. Courageously and with unbelievable determination, Petty Officer Caron continued his attempt to reach the third Marine. until he himself was killed by an enemy rocket round. His inspiring valor, steadfast determination, and selfless dedication in the face of extreme danger sustain and enhance the finest traditions of the United States Naval Service.

***Carter, Bruce Wayne.** Private First Class, U.S. Marine Corps, Company H, 2nd Battalion, 3rd Marines, 3rd Marine Division (Rein), FMF. *Place and date:* Quang Tri Province, Republic of Vietnam, 7 August 1969. *Entered service at:* Jacksonville, FL.

Bruce Wayne Carter

Date and place of birth: 7 May 7, 1950, Schenectady, NY. *Citation:* For conspicuous gallantry and at the risk of his life above and beyond the call of duty while serving as Grenadier with Company H, 2nd Battalion, 3rd Marines, 3rd Marine Division in connection with combat operations against the enemy in the Republic of Vietnam. On 7 August 1969, Private First Class Carter's unit was maneuvering against the enemy during Operation IDAHO CANYON and came under a heavy volume of fire from a numerically superior hostile force. The lead element soon became separated from the main body of the squad by a brush fire. Private First Class Carter and his fellow Marines were pinned down by vicious crossfire when, with complete disregard for his own safety, he stood in full view of the North Vietnamese Army soldiers to deliver a devastating volume of fire at their positions. The accuracy and aggressiveness of his attack caused several enemy casualties and forced the remainder of the soldiers to retreat from the immediate area. Shouting directions to the Marines around him, Private First Class Carter then commenced leading them from the path of the rapidly approaching brush fire when he observed a hostile grenade land between him and his companions. Fully aware of the probable consequences of his action but determined to protect the men following him, he unhesitatingly threw himself over the grenade, absorbing the full effects of its detonation with his own body. Private First Class Carter's indomitable courage, inspiring initiative, and selfless devotion to duty upheld the highest traditions of the Marine Corps and of the United States Naval Service. He gallantly gave his life in the service of his country.

Raymond Michael Clausen

Clausen, Raymond Michael. Private First Class, U.S. Marine Corps, Marine Medium Helicopter Squadron 263, Marine Aircraft Group 16, 1st Marine Aircraft Wing. *Place and date:* Republic of Vietnam, 31 January 1970. *Entered service at:* New Orleans, LA. *Date and place of birth:* 14 October 1947, New Orleans, LA. *Citation:* For conspicuous gallantry and intrepidity at the risk of his life above and beyond the call of duty while serving with Marine Medium Helicopter Squadron 263, Marine Aircraft Group 16, 1st Marine Aircraft Wing, during operations against enemy forces in the Republic of Vietnam on 31 January 1970. Participating in a helicopter rescue mission to extract elements of a platoon which had inadvertently entered a minefield while attacking enemy positions, Private First Class Clausen skillfully guided the helicopter pilot to a landing in an area cleared by one of several mine explosions. With eleven Marines wounded, one dead, and the remaining eight Marines holding their positions for fear of detonating other mines, Private First Class Clausen quickly leaped from the helicopter and, in the face of enemy fire, moved across the extremely hazardous, mine-laden area to assist in carrying casualties to the waiting helicopter and in placing them aboard. Despite the ever-present threat of further mine explosions, he continued valiant efforts, leaving the comparatively safe area of the helicopter six separate occasions to carry out his rescue efforts. On one occasion, while he was carrying one of the wounded, another mine detonated, killing a corpsman and wounding three other men. Only when he was certain that all Marines were safely aboard did he signal pilot to lift the helicopter. By the courageous, determined and inspiring efforts in the face of the utmost danger, Private First Class Clausen upheld the highest traditions of the Marine Corps and of the United States Naval Service.

Ronald L. Coker

*Coker, Ronald L. Private First Class, U.S. Marine Corps, Company M, 3rd Battalion, 3rd Marine Division (Rein), FMF. *date:* Quang Tri Province, Republic of Vietnam, 24 March 1969. *Entered service at:* Denver, CO. *Date and place of birth:* 9 August 1947, Alliance, NE. *Citation:* For conspicuous gallantry and intrepidity at the risk of his life above and beyond the call of duty while serving as a Rifleman with Company M, 3rd Battalion, 3rd Division in action against enemy forces in the Republic of Vietnam. On 24 March 1969, while serving as Point Man for the 2d Platoon, Private First Class Coker was leading his patrol when he encountered five enemy soldiers on a narrow jungle trail. Private First Class Coker's squad aggressively pursued them to a cave. As the squad neared the cave, it came under intense hostile fire, wounding one Marine and forcing the others to take cover. Observing the wounded man lying exposed to continuous enemy fire, Private First Class Coker disregarded his own safety and moved across the fire-swept terrain toward his companion. Although wounded by enemy small arms fire, he continued to crawl across the hazardous area and skillfully threw a hand grenade into the enemy positions, suppressing the hostile fire sufficiently to enable him to reach the man. As he began to drag his injured comrade towards safety, a grenade landed on the wounded Marine. Unhesitatingly, Private First Class Coker grasped it with both hands and turned away from his wounded companion, but before he could dispose of the grenade it exploded. Severely wounded, but undaunted, he refused to abandon his comrade. As he moved toward friendly lines, two more enemy grenades exploded near him, inflicting still further injuries. Concerned only for the safety of his comrade, Private First Class Coker, with supreme effort continued to crawl and pull the wounded Marine with him. His heroic deeds inspired his fellow Marines to such aggressive action that the enemy fire was suppressed sufficiently for others to reach him and carry him to a relatively safe area where he succumbed to his extensive wounds. Private First Class Coker's indomitable courage, inspiring initiative and selfless devotion upheld the highest traditions of the Marine Corps and of the United States Naval Service. He gallantly gave his life for his country.

*Connor, Peter Spencer. Staff Sergeant, U.S. Marine Corps, Company F, 2nd Battalion, 3rd Marines, 1st Marine Division (Reinforced), Fleet Marine Force, *Place and date:* Quang Ngai Province, Republic of Vietnam, 25 February 1966. *Entered service at:* South Orange, NJ. *Date and place of birth:* 4 September 1932, Orange, NJ. *Citation:* For conspicuous gallantry and intrepidity in action against enemy Viet Cong forces at the risk of his life above and beyond the call of duty. Leading his platoon on a search and destroy operation in an area made particularly hazardous by extensive cave and tunnel complexes, Sergeant Connor maneuvered his unit aggressively forward under intermittent enemy small-arms fire. Exhibiting particular alertness and keen observation, he spotted an enemy spider hole emplacement approximately fifteen meters to his front. He pulled the pin from a fragmentation grenade intending to charge the hole boldly and drop the missile into its depths. Upon pulling the pin he realized that the firing mechanism was faulty, and that even as he held the safety device firmly in place, the fuze charge was already activated. With only precious seconds to decide, he further realized that he could not cover the distance to the small opening of the spider hole in sufficient time, and that to hurl the deadly bomb in any direction would result in death or injury to some of his comrades tactically deployed near him. Manifesting extraordinary gal-

Peter Spencer Connor

lantry and wit utter disregard for his personal safety, he chose to hold the grenade against his own body in order to absorb the terrific explosion and spare his comrades. His act of extreme valor and selflessness in the face of virtually certain death, although leaving him mortally wounded, spared many of his fellow Marines from death or injury. His gallant action in giving his life in the cause of freedom reflects the highest credit upon the Marine Corps and the Armed Forces of the United States.

*Cook, Donald Gilbert. Colonel (then Captain), U.S. Marine Corps, Advisor, Republic of Vietnam. *Place and date:* Republic of Vietnam, vicinity of Benh Gia, Phouc Tuy Province, 31 December 1964 to 8 December 1967. *Entered service at:* Brooklyn, NY, January 1957. *Date and place of birth:* 9 August 1934, Brooklyn, NY. *Citation:* For conspicuous gallantry and intrepidity at the risk of his life above and beyond the call of duty while interned as a Prisoner of War by the Viet Cong in the Republic of Vietnam during the period 31 December 1964 to 8 December 1967. Despite the fact that by so doing he would bring about harsher treatment for himself, Colonel (then Captain) Cook established himself as the senior prisoner, even though in actuality he was not. Repeatedly assuming more than his share of their health, Colonel Cook willingly and unselfishly put

Donald Gilbert Cook

the interests of his comrades before that of his own well-being and, eventually, his life. Giving more needy men his medicine and drug allowance while constantly nursing them, he risked infection from contagious diseases while in a rapidly deteriorating state of health. This unselfish and exemplary conduct, coupled with his refusal to stray even the slightest from the Code of Conduct, earned him the deepest respect from not only his fellow prisoners, but his captors as well. Rather than negotiate for his own release or better treatment, he steadfastly frustrated attempts by the Viet Cong to break his indomitable spirit. and passed this same resolve on to the men whose well-being he so closely associated himself. Knowing his refusals would prevent his release prior to the end of the war, and also knowing his chances for prolonged survival would be small in the event of continued refusal, he chose nevertheless to adhere to a Code of Conduct far above that which could be expected. His personal valor and exceptional spirit of loyalty in the face of almost certain death reflected the highest credit upon Colonel Cook, the Marine Corps, and the United States Naval Service [late Vietnam award].

Thomas E. Creek

*Creek, Thomas E. Lance Corporal, U.S. Marine Corps, Company I, 3rd Battalion, 9th Marines, 3rd Marine Division (Rein), FMF. *Place and date:* Near Cam Lo, Republic of Vietnam, 13 February 1969. *Entered service at:* San Diego, CA. Date *and place of birth:* 7 April 1950, Joplin, MO. *Citation:* For conspicuous gallantry and intrepidity at the risk of his life above and beyond the call of duty while serving as a Rifleman with Company I, 3rd Battalion, 9th Marines, 3rd Marine Division in action against enemy forces in the Republic of Vietnam. On 13 February 1969, Lance Corporal Creek's squad was providing security for a convoy moving to supply the Vandegrift Command Base when an enemy command detonated mine destroyed one of the vehicles and halted the convoy near the Cam Lo Resettlement Village. Almost immediately, the Marines came under a heavy volume of hostile mortar fire followed by intense small arms fire from a well-concealed enemy force. As his squad deployed to engage the enemy, Lance Corporal Creek quickly moved to a fighting position and aggressively engaged in the fire fight. Observing a position from which he could more effectively deliver fire against the hostile force, he completely disregarded his own safety as he fearlessly dashed across the fire-swept terrain and was seriously wounded by enemy fire. At the time, an enemy grenade was thrown into the gully where he had fallen, landing between him and several companions. Fully realizing inevitable results of his action, Lance Corporal Creek rolled on the grenade and absorbed the full force of the explosion with his own body, thereby saving the lives of five of his fellow Marines. As a result of his heroic action, his men were inspired to such aggressive action that the enemy was defeated and the convoy was able to continue its vital mission. Lance Corporal Creek's indomitable courage, inspired Marine Corps and the United States Naval Service. He gallantly gave his life for his country.

*Davis, Rodney Maxwell. Sergeant, U.S. Marine Corps, Company B, 1st Battalion, 5th Marine, 1st Marine Division. *Place and date:* Quang Nam Province, Republic of Vietnam, 6 September 1967. *Entered service at:* Macon, GA. *Date and place of birth:* 7 April 1942, Macon, GA. *Citation:* For conspicuous gallantry and intrepidity at the risk of his life above and beyond the call of duty while serving as the right guide of the 2nd Platoon, Company B, 1st Battalion, 5th Marines, 1st Marine Division, in action against enemy forces in Quang Nam Province, Republic of Vietnam, on 6 September 1967. Elements of the 2nd Platoon were pinned down by a numerically superior force of attacking North Vietnamese Army Regulars. Remnants of the platoon were located in a trench line where Sergeant Davis was directing the fire of his men in an attempt to repel the enemy attack. Disre-

Rodney Maxwell Davis

garding the enemy hand grenades and high volume of small arms and mortar fire, Sergeant Davis moved from man to man shouting words of encouragement to each of them while firing and throwing grenades at the onrushing enemy. When an enemy grenade landed in the trench in the midst of his men, Sergeant Davis, realizing the gravity of the situation, and in a final valiant act of complete self-sacrifice, instantly threw himself upon the grenade, absorbing with his own body the full and terrific force of the explosion. Through his extraordinary initiative and inspiring valor in the fact of almost certain death, Sergeant Davis saved his comrades from injury and possible loss of life, enabled his platoon to hold its vital position, and upheld the highest traditions of the Marine Corps and the United States Naval Service. He gallantly gave his life for his country.

*De La Garza, Emilio Albert, Jr. Lance Corporal, U.S. Marine Corps, Company E, 2nd Battalion, 1st Marines, 1st Marine Division. *Place and date:* Near Da Nang, Republic of Vietnam, 11 April 1970. *Entered service at:* Chicago, IL. *Date and place of birth:* 23 June 1949, East Chicago, IN. *Citation:* For conspicuous gallantry and intrepidity at the risk of his life above and beyond the call of duty while serving as a machine gunner with Company E, 2nd Battalion, 1st Marines, 1st Marine Division, in the Republic of Vietnam on April 11, 1970. Returning with his squad from a

Emilio Albert De La Garza, Jr.

night ambush operation, Lance Corporal De La Garza joined his platoon commander and another Marine in searching for two enemy soldiers who had been observed fleeing for cover toward a small pond. Moments later, he located one of the enemy soldiers hiding among the reeds and brush. As the three Marines attempted to remove the resisting soldier from the pond, Lance Corporal De La Garza observed him pull the pin on a grenade. Shouting a warning, Lance Corporal De La Garza placed himself between the other two Marines and the ensuing blast from the grenade, thereby saving the lives of his comrades at the sacrifice of his own. By his prompt and decisive action, and his great personal valor in the face of almost certain death, Lance Corporal De La Garza upheld and further enhanced the finest traditions of the Marine Corps and the United States Naval Service.

Ralph Ellis Dias

*Dias, Ralph Ellis.** Private First Class, U.S. Marine Corps, 3d Platoon, Company D, 1st Battalion, 7th Marines, 1st Marine Division (Rein), FMF. *Place and date:* Que Son Mountain, Republic of Vietnam, 12 November 1969. *Entered service at:* Pittsburgh, PA, 9 October 1967. *Date and place of birth:* 15 July 1950, Shelocta, Indiana County, PA. *Citation:* As a member of a reaction force which was pinned down by enemy fire while assisting a platoon in the same circumstance, Pfc. Dias, observing that both units were sustaining casualties, initiated an aggressive assault against an enemy machine gun bunker which was the principal source of hostile fire. Severely wounded by enemy snipers while charging across the open area, he pulled himself to the shelter of a nearby rock. Braving enemy fire for a second time, Pfc. Dias was again wounded. Unable to walk, he crawled 15 meters to the protection of a rock located near his objective and, repeatedly exposing himself to intense hostile fire, unsuccessfully threw several hand grenades at the machine gun emplacement. Still determined to destroy the emplacement, Pfc. Dias again moved into the open and was wounded a third time by sniper fire. As he threw a last grenade which destroyed the enemy position, he was mortally wounded by another enemy round. Pfc. Dias' indomitable courage, dynamic initiative, and selfless devotion to duty upheld the highest traditions of the Marine Corps and the U.S. Naval Service. He gallantly gave his life in the service to his country [late Vietnam award].

Dickey, Douglas Eugene. Private First Class, U.S. Marine Corps, Company C, 1st Battalion, 4th Marines 9th Marine Amphibious Brigade, 3rd Marine Division (Rein). *Place and date:* Republic of Vietnam, 26 March 1967. *Entered service at:* Cincinnati, OH. *Date and place of birth:* 24 December 1946, Greenville, Darke, Ohio, *Citation:* For conspicuous gallantry and intrepidity at the risk of his life above and beyond the call of duty. While participating in Operation BEACON HILL 1, the 2nd Platoon was engaged in a fierce battle with the Viet Cong at close range in dense jungle foliage. Private First Class Dickey had come forward to replace a radio operator who had been wounded in this intense action and was being treated by a medical corpsman. Suddenly an enemy grenade landed in the midst of a group of Marines, which included the wounded radio operator who was immobilized. Fully realizing the inevitable result of his actions, Private

Douglas Eugene Dickey

First Class Dickey, in a final valiant act, quickly and unhesitatingly threw himself upon the deadly grenade, absorbing with his own body the full and complete force of the explosion. Private First Class Dickey's personal heroism, extraordinary valor and selfless courage saved a number of his comrades from certain injury and possible death at the cost of his own life. His actions reflected great upon himself, the Marine Corps and the United States Naval Service. He gallantly gave his life for his country.

Foster, Paul Hellstrom. Sergeant, U.S. Marine Corps Reserve, 2nd Battalion, 4th Marines, 3rd Marine Division. *Place and date:* Near Con Thien, Republic of Vietnam, 14 October 1967. *Entered service at:* San Francisco, CA. *Date and place of birth:* 17 April 1939, San Mateo, CA. *Citation:* For conspicuous gallantry and intrepidity at the risk of his life above and beyond the call of duty while serving as an Artillery Liaison Operations Chief with the 2nd Battalion, 4th Marines, 3rd Marine Division, near Con Thien in the Republic of Vietnam. In the early morning hours of 14 October 1967, the 2nd Battalion was occupying a defensive position which protected a bridge on the road leading from Con Thien to Cam Lo. Suddenly, the Marines' position came under a heavy volume of mortar and artillery fire, followed by an aggressive enemy ground assault. In the ensuing engagement, the hostile force penetrated the perimeter and brought a heavy concentration of small arms, automatic weapons, and rocket fire to bear on the Battalion Command Post. Although his position in the

Fire Support Coordination Center was dangerously exposed to enemy fire and he was wounded when an enemy hand grenade exploded near his position, Sergeant Foster resolutely continued to direct accurate mortar and artillery fire on the advancing North Vietnamess troops. As the attack continued, a hand grenade landed in the midst of Sergeant Foster and his five companions. Realizing the danger he shouted a warning, threw his armored vest over the grenade, unhesitatingly placed his own body over the armored vest. When grenade exploded, Sergeant Foster absorbed the entire blast with own body and was mortally wounded. His heroic actions undoubtedly saved his comrades from further injury or possible death. Sergeant Foster's courage, extraordinary heroism, and unfaltering devotion to duty reflected great credit upon himself and the Marine Corps and upheld the highest traditions of the United States Naval Service. He gallantly gave his life for his country.

Fox, Wesley L. Captain, U.S. Marine Corps, Company A, 1st Battalion, 9th Marines, 3rd Marine Division. *Place and date:* Quang Tri Province, Republic of Vietnam, 22 February 1969. *Entered service at:* Leesburg, VA. *Date* and *place of birth:* 30 September 1931, Herndon, VA. *Citation:* For conspicuous gallantry and intrepidity at the risk of his life above and beyond the call of duty while serving as Commanding Officer of Company A, 1st Battalion, 9th Marines, 3rd Marine Division, in action against the enemy in the northern A Shau Valley, Quang Tri Province, Republic of Vietnam, on 22 February 1969. Captain (then First Lieutenant) Fox's company came under intense fire from a large well concealed enemy force. Captain Fox maneuvered to a position from which he could assess the situation and confer with his platoon leaders. As they departed to execute the plan he had devised, the enemy attacked and Captain Fox was wounded along with all of the other members of the command

Wesley L. Fox

group, except the executive officer. Captain Fox continued to direct the activity of his company. Advancing through heavy enemy fire, he personally neutralized one enemy position and calmly ordered an assault against the hostile emplacements. He then moved through the hazardous area coordinating aircraft support with the activities of his men. When his executive officer was mortally wounded, Captain Fox reorganized the company and directed the fire of his men as they hurled grenades against the enemy and drove the hostile forces into retreat. Wounded again in the final assault, Captain Fox refused medical attention, established a defensive posture, and supervised the preparation of casualties for medical evacuation. His indomitable courage, inspiring initiative, and unwavering devotion to duty in the face of grave personal danger inspired his Marines to such aggressive actions that they overcame all enemy resistance and destroyed a large bunker complex. Captain Fox's heroic actions reflect great credit upon himself and the Marine Corps, and uphold the highest traditions of the United States Naval Service. [*Other Navy award: Bronze Star w/V. He retired as a colonel in September 1993.*]

*Gonzalez, Alfredo. Sergeant, U.S. Marine Corps, Company A, 1st Battalion, 1st Marines, 1st Marine Division (Rein), FMF. *Place and date:* Near Thua Thien, Republic of Vietnam, 4 February 1968. *Entered service at:* San Antonio, TX. *Date and place of birth:* 23 May 1946, Edinburg, TX. *Citation:* For conspicuous gallantry and intrepidity at the risk of his life above and beyond the call of duty while serving as Platoon Commander, 3rd Platoon, Company A, 1st Battalion, 1st Marines, 1st Marine Division, in the Republic of Vietnam. On 31 January 1968, during the initial phase of Operation HUE CITY Sergeant Gonzalez' unit was formed as a reaction force and deployed to Hue to relieve the pressure on the beleaguered city. While moving by truck convoy along Route No. 1, near the village of Lang Van Lrong, the Marines received a heavy volume of enemy fire. Sergeant Gonzalez aggres-

Alfredo Gonzalez

sively maneuvered the Marines in his platoon, and directed their fire until the area was cleared of snipers. Immediately after crossing a river south of Hue, the column was again hit by intense enemy fire. One of the Marines on top of a tank was wounded and fell to the ground in an exposed position. With complete disregard for his own safety, Sergeant Gonzalez ran through the fire-swept area to the assistance of his injured comrade. He lifted him up and though receiving fragmentation wounds during the rescue, he carried the wounded Marine to a covered position for treatment. Due to the increased volume and accuracy of enemy fire from a fortified machine gun bunker on the side of the road, the company was temporarily halted. Realizing the gravity of the situation, Sergeant Gonzalez exposed himself to the enemy fire and moved his platoon along the east side of a bordering rice paddy to a dike directly across from the bunker. Though fully aware of the danger involved, he moved to the fire-swept road and destroyed the hostile position with hand grenades. Although seriously wounded again on 3 February, he steadfastly refused medical treatment and continued to supervise his men and lead the attack. On 4 February, the enemy had again pinned the company down, inflicting heavy casualties with automatic weapons and rocket fire. Sergeant Gonzalez, utilizing a number of light antitank assault weapons, fearlessly moved from position to position firing numerous rounds at the heavily fortified enemy emplacements. He successfully knocked out a rocket position and suppressed much of the enemy fire before falling mortally wounded. The heroism, courage, and dynamic leadership displayed by Sergeant Gonzalez reflected great credit upon himself and the Marine Corps, and were in keeping with the highest traditions of the United States Naval Service. He gallantly gave his life for his country.

*Graham, James Albert.** Captain, U.S. Marine Corps, Company F, 2nd Battalion, 5th Marines, 1st Marine Division. *Place and date:* Republic of Vietnam, 2 June 1967. *Entered service at:* Prince Georges, MD. *Date and place of birth:* 25 August 1940, Wilkinsburg County, PA. *Citation:* For conspicuous gallantry and intrepidity at the risk of his life above and beyond the call of duty. During Operation UNION II, the First Battalion, Fifth Marines, consisting of Companies A and D, with Captain Graham's company attached, launched an attack against an enemy occupied position, with two companies assaulting and one in reserve. Company F, a leading company, was proceeding across a clear paddy area one thousand meters wide, attacking toward the assigned objective, when it came under fire from mortars and small arms which immediately inflicted large number of casualties. Hardest hit by the enemy fire was the 2nd platoon of Company F, which was pinned down in the open

James Albert Graham

paddy area by intense fire from two concealed machine guns. Forming an assault unit from members of his small company headquarters, Captain Graham boldly led a fierce assault through the second platoon's position, forcing the enemy to abandon the first machine gun position, thereby relieving some of the pressure on his second platoon, and enabling evacuation of the wounded to a more secure area. Resolute to silence the second machine gun, which continued its devastating fire, Captain Graham's small force stood steadfast in its hard won enclave. Subsequently, during the afternoon's fierce fighting, he suffered two minor wounds while personally accounting for an estimated fifteen enemy killed. With the enemy position remaining invincible upon each attempt to withdraw to friendly lines, and although knowing that he had no chance of survival, he chose to remain with one man who could not be moved due to the seriousness of his wounds. The last radio transmission from Captain Graham reported that he was being assaulted by a force of twenty-five enemy; he died while protecting himself and the wounded man he chose not to abandon. Captain Graham's actions throughout the day were a series of heroic achievements. His outstanding courage, superb leadership and indomitable fighting spirit undoubtedly saved the second platoon from annihilation and reflected great credit upon himself, the Marine Corps, and the United States Naval Service. He gallantly gave his life for his country.

*Graves, Terrence Collinson. Second Lieutenant, U.S. Marine Corps, 3rd Force Reconnaissance Company, 3rd Reconnaissance Battalion, 3rd Marine Division (Rein), FMF. *Place and date:* Quang Tri Province, Republic of Vietnam, 16 February 1968. *Entered* service *at:* Miami. FL. *Date and place of birth:* 6 July 1945, Corpus Christi. TX. *Citation:* For conspicuous gallantry and intrepidity at. the risk of his life, above and beyond the call of duty as a Platoon Commander with the 3rd Force Reconnaissance Company, 3rd Reconnaissance Battalion, 3rd Marine Division. in the Republic of Vietnam on 16 February 1968. While on a long-range reconnaissance mission. Lieutenant Graves' eight-man patrol observed seven enemy soldiers approaching their position. Reacting instantly, he deployed his men and directed their fire on the approaching enemy. After the fire had

Terrence C. Graves

ceased, he and two patrol members commenced a search of the area, and suddenly came under a heavy volume of hostile small arms and automatic weapons fire from a numerically superior enemy force. When one of his men was hit by the enemy fire, Lieutenant Graves moved through the fire-swept area to his radio and, while directing suppressive fire from his men, requested air support and adjusted a heavy volume of artillery and helicopter gun-ship fire upon the enemy. After attending the wounded, Lieutenant Graves, accompanied by another Marine, moved from his relatively safe position to confirm the results of the earlier engagement. Observing that several of the enemy were still alive, he launched a determined assault, eliminating the remaining enemy troops. He then began moving the patrol to a landing zone for extraction, when the unit again came under intense fire which wounded two more Marines and Lieutenant Graves. Refusing medical attention, he once more adjusted air strikes and artillery fire upon the enemy while directing the fire of his men. He led his men to a new landing site into which he skillfully guided the incoming aircraft and boarded his men while remaining exposed to the hostile fire. Realizing that one of the wounded had not embarked, he directed the aircraft to depart and, along with another Marine, moved to the side of the casualty. Confronted with a shortage of ammunition, Lieutenant Graves utilized supporting arms and directed fire until a second helicopter arrived. At this point, the volume of enemy fire intensified, hitting the helicopter and causing it to crash shortly after liftoff. All aboard were killed. Lieutenant Graves' outstanding courage, superb leadership and indomitable fighting spirit throughout the day were in keeping with the highest traditions of the Marine Corps and the United States Naval Service. He gallantly gave his life for his country.

Howard, Jimmie E. Gunnery Sergeant (then Staff Sergeant), U.S. Marine Corps, Company C, 1st Reconnaissance Battalion, 1st Marine Division. *Place and date:* Republic of Vietnam, 16 June 1966. *Entered service at:* Burlington, Iowa. *Date and place of birth:* 27 July 1929, Burlington, Iowa. *Citation:* For conspicuous gallantry and intrepidity at the risk of his life above and beyond the call of duty. Gunnery Sergeant (then Staff Sergeant) Howard and his eighteen-man platoon were occupying an observation post deep within enemy-controlled territory. Shortly after midnight on 16 June 1966, a Viet Cong force of estimated at battalion size approached the Marines' position and launched a vicious attack with small arms, automatic weapons, and mortar fire. Reacting swiftly and fearlessly in the face of the overwhelming odds, Gunnery Sergeant Howard skillfully organized his small but determined force into a tight perimeter defense and calmly

Jimmie E. Howard

moved from position to position to direct his men's fire. Throughout the night, during assault after assault, his courageous example and firm leadership inspired and motivated his men to withstand the unrelenting fury of the hostile fire in the seemingly hopeless situation. He constantly shouted encouragement to his men and exhibited imagination and resourcefulness in directing their return fire. When fragments of an exploding enemy grenade wounded him severely and prevented him from moving his legs, he distributed his ammunition to the remaining members of his platoon and proceeded to maintain radio communications and direct air strikes on the enemy with uncanny accuracy. At dawn, despite the fact that five men were killed and all but one wounded, his beleaguered platoon was still in command of its position. When evacuation helicopters approached his position, Gunnery Sergeant Howard warned them away and called for additional air strikes and directed devastating small arms fire and air strikes against enemy automatic weapons positions in order to make the landing zone as secure as possible. Through his extraordinary courage and resolute fighting spirit. Gunnery Sergeant Howard was largely responsible for preventing the loss of his entire platoon. His valiant leadership and courageous fighting spirit served to inspire the men of his platoon to heroic endeavor in the face of overwhelming odds, and reflect the highest credit upon Gunnery Sergeant Howard, the Marine Corps, and the United States Naval Service. [*Other Navy award: Silver Star.*]

*****Howe, James Donnie.** Lance Corporal, U.S. Marine Corps, Company I, 3rd Battalion, 7th Marines, 1st Marine Division. *Place and date:* Republic of Vietnam, 6 May 1970. *Entered service at:* Fort Jackson, SC. *Date and place of birth:* 17 December 1948, Six Mile, Pickens, SC. *Citation:* For conspicuous gallantry and intrepidity at

James Donnie Howe

the risk of his life above and beyond the call of duty while serving as a Rifleman with Company I, 3rd Battalion, 7th Marines, 1st Marine Division during operations against enemy forces in the Republic of Vietnam. In the early morning hours of 8 May 1970, Lance Corporal Howe and two other Marines were occupying a defensive position in a sandy beach area fronted by bamboo thickets. Enemy sappers suddenly launched a grenade attack against the position, utilizing the cover of darkness to carry out their assault. Following the initial explosions of the grenades, Lance Corporal Howe and his two comrades moved to a more advantageous position in order to return suppressive fire. When an enemy grenade landed in their midst,. Lance Corporal Howe immediately shouted a warning and then threw himself upon the deadly missile, thereby protecting the lives of the fellow Marines . His heroic and selfless action was in keeping with the finest traditions of the Marine Corps and of the United States; Naval Service. He valiantly gave his life in the service of his country.

Ingram, Robert R. Corpsman, Petty Officer, U.S. Navy. Serving with Company C, First Battalion, Seventh Marines, Republic of Vietnam. *Citation:* For conspicuous gallantry and intrepidity at the risk of his life above and beyond the call of duty while serving as Corpsman with Company C, First Battalion, Seventh Marines against elements of a North Vietnam Aggressor (NVA) battalion in Quang Ngai Province Republic of Vietnam on 28 March 1966. Petty Officer Ingram accompanied the point platoon as it aggressively dispatched an outpost of an NVA battalion. The momentum of the attack rolled off a ridge line down a tree covered slope to a small paddy and a village beyond. Suddenly, the village tree line exploded with an intense hail of automatic rifle fire from approximately 100 North Vietnamese regulars. In mere moments, the platoon ranks were decimated. Oblivious to the danger, Petty Officer Ingram crawled across the bullet spattered terrain to reach a downed Marine. As he administered aid, a bullet went through the palm of his hand. Calls for 'CORPSMAN' echoed across the ridge. Bleeding, he edged across the fire swept landscape, collecting ammunition from the dead and administering aid to the wounded. Receiving two more wounds before realizing the third wound was life-threatening, he looked for a way off the face of the ridge, but again he heard the call for corpsman and again, he resolutely answered. Though severely wounded three times, he rendered aid to those incapable until he finally reached the right flank of the platoon. While dressing the head wound of another corpsman, he sustained his fourth bullet wound. From sixteen hundred hours until just prior to sunset, Petty Officer Ingram pushed, pulled, cajoled, and doctored his Marines. Enduring the pain from his many wounds and disregarding the probability of his demise, Petty Officer Ingram's intrepid actions saved many lives that day. By his indomitable fighting spirit, daring initiative, and unfaltering dedications to duty, Petty Officer Ingram reflected great credit upon himself and upheld the highest traditions of the United States Naval Service [late Vietnam award, at White House on 10 July 1998].

Robert H. Jenkins, Jr.

*Jenkins, Robert H., Jr. Private First Class, U.S. Marine Corps, 3rd Reconnaissance Battalion, 3rd Marine Division (Rein), FMF. *Place and date:* Fire Support Base Argonne, Republic of Vietnam, 5 March 1969. *Entered service at:* Jacksonville, FL. *Date and place of birth:* 1 June 1948, Interlachen, FL. *Citation:* For conspicuous gallantry and intrepidity at the risk of his life above and beyond the call of duty while serving as a machine gunner with Company C, 3rd Reconnaissance Battalion, 3rd Marine Division in connection with. operations against enemy forces in the Republic of Vietnam. Early on the morning of 5 March 1969, Private First Class Jenkins' twelve-man reconnaissance team was occupying a defensive position at Fire Support Base Argonne south of the Demilitarized Zone. Suddenly, the Marines were assaulted by a North Vietnamese Army platoon employing mortars, automatic weapons, and hand grenades. Reacting instantly, Private First Class Jenkins and another Marine quickly moved into a two-man fighting emplacement, and as they boldly delivered accurate machine gun fire against the enemy, a North Vietnamese soldier threw a hand grenade into the friendly emplacement. Fully realizing the inevitable results of his actions, Private First Class Jenkins quickly seized his comrade, and pushing the man to the ground, he leaned on top of the Marine to shield him from the explosion. Absorbing the full impact of the detonation, Private First Class Jenkins was seriously injured and subsequently succumbed to his wounds. His courage, inspiring valor and selfless devotion to duty saved a fellow Marine from serious injury or possible death and upheld the highest traditions of the Marine Corps and the United States Naval Service. He gallantly gave his life for his country.

*Jimenez, Jose Francisco. Lance Corporal, U.S. Marine Corps, Company K, 3rd Battalion, 7th Marines, 1st Marine Division. *Place and date:* Quang Nam Province, Republic of Vietnam, 28 August 1969. *Entered service at:* Phoenix, AZ. *Date and place of birth:* 20 March 1946, Mexico City, Mexico. *Citation:* For conspicuous gallantry and intrepidity at the risk of his life above and beyond the call of duty while serving as a Fire Team Leader with Company K, 3rd Battalion, 7th Marines, 1st

Jose Francisco Jimenez

Marine Division in operations against the enemy in the Republic of Vietnam on 28 August 1969. On that date Lance Corporal Jimenez' unit came under heavy attack by North Vietnamese Army soldiers concealed in well camouflaged emplacements. Lance Corporal Jimenez reacted by seizing the initiative and plunging forward toward the enemy positions. He personally destroyed several enemy personnel and silenced an antiaircraft weapon. Shouting encouragement to his companions, Lance Corporal Jimenez continued his aggressive forward movement. He slowly maneuvered to within ten feet of hostile soldiers who were firing automatic weapons from a trench and, in the face of vicious enemy fire, destroyed the position. Although he was by now the target of concentrated fire from hostile gunners intent upon halting his assault, Lance Corporal Jimenez continued to press forward. As he moved to attack another enemy soldier, he was mortally wounded. Lance Corporal Jimenez' indomitable courage, aggressive fighting spirit and unfaltering devotion to duty upheld the highest traditions of the Marine Corps and the United States Naval Service.

Ralph H. Johnson

*Johnson, Ralph H. Private First Class, U.S. Marine Corps, Company A, 1st Reconnaissance Battalion, 1st Marine Division (Rein), FMF. *Place and date:* Near the Quan Due Duc Valley, Republic of Vietnam, 5 March 1968. *Entered service at:* Oakland, CA. *Date and place of birth:* 11 January 1949, Charleston, SC. *Citation:* For conspicuous gallantry and intrepidity at the risk of his life above and beyond the call of duty while serving as a Reconnaissance Scout with Company A, 1st Reconnaissance Battalion, 1st Marine Division in action against the North Vietnamese Army and Viet Cong forces in the Republic of Vietnam. In the early morning hours of 5 March 1968, during Operation ROCK, Private First class Johnson was a member of a fifteen-man reconnaissance patrol manning an observation post on Hill 146 overlooking the Quan Due Duc Valley deep in enemy controlled territory. They were attacked by a platoon-size hostile force employing automatic weapons, satchel charges and hand grenades. Suddenly, a hand grenade landed in the three-man fighting hole occupied by Private Johnson and two fellow Marines. Realizing the inherent danger to his two comrades, he shouted a warning and unhesitatingly hurled himself upon the explosive device. When the grenade exploded, Private

Johnson absorbed the blast and was killed instantly. His prompt and heroic act saved the life of one Marine at the cost of his own and undoubtedly prevented the enemy from penetrating his sector of the patrol's perimeter. Private Johnson's courage, inspiring valor and selfless devotion to duty were in keeping with the highest traditions of the United States Naval Service. He gallantly gave his life for his country.

*Keith, Miguel. Lance Corporal, U.S. Marine Corps, Combined Action Platoon 1–3–2, III Marine Amphibious Force. *Place and date:* Quang Ngai Province, Republic of Vietnam, 8 May 1970. *Entered service at:* Omaha, NE. *Date and place of birth:* 2 June 1951, San Antonio, TX. *Citation:* For conspicuous gallantry and intrepidity at the risk of his life above and beyond the call of duty while serving as a machine gunner with Combined Action Platoon 1–3–2, III Marine Amphibious Force, operating in Quang Ngai Province, Republic of Vietnam. During the early morning of 8 May 1970, Lance Corporal Keith was seriously wounded when his platoon was subjected to a heavy ground attack by a greatly outnumbering enemy force. Despite his painful wounds he ran across the fire-swept terrain to check the security of vital defensive positions and then, while completely exposed to view, pro-

Miguel Keith

ceeded to deliver a hail of devastating machine gun fire against the enemy. Determined to stop five of the enemy approaching the command post, he rushed forward, firing as he advanced. He succeeded in disposing of three of the attackers and in dispersing the remaining two. At this point, a grenade detonated near Lance Corporal Keith, knocking him to the ground and inflicting further severe wounds. Fighting pain and weakness from loss of blood, he again braved the concentrated hostile fire to charge an estimated twenty-five enemy soldiers who were massing to attack. The vigor of his assault and his well placed fire eliminated four of the enemy while the remainder fled for cover. During this valiant effort, he was mortally wounded by an enemy soldier. By his courageous and inspiring performance in the face of almost overwhelming odds, Lance Corporal Keith contributed in large measure to the success of his platoon in routing a numerically superior enemy force, and upheld the finest traditions of the Marine Corps and of the United States Naval Service.

Kellogg, Allan Jay, Jr. Gunnery Sergeant, U.S. Marine Corps (then Staff Sergeant), Company G, 2nd Battalion, 5th Marines, 1st Marine Division. *Place and date:* Quang Nam Province, Republic of Vietnam, 11 March 1970. *Entered service at:* Bridgeport, CT. *Date and place of birth:* 1 October 1943, Bethel, CT. *Citation:* For conspicuous gallantry and intrepidity at the risk of his life above and beyond the call of duty while serving as a Platoon Sergeant with Company G, 2nd Battalion, 5th

Marines, 1st Marine Division, in connection with combat operations against the enemy in the Republic of Vietnam on the night of 11 March 1970. Under the leadership of Gunnery Sergeant (then Staff Sergeant) Kellogg, a small unit from Company G was evacuating a fallen comrade when the unit came under a heavy volume of small arms and automatic weapons fire from a numerically superior enemy force occupying well-concealed emplacements in the surrounding jungle. During the ensuing fierce engagement, an enemy soldier managed to maneuver through the dense foliage to a position near the Marines and hurled a hand grenade into their midst which glanced off the chest of Gunnery Sergeant Kellogg. Quick to act, he forced the grenade into the mud in which he was standing, threw himself over the lethal weapon, and absorbed the full effects of its det-

Allan Jay Kellogg, Jr.

onation with his body, thereby preventing serious injury or possible death to several of his fellow Marines. Although suffering multiple injuries to his chest and his right shoulder and arm, Gunnery Sergeant Kellogg resolutely continued to direct the efforts of his men until all were able to maneuver to the relative safety of the company

perimeter. By his heroic and decisive action in risking his own life to save the lives of his comrades, Gunnery Sergeant Kellogg reflected the highest credit upon himself and upheld the finest traditions of the Marine Corps and the United States Naval Service. [*Other Navy award: Bronze Star w/V. Retired a sergeant major in October 1990.*]

Lee, Howard Vincent. Major, U.S. Marine Corps, Company E, 2nd Battalion, 4th Marines, 3rd Marine Division (Reinforced). *Place and date:* Near Cam Lo, Republic of Vietnam, 8 and 9 August 1966. *Entered service at:* Dumfries, VA. *Date and place of birth:* 1 August 1933, New York, NY. *Citation:* For conspicuous gallantry and intrepidity at the risk of his life above and beyond the call of duty. A platoon of Major (then Captain) Lee's company, while on an operation

Howard Vincent Lee

deep in enemy territory, was attacked and surrounded by a large Vietnamese force. Realizing that the unit had suffered numerous casualties, depriving it of effective leadership, and fully aware that the platoon was even then under heavy attack by the enemy, Major Lee took seven men and proceeded by helicopter to reinforce the beleaguered platoon. Major Lee disembarked from the helicopter with two of his men and, braving withering enemy fire, led them into the perimeter, where he fearlessly moved from position to position, directing and encouraging the overtaxed troops. The enemy then launched a massive attack with the full might of their forces. Although painfully wounded by fragments from an enemy grenade in several areas of his body, including his eye, Major Lee continued undauntedly throughout the night to direct the valiant defense, coordinate supporting fires, and apprise higher headquarters of the plight of the platoon. The next morning he collapsed from his wounds and was forced to relinquish command. However the small band of Marines had held their position and repeatedly fought off many vicious enemy attacks for a grueling six hours until their evacuation was effected the following morning. Major Lee's actions saved his men from capture, minimized the loss of lives, and dealt the enemy a severe defeat. His indomitable fighting spirit, superb leadership, and great personal valor in the face of tremendous odds, reflect great credit upon himself and are in keeping with the highest traditions of the Marine Corps and the United States Naval Service. [*Other Navy award: Silver Star.*]

Livingston, James E. Captain, U.S. Marine Corps, Company E, 2nd Battalion, 4th Marines, 9th Marine Amphibious Brigade, *Place and date:* Dai Do, Republic of Vietnam, 2 May 1968. *Entered service* at: Auburn, AL. *Date and place of birth.:* 12 January 1940, Towns, Telfair County, GA. *Citation:* For conspicuous gallantry and intrepidity at the risk of his life above and beyond the call of duty while serving as Commanding Officer, Company E, 2nd Battalion, 4th Marines, 9th Marine Amphibious Brigade in action against enemy forces in the Republic of Vietnam. On 2 May 1968, Company E launched a determined assault on the heavily fortified village of Dai Do, which had been seized by the enemy on the preceding evening isolating a Marine company from the remainder of the battalion. Skillfully employing screening agents, Captain Livingston maneuvered his men to assault

James E. Livingston

positions across 500 meters of dangerous open rice paddy while under intense enemy fire. Ignoring hostile rounds impacting near him, he fearlessly led his men in a savage assault against enemy emplacements within the village. While adjusting supporting arms fire, Captain Livingston moved to the points of heaviest resistance, shouting words of encouragement to his Marines, directing their fire, and spurring the dwindling momentum of the attack on repeated occasions. Although twice painfully wounded by grenade fragments, he refused medical treatment and courageously led his men in the destruction of over 100 mutually supporting bunkers, driving the remaining enemy from their positions, and relieving the pressure on the stranded Marine company. As the two companies consolidated positions and evacuated casualties, a third company passed through the friendly lines launching an assault on the adjacent village of Dinh To, only to be halted by a furious counter-attack of an enemy battalion. swiftly assessing the situation and disregarding the heavy volume of enemy fire, Captain Livingston boldly maneuvered the remaining effective men of his company forward, joined forces with the heavily engaged Marines, and halted the enemy's counterattack. Wounded a third time and unable to walk, he steadfastly remained in the dangerously exposed area, deploying his men to more tenable positions and supervising the evacuation of casualties. Only when assured of the safety of his men did he allow himself to be evacuated. Captain Livingston's gallant actions uphold the highest traditions of the Marine Corps and the United States Naval Service. [*Other Navy awards: Distinguished Service Medal, Silver Star, Bronze Star w/V. He retired as a major general.*]

*Martini, Gary Wayne. Private First Class U.S. Marine Corps, Company F, 2nd Battalion, 1st Marines, 1st Marine Division. *Place and date:* Binh Son, Republic of Vietnam, 21 April 1967. *Entered service* at: Portland, OR. *Date and place of birth:* 21 September 1948, Rockbridge Baths, VA. *Citation:* For conspicuous gallantry and at the risk of his life above and beyond the call of duty. On 21 April 1967, during Operation UNION, elements of Company F, conducting offensive operations at Binh Son, encountered a firmly entrenched enemy force and immediately deployed to engage them. The Marines in Private Martini's platoon assaulted across an open rice paddy to within twenty meters of the enemy trench line where they were suddenly struck by hand grenades, intense small arms, automatic weapons, and mortar fire. The enemy onslaught killed 14 and wounded 18

Gary Wayne Martini

Marines, pinning the remainder of the platoon down behind a low paddy dike. In the face of imminent danger, Private Martini immediately crawled over the dike to a forward open area within 15 meters of the enemy position where, continuously exposed to the hostile fire, he hurled hand grenades, killing several of the enemy. Crawling back through the intense fire, he rejoined his platoon which had moved to the relative safety of a trench line. From this position he observed several of his wounded comrades lying helpless in the fire-swept paddy. Although he knew that one man had been killed attempting to assist the wounded, Private Martini raced through the open area and dragged a comrade back to a friendly position. In spite of a serious wound received during this first daring rescue, he again braved the unrelenting fury of the enemy fire to aid another companion lying wounded only 20 meters in front of the enemy trench line. As he reached the fallen Marine, he received a mortal wound, but disregarding his own condition, he began to drag the Marine toward his platoon's position. Observing men from his unit attempting to leave the security of their position to aid him, concerned only for their safety, he called to them to remain under cover, and through a final supreme effort, moved his injured comrade to where he could be pulled to safety, before he fell, succumbing to his wounds. Stouthearted and indomitable, Private Martini unhesitatingly yielded his life to save two of his comrades and insure the safety of the remainder of his platoon. His outstanding courage, valiant fighting spirit and selfless devotion to duty reflected the highest credit upon himself, the Marine Corps, and the United States Naval Service. He gallantly gave his life for his country.

*Maxam, Larry Leonard.** Corporal U.S. Marine Corps, Company D, 1st Battalion, 4th Marines, 3rd Marine Division (Rein), FMF. *Place and date:* Quang Tri Province, Republic of Vietnam, 2 February 1968. *Entered service at:* Los Angeles, CA. *Date and place of birth* : 9 January 1948, Glendale, CA. *Citation:* For conspicuous gallantry and intrepidity at the risk of his life above and beyond the call of duty while serving as a Fire Team Leader with Company D, 1st Battalion, 4th. Marines, 3rd Marine Division in the Republic of Vietnam. On 2 February 1968, the Cam Lo District Headquarters came under extremely heavy rocket, artillery, mortar, and recoilless rifle fire from a numerically superior enemy force, destroying a portion of the defensive perimeter. Corporal Maxam, observing the enemy massing for an assault into the compound across the remaining defensive wire, instructed his Assistant Fire Team Leader to take charge of

Larry Leonard Maxam

the fire team, and unhesitatingly proceeded to the weakened section of the perimeter. Completely exposed to the concentrated enemy fire, he sustained multiple fragmentation wounds from exploding grenades as he ran to an abandoned machine gun position. Reaching the emplacement, he grasped the machine gun and commenced to deliver effective fire on the advancing enemy. As the enemy directed maximum fire power against the determined Marine, Corporal Maxam's position received a direct hit from a rocket propelled grenade, knocking him backwards and inflicting severe fragmentation wounds to his face and right eye. Although momentarily stunned and in intense pain, Corporal Maxam courageously resumed his firing position and subsequently was struck again by small-arms fire. With resolute determination, he gallantly continued to deliver intense machine gun fire, causing the enemy to retreat through the defensive wire to positions of cover. In a desperate attempt to silence his weapon, the North Vietnamese threw hand grenades and directed recoilless rifle fire against him inflicting two additional wounds. Too weak to reload his machine gun, Corporal Maxam fell to a prone position and valiantly continued to deliver effective fire with his rifle. After one and a half hours, during which he was hit repeatedly by fragments from exploding grenades and concentrated small-arms fire, he succumbed to his wounds, having successfully defended nearly one half of the perimeter single-handedly. Corporal Maxam's aggressive fighting spirit, inspiring valor and selfless devotion to duty reflected great credit upon himself and the Marine Corps and upheld the highest traditions of the United States Naval Service. He gallantly gave his life for his country.

John James McGinty III

McGinty, John James, III. Second Lieutenant (then Staff Sergeant), U.S. Marine Corps, Company K, 3rd Battalion, 4th Marines, 3rd Marine Division, Fleet Marine Force. *Place and date:* Republic of Vietnam, 18 July 1966. *Entered service at:* Laurel Bay, SC. *Date and place of birth:* 21 January 1940, Boston, MA. *Citation:* For conspicuous gallantry and intrepidity at the risk of his life above and beyond the call of duty. Second Lieutenant (then Staff Sergeant) McGinty's platoon, which was providing rear security to protect the withdrawal of the Battalion from a position which had been under attack for three days, came under heavy small arms, automatic weapons and mortar fire from an estimated enemy regiment. With each successive human wave which assaulted his thirty-two-man platoon during the four-hour battle, Second Lieutenant McGinty rallied his men to beat off the enemy. In one bitter assault, two of the squads became separated from the remainder of the platoon. With complete disregard for his safety, Second Lieutenant McGinty charged through intense automatic weapons and mortar fire to their position. Finding twenty men wounded and the Medical Corpsman killed, he quickly reloaded ammunition magazines and weapons for the wounded men and directed their fire upon the enemy. Although he was painfully wounded as he moved to care for the disabled men, he continued to shout encouragement to his troops and to direct their fire so effectively that the attacking hordes were beaten off. When the enemy tried to out-flank his position, he killed five of them at point-blank range with his pistol. When they again seemed on the verge of overrunning the small force, he skillfully adjusted artillery and air strikes within fifty yards of his position. This destructive fire power routed the enemy, who left an estimated 500 bodies on the battlefield. Second Lieutenant McGinty's personal heroism, indomitable leadership, selfless devotion to duty, and bold fighting spirit inspired his men to resist the repeated attacks by a fanatical enemy, reflected great credit upon himself, and upheld the highest traditions of the Marine Corps and the United States Naval Service. [*He retired a captain in October 1976.*]

Modrzejewski, Robert Joseph. Major (then Captain), U.S. Marine Corps, Company K, 3rd Battalion, 4th Marines, 3rd Marine Division, FMF. *Place and date:* Republic of Vietnam, 15 to 18 July 1966. *Entered service at:* Annapolis, MD. *Date and place of birth:* 3 July 1934, Milwaukee, WI. *Citation:* For conspicuous gallantry and intrepidity at the risk of his life above and beyond the call of duty. On 15 July, during Operation HASTINGS, Company K was landed in an enemy-infested jungle area to establish a blocking position at a major enemy trail network. Shortly after landing, the company encountered a reinforced enemy platoon in a well-organized, defensive position. Major (then Captain) Modrzejewski led his men in the successful seizure of the enemy redoubt, which contained large quantities of ammunition and supplies. That evening, a numerically superior enemy force counterattacked in an effort to retake the vital supply area, thus set-

Modrzejewski, Robert Joseph

ting the pattern of activity for the next two and one-half days. In the first series of attacks, the enemy assaulted repeatedly in overwhelming numbers but each time was repulsed by the gallant Marines. The second night, the enemy struck in battalion strength, and Major Modrzejewski was wounded in this intensive action which was fought at close quarters. Although exposed to enemy fire, and despite his painful wounds, he crawled 200 meters to provide critically needed ammunition to an exposed element of his command and was constantly present wherever the fighting was heaviest despite numerous casualties, a dwindling supply of ammunition and the knowledge that they were surrounded, he skillfully directed artillery fire to within a few meters of his position and courageously inspired the efforts of his Company in repelling the aggressive enemy attack. On 18 July, Company K was attacked by a reg-imental size enemy force. Although his unit was vastly outnumbered and weakened by the previous fighting, Major Modrzejewski reorganized his men and calmly moved among them to encourage and direct their efforts to heroic limits as they fought to overcome the vicious enemy onslaught. Again he called in air and artillery strikes at close range with devastating effect on the enemy, which together with the bold and determined fighting of the men of Company K, repulsed the fanatical attack of the larger North Vietnamese force. His unparalleled personal heroism and indomitable leadership inspired his men to a significant victory over the enemy force and reflected great credit up on himself, the Marine Corps, and the United States Naval Service. [*He retired in August 1986.*]

William D. Morgan

***Morgan, William D.** Corporal, U.S. Marine Corps, Company H, 2nd Battalion, 9th Marines, 3rd Marine Division. *Place* and *date:* Quang Tri Province, Republic of Vietnam, 25 February 1969. *Entered service at:* Pittsburgh, PA. *Date and place of birth:* 17 September 1947, Pittsburgh, PA. *Citation:* For conspicuous gallantry and intrepidity at the risk of his life above and beyond the call of duty while serving as a Squad Leader with Company H, 2nd Battalion, 9th Marines, 3rd Marine Division in operations against the enemy in the Quang Tri Province, Republic of Vietnam. on 25 February 1969, while participating in Operation DEWEY CANYON southeast of Vandergrift Combat. Base, one of the squads of Corporal Morgan's platoon was temporarily pinned down and sustained several casualties while attacking a North Vietnamese Army force occupying a heavily fortified bunker complex. Observing that two of the wounded Marines had fallen in a position dangerously exposed to the enemy fire and that all attempts to evacuate them were halted by a heavy volume of automatic weapons fire and rocket-propelled grenades, Corporal Morgan unhesitatingly maneuvered through the dense jungle undergrowth to a road that passed in front of a hostile emplacement which was the principal source of enemy fire. Fully aware of the possible consequences of his valiant action, but thinking only of the welfare of his injured companions, Corporal Morgan shouted words of encouragement to them as he initiated an aggressive assault against the hostile bunker. While charging across the open road, he was clearly visible to the hostile soldiers who turned their fire in his direction and mortally wounded him, but his diversionary tactic enabled the remainder of his squad to retrieve their casualties and overrun the North Vietnamese Army position. His heroic and determined actions saved the lives of two fellow Marines and were instrumental in the subsequent defeat of the enemy. Corporal Morgan's indomitable courage, inspiring initiative and selfless devotion to duty upheld the highest traditions of the Marine Corps and of the United States Naval Services. He gallantly gave his life for his country.

Melvin Earl Newlin

*Newlin, Melvin Earl. Private First Class, U.S. Marine Corps, 2nd Battalion, 5th Marines, 1st Marine Division (Rein), FMF. *Place and date:* Quang Nam Province, Republic of Vietnam, 4 July 1967. *Entered service at:* Cleveland, OH. *Date and place of birth.:* 27 September 1948, Wellsville, OH. *Citation:* For conspicuous gallantry and intrepidity at the risk of his life above and beyond the call of duty while serving as a machine gunner attached to the 1st Platoon, Company F, 2nd Battalion, 5th Marines, 1st Marine Division, in the Republic of Vietnam on 3 and 4 July 1967. Private Newlin. with four other Marines, was manning a key position on the perimeter of the Nong Son outpost when the enemy launched a savage and well coordinated mortar and infantry assault, seriously wounding him and killing his four comrades. Propping himself against his machine gun, he poured a deadly accurate stream of fire into the charging ranks of the Viet Cong. Though repeatedly hit by small-arms fire, he twice repelled enemy attempts to overrun his position. During the third attempt, a grenade explosion wounded him again and knocked him to the ground unconscious. The Viet Cong guerrillas, believing him dead, bypassed him and continued their assault on the main force. Meanwhile, Private Newlin regained consciousness, crawled back to his weapon, and brought it to bear on the rear of the enemy causing havoc and confusion among them. Spotting the enemy attempting to bring a captured 106 recoilless weapon to bear on other Marine positions, he shifted his fire, inflicting heavy casualties on the enemy and preventing them from firing the captured weapon. He then shifted his fire back to the primary enemy force, causing the enemy to stop their assault on the Marine bunkers and to once again attack his machine gun position. Valiantly fighting off two more enemy assaults, he firmly held his ground until mortally wounded. Private Newlin had single-handedly broken up and disorganized the entire enemy assault force, causing them to lose momentum and delaying them long enough for his fellow Marines to organize a defense and beat off their secondary attack. His indomitable courage, fortitude, and unwavering devotion to duty in the face of almost certain death reflect great credit upon himself and the Marine Corps and upheld the highest traditions of the United States Naval Service.

*Noonan, Thomas P., Jr. Lance Corporal, U.S. Marine Corps, Company G, 2nd Battalion, 9th Marines, 3rd Marine Division. *Place and date:* Near Vandergrift

Combat Base, A Shau Valley, Republic of Vietnam, 5 February 1969. *Entered service at:* Brooklyn, NY. *Date and place of birth.:* 18 November 1948, Brooklyn, NY. *Citation:* For conspicuous gallantry and intrepidity at the risk of his life above and beyond the call of duty while serving as a Fire Team Leader with Company G, 2nd Battalion, 9th Marines, 3rd Marine Division, in operations against the enemy in Quang Tri Province in the Republic of Vietnam. On 5 February 1969, Company G was directed to move from a position which they had been holding southeast of the Vandergrift Combat Base in A Shau Valley to an alternate location. As the Marines commenced a slow and difficult descent down the side of the hill made extremely slippery by the heavy rains, the leading element came under a heavy fire from a North Vietnamese Army unit occupying well concealed positions in the rocky

Thomas P. Noonan, Jr.

terrain. Four men were wounded, and repeated attempts to recover them failed because of the intense hostile fire. Lance Corporal Noonan moved from his position of relative security and, maneuvering down the treacherous slope to a location near the injured men, took cover behind some rocks. Shouting words of encouragement to the wounded men to restore their confidence, he dashed across the hazardous terrain and commenced dragging the most seriously wounded man away from the fire-swept area. Although wounded and knocked to the ground by an enemy round Lance Corporal Noonan recovered rapidly and resumed dragging the man toward the marginal security of a rock. He was, however, mortally wounded before he could reach his destination. His heroic actions inspired his fellow Marines to such aggressiveness that they initiated a spirited assault which forced the enemy soldiers to withdraw. Lance Corporal Noonan's indomitable courage, inspiring initiative, and selfless devotion to duty upheld the highest traditions of the Marine Corps and the United States Naval Service. He gallantly gave his life for his country.

O'Malley, Robert Emmet. Sergeant, U.S. Marine Corps, Company I, 3rd Battalion, 3rd Marine Regiment, 3rd Marine Division (Reinforced). *Place and date:* Near An Cu'ong 2 South Vietnam, 18 August 1965. *Entered service at:* Charlotte, NC. *Date and place of birth:* 3 June 1943, New York, NY. *Citation:* For conspicuous gallantry and intrepidity in action against the communist (Viet Cong) forces at the risk of his own life above and beyond the call of duty. While leading his squad in the assault against a strongly entrenched enemy force, his unit came under intense small arms fire. With complete disregard for his personal safety, Corporal O'Malley raced across an open rice paddy to a trench line where the enemy forces were located. Jumping

Robert Emmet O'Malley

into the trench, he attacked the Viet Cong with his rifle and grenades, and singly killed eight of the enemy. He then led his squad to the assistance of an adjacent Marine unit which was suffering heavy casualties. Continuing to press forward, he reloaded his weapon and fired with telling effect into the enemy emplacement. He personally assisted in the evacuation of several wounded Marines, and again regrouping the remnants of his squad, he returned to the point of the heaviest fighting. Ordered to an evacuation point by an officer, Corporal O'Malley gathered his besieged and badly wounded squad, and boldly led them under fire to a helicopter for withdrawal. Although three times wounded in this encounter, and facing imminent death from a fanatic and determined enemy, he steadfastly refused evacuation and continued to cover his squad's boarding of the helicopters while, from an exposed position, he delivered fire against the enemy until his wounded men were evacuated. Only then, with his last mission accomplished, did he permit himself to be removed from the battlefield. By his valor, leadership, and courageous efforts in behalf of his comrades, he served as an inspiration to all who observed him and reflected the highest credit upon the Marine Corps and the United States Naval Service.

*Paul, Joe C. Lance Corporal, U.S. Marine Corps, Company H, 2nd Battalion, 4th Marines (Rein), 3rd Marine Division (Rein). *Place and date:* near Chu Lai, Republic of Vietnam, 18 August 1965. *Entered service at:* Dayton, OH. *Date and place of birth:* 23 April 1946, Williamsburg, KY. *Citation:* For conspicuous gallantry and intrepidity at the risk of his life above and beyond the call of duty. In violent battle, Corporal Paul's platoon sustained five casualties as it was temporarily pinned down, by devastating mortar, recoilless rifle, automatic weapons, and rifle fire delivered by insurgent communist (Viet Cong) forces in well entrenched positions. The wounded Marines were unable to move from their perilously exposed positions forward of the remainder of their platoon, and were suddenly subjected to a barrage of white phosphorous rifle grenades. Corporal Paul, fully aware that his tactics would almost certainly result in serious injury or death to himself, chose to disregard his

Joe C. Paul

own safety and boldly dashed across the fire-swept rice paddies, placed himself between his wounded comrades and the enemy, and delivered effective suppressive fire with his automatic weapon in order to divert the attack long enough to allow the casualties to be evacuated. Although critically wounded during the course of the battle, he resolutely remained in his exposed position and continued to fire his rifle until he collapsed and was evacuated. By his fortitude and gallant spirit of self-sacrifice in the face of almost certain death, he saved the lives of several of his fellow Marines. His heroic action served to inspire all who observed him and reflect the highest credit upon himself, the Marine Corps and the United States Naval Service. He gallantly gave his life in the cause of freedom.

William Thomas Perkins, Jr.

*Perkins, William Thomas, Jr. Corporal, U.S. Marine Corps, Company C, 1st Battalion, 1st Marines, 1st Marine Division. *Place and date:* Quang Tri Province, Republic of Vietnam, 12 October 1967. *Entered service at:* San Francisco, CA. *Date and place of birth:* 10 August 1947, Rochester, NY. *Citation:* For conspicuous gallantry and intrepidity at the risk of his life above and beyond the call of duty while serving as a combat photographer attached to Company C, 1st Battalion, 1st Marines, 1st Marine Division, in the Republic of Vietnam on 12 October 1967. During Operation MEDINA, a major reconnaissance in force southwest of Quang Tri, Company C made heavy combat contact with a numerically superior North Vietnamese Army force estimated at from two to three companies. The focal point of the intense fighting was a helicopter landing zone which was also serving as the Command Post of Company C. In the course of a strong hostile attack, an enemy grenade landed in the immediate area occupied by Corporal Perkins and three other Marines. Realizing the inherent danger, he shouted the warning, "Incoming Grenade" to his fellow Marines, and in a valiant act of heroism, hurled himself upon the grenade absorbing the impact of the explosion with his own body, thereby saving the lives of his comrades at the cost of his own. Through his exceptional courage and inspiring valor in the face of certain death, Corporal Perkins reflected great credit upon himself and the Marine Corps and upheld the highest traditions of the United States Naval Service. He a gallantly gave his life for his country.

*Peters, Lawrence David. Sergeant, U.S. Marine Corps, Company M, 3rd Battalion, 5th Marines, 1st Marine Division. *Place and date:* Quang Tin Province, Republic of Vietnam, 4 September 1967. *Entered service at:* Binghamton, NY. *Date and place of birth:* 16 September 1946, Johnson City, NY. *Citation:* For conspicuous gallantry and intrepidity at the risk of his life above and beyond the call of duty while serving as a squad leader with Company M, 3rd Battalion, 5th Marines, 1st Marine Division, in the Republic of Vietnam on 4 September 1967. During Operation SWIFT, in the province of Quang Tin, the Marines of the 2nd platoon of Company M were struck by intense mortar, machine gun, and small-arms fire from an entrenched enemy force. As the company rallied its forces, Sergeant Peters maneuvered his squad in an assault on an enemy defended knoll. Disregarding his own safety, as enemy rounds hit all about him, he stood in the open, pointing out enemy positions until he was painfully wounded in the leg. Disregarding his wound, he moved forward and continued to lead his men. As the enemy fire increased in accuracy and volume, his squad lost its momentum and was temporarily pinned down. Exposing himself to devastating enemy fire, he consolidated his position to render more effective fire. While directing the base of fire, he was wounded a

Lawrence David Peters

second time in the face and neck from an exploding mortar round. As the enemy attempted to infiltrate the position of an adjacent platoon, Sergeant Peters stood erect in the full view of the enemy firing burst after burst forcing them to disclose their camouflaged positions. Sergeant Peters steadfastly continued to direct his squad in spite of two additional wounds, persisted in his efforts to encourage and supervise his men until lie lost consciousness and succumbed. Inspired by his selfless actions, the squad regained fire superiority and once again carried the assault to the enemy. By his outstanding valor, indomitable fighting spirit and tenacious determination in the face of overwhelming odds, Sergeant Peters upheld the highest traditions of the Marine Corps and the United States Naval Service. He gallantly gave his life for his country.

*Phipps, Jimmy W.   Private 1st Class, U.S. Marine Corps. Company B, 1st Engineer Battalion, 1st Marine Division (Rein), FMF. *Place and date:* Near An Hoa, Republic of Vietnam. 27 May 1969. *Entered service at:* 3 January 1968, Los Angeles. CA. *Date and place of birth:* November 1, 1950, Santa Monica, CA. *Citation:* For conspicuous gallantry and intrepidity at the risk of his life above and beyond the call of duty while serving as a Combat Engineer with Company B, 1st Engineer Battalion, 1st Marine Division in connection with combat operations against the enemy in the Republic of Vietnam. On 27 May 1969. Private First Class Phipps was a member of a two-man combat engineer demolition team assigned to locate and destroy enemy artillery ordnance and concealed firing devices. After he had expended all of his explosives and blasting caps, Private First Class Phipps discovered a 175mm high explosive artillery round in a rice paddy. Suspecting that the enemy had attached the artillery round to

Jimmy W. Phipps

a secondary explosive device, he warned other Marines in the area to move to covered positions and prepared to destroy the round with a hand grenade. As he was attaching the hand grenade to a stake beside the artillery round, the fuse of the enemy's secondary explosive device ignited. Realizing that his assistant and the platoon commander were both within a few meters of him and that the imminent explosion could kill all three men, Private First Class Phipps grasped the hand grenade to his chest and dived forward to cover the enemy's explosive and the artillery round with his body, thereby shielding his companions from the detonation while absorbing the full and tremendous impact with his own body. Private First Class Phipps' indomitable courage, inspiring initiative, and selfless devotion to duty saved the lives of two Marines and upheld the highest traditions of the Marine Corps and the United States Naval Service, he gallantly gave his life for his country.

Pittman, Richard Allen. Sergeant, U.S. Marine Corps, Company I, 3rd Battalion, 5th Marines, 1st Marine Division (Rein.) FMF. *Place and date:* near the Demilitarized Zone, Republic of Vietnam, 24 July 1966. *Entered service at:* Stockton, CA. *Date and place of birth:* 26 May 1945, French Camp, San Joaquin, CA. *Citation:* For conspicuous gallantry and intrepidity at the risk of his life above and beyond the call of duty. On 24 July 1966, while Company I was conducting an operation along the axis of a narrow jungle trail, the leading company elements suffered numerous casualties when they suddenly came under heavy fire from a well concealed and numerically superior enemy force. Hearing the engaged Marines' calls for more firepower, Sergeant (then Lance Corporal) Pittman quickly exchanged his rifle for a machine

Richard Allen Pittman

gun and several belts of ammunition, left the relative safety of his platoon, and unhesitatingly rushed forward to aid his comrades. Taken under intense enemy small-arms fire at point blank range during his advance, he returned the fire, silencing the enemy position. As Sergeant Pittman continued to forge forward to aid members of the leading platoon, he again came under heavy fire from two automatic weapons which he promptly destroyed. Learning that there were additional wounded Marines fifty yards further along the trail, he braved a withering hail of enemy mortar and small-arms fire to continue onward. As he reached the position where the leading Marines had fallen, he was suddenly confronted with a bold frontal attack by 30 to 40 enemy. Totally disregarding his own safety, he calmly established a position in the middle of the trail and raked the advancing enemy with devastating machine gun fire. His weapon rendered ineffective, he picked up an enemy submachine gun and, together with a pistol seized from a fallen comrade, continued his lethal fire until the enemy force had withdrawn. Having exhausted his ammunition except for a grenade which he hurled at the enemy, he then rejoined his own platoon. Sergeant Pittman's daring initiative, bold fighting spirit and selfless devotion to duty inflicted many enemy casualties, disrupted the enemy attack and saved the lives of many of his wounded comrades. His personal valor at grave risk to himself reflects the highest credit upon himself, the Marine Corps, and the United States Naval Service. [*He retired as a master sergeant in November 1988.*]

Pless, Stephen Wesley. Major, U.S. Marine Corps, VMD-6, Mag-36, 1st Marine Aircraft Wing. *Place and date:* Near Quang Ngai, Republic of Vietnam, 19 August 1967. *Entered service at:* Atlanta, GA. *Date and place of birth:* 6 September 1939, Newman, GA. *Citation:* For conspicuous gallantry and intrepidity at the risk of his life above and beyond the call of duty while serving as a helicopter gunship pilot attached to Marine Observation Squadron Six in action against enemy forces near Quang Ngai, Republic of Vietnam, on 19 August 1967. During an escort mission Major (then Captain) Pless monitored an emergency call that four American soldiers stranded on a nearby beach were being overwhelmed by a large Viet Cong force. Major Pless flew to the scene and found 30 to 50 enemy soldiers in the open. Some of the enemy were bayoneting and beating the downed Americans. Major Pless

Stephen Wesley Pless

displayed exceptional airmanship as he launched a devastating attack against the enemy force, killing or wounding many of the enemy and driving the remainder back into a tree line. His rocket and machine gun attacks were made at such low levels that the aircraft flew through debris created by explosions from its rockets. Seeing one of the wounded soldiers gesture for assistance, he maneuvered his helicopter into a position between the wounded men and the enemy, providing a shield which permitted his crew to retrieve the wounded. During the rescue the enemy directed intense fire at the helicopter and rushed the aircraft again and again, closing to within a few feet before being beaten back. When the wounded men were aboard, Major Pless maneuvered the helicopter out to sea. Before it became safely airborne, the overloaded aircraft settled four times into the water. Displaying superb airmanship, he finally got the helicopter aloft. Major Pless' extraordinary heroism coupled with his outstanding flying skill prevented the annihilation of the tiny force. His courageous actions reflect great credit upon himself and uphold the highest traditions of the Marine Corps and the United States Naval Service. [*Other Navy awards: Silver Star, Distinguished Flying Cross, Bronze Star, nine Air Medals, seven silver, two gold. He died on active service in 1967.*]

William R. Prom

*Prom, William R. Lance Corporal, U.S. Marine Corps, Company I, 3rd Battalion, 3rd Marines, 3rd Marine Division (Rem), FMF. *Place and date:* Near An Hoa, Republic of Vietnam, 9 February 1969. *Entered service at:* Pittsburgh, PA. *Date and place of birth:* 17 November 1948, Pittsburgh, PA. *Citation:* For conspicuous gallantry and intrepidity at the risk of his life above and beyond the call of duty while serving as a Machine Gun Squad Leader with Company I, 3rd Battalion, 3rd Marines, 3rd Marine Division in action against the enemy in the Republic of Vietnam. While returning from a reconnaissance operation on 9 February 1969 during Operation TAYLOR COMMON, two platoons of Company I came under an intense automatic weapons fire and grenade attack from a well concealed North Vietnamese Army force in fortified positions. The leading element of the platoon was isolated and several Marines were wounded. Lance Corporal Prom immediately assumed control of one of his machine guns and began to deliver return fire. Disregarding his own safety he advanced to a position from which he could more effectively deliver covering fire while first aid was administered to the wounded men. Realizing that the enemy would have to be destroyed before the injured Marines could be evacuated, Lance Corporal Prom again moved forward and delivered a heavy volume of fire with such accuracy that he was instrumental in routing the enemy, thus permitting his men to regroup and resume their march. Shortly thereafter, the platoon again came under heavy fire in which one man was critically wounded. React-ing instantly, Lance Corporal Prom moved forward to protect his injured comrade. Unable to continue his own fire because of his severe wounds, he continued to advance to within a few yards to the enemy positions. There, standing in full view of the enemy, he accurately directed the fire of his Support elements until he was mor-tally wounded. Inspired by his heroic actions, the Marines launched an assault that destroyed the enemy. Lance Corporal Prom's indomitable courage, inspiring initia-tive and selfless devotion to duty upheld the highest traditions of the. Marine Corps and the United States Naval Service. He gallantly gave his life for his country.

*Ray, David Robert.** Hospital Corpsman Second Class, United States Navy, 2nd Battalion, 11th Marines, 1st Marine Division (Rein), FMF. *Place and date:* Quang Nam Province, Republic of Vietnam, 19 March 1969. *Entered service at:* Nashville, TN. *Date and place of birth:* 14 February 1945, McMinnville, TN. *Citation:* For con-spicuous gallantry and intrepidity at the risk of his life above and beyond the call of duty while serving as a Corpsman with Battery D, 2nd Battalion, 11th Marines, 1st Marine Division, at Phu Loc 6, near An Hoa, Quang Nam Province, in the Repub-lic of Vietnam, on 19 March 1969. During the early morning hours, an estimated bat-talion-sized enemy force launched a determined assault against the Battery's position, and succeeded in effecting a penetration of the barbed-wire perimeter. The initial burst of enemy fire caused numerous casualties among the Marines who had imme-diately manned their howitzers during the rocket and mortar attack. Undaunted by the intense hostile fire, Petty Officer Ray moved from parapet to parapet, rending emergency medical treatment to the wounded. Although seriously wounded himself while administering first aid to a Marine casualty, he refused medical aid and con-tinued his lifesaving efforts. While he was bandaging and attempting to comfort another wounded Marine, Petty Officer Ray was forced to battle two enemy soldiers who attacked his position, personally killing one and wounding the other. Rapidly losing his strength as a result of his own severe wounds, he nonetheless managed to move through the hail of enemy fire to other casualties. Once again, he was faced with the intense fire of oncoming enemy troops and, despite the grave personal dan-ger and insurmountable odds, succeeded in treating the wounded and holding off the enemy until he ran out of ammunition, at which time he sustained fatal wounds. Petty Officer Ray's final act of heroism was to protect the patient he was treating. He threw himself upon the wounded Marine, thus saving the man's life when an enemy grenade exploded nearby. By his determined and persevering actions, courageous spirit, and selfless devotion to the welfare of his Marine Comrades, Petty Officer Ray served to inspire the men of Battery D to heroic efforts in defeating the enemy. Ths conduct throughout was in keeping with the finest traditions of the United States Naval Service.

*Reasoner, Frank Stanley.** First Lieutenant, U.S. Marine Corps, Company A, 3rd Reconnaissance Battalion, 3rd Marine Division. *Place and date:* near Da Nang, Vietnam, 12 July 1965. *Entered service at:* Kellogg, Idaho. *Date and place of birth:* 16 September 1937, Spokane, WA. *Citation:* For conspicuous gallantry and intrepidity at the risk of his life above and beyond the call of duty. The reconnaissance patrol

led by Lieutenant Reasoner had deeply penetrated heavily controlled enemy territory
when it came under extremely heavy fire from
an estimated 50 to 100 Viet Cong insurgents.
Accompanying the advance party and the
point that consisted of five men, he immediately deployed his men for an assault after the
Viet Cong had opened fire from numerous
concealed positions. Boldly shouting encouragement, and virtually isolated from the
main body, he organized a base of fire for an
assault on the enemy positions. The slashing
fury of the Viet Cong machine gun and automatic weapons fire made it impossible for
the main body to move forward. Repeatedly
exposing himself to the devastating attack he
skillfully provided covering fire, killing at
least two Viet Cong and effectively silencing
an automatic weapons position in a valiant
attempt to effect evacuation of a wounded
man. As casualties began to mount his radio

Frank Stanley Reasoner

operator was wounded and Lieutenant Reasoner immediately moved to his side and
tended his wounds. When the radio operator was hit a second time while attempting to reach a covered position, Lieutenant Reasoner courageously running to his
aid through the grazing machine-gun fire fell mortally wounded. His indomitable
fighting spirit, valiant leadership and unflinching devotion to duty provided the
inspiration that was to enable the patrol to complete its mission without further
casualties. In the face of almost certain death he gallantly gave his life in the service
of his country. His actions upheld the highest traditions of the Marine Corps and the
United States Naval Service.

*Singleton, Walter K. Sergeant, U.S. Marine Corps, Company A, 1st Battal-
ion, 9th Marines, 3rd Marine Division. *Place and date:* Gio Linh District, Quang Tri
Province, Republic of Vietnam, 24 March 1967. *Entered service at:* Memphis, TN.
Date and place of birth: 7 December 1944, Memphis, TN. *Citation:* For conspicuous
gallantry and intrepidity at the risk of his life above and beyond the call of duty.
Sergeant Singleton's Company was conducting combat operations in Gio Linh District, Quang Tri Province, Republic of Vietnam, when the lead platoon received
intense small arms, automatic weapons, rocket, and mortar fire from a well
entrenched enemy force. As the company fought its way forward, the extremely heavy
enemy fire caused numerous friendly casualties. Sensing the need for early treatment
of the wounded, Sergeant Singleton quickly moved from his relatively safe position
in the rear of the foremost point of the advance and made numerous trips through
the enemy killing tone to move the injured men out of the danger area. Noting that
a large part of the enemy fine was coming from a hedgerow, he seized a machine-

gun and assaulted the key enemy location, delivering devastating fire as he advanced. He forced his way through the hedgerow directly into the enemy strong point. Although he was mortally wounded, his fearless attack killed eight of the enemy and drove the remainder from the hedgerow. Sergeant Singleton's bold actions completely disorganized the enemy defense and saved the lives of many of his comrades. His daring initiative, selfless devotion to duty and indomitable fighting spirit reflected great credit upon himself and the Marine Corps, and his performance upheld the highest traditions of the United States Naval Service.

*Smedley, Larry Eugene. Corporal, U.S. Marine Corps, Company D, 1st Battalion, 7th Marines, 1st Marine Division. *Place and date:* Quang Nam Province, Republic of Vietnam, 21 December 1967. *Entered service* at: Orlando, FL. *Date and place of birth:* 4 March 1949, Front Royal, VA. *Citation:* For conspicuous gallantry and intrepidity at the risk of his life above and beyond the call of duty while serving as a squad leader with company D, 1st Battalion, 7th Marines, 1st Marine Division in connection with operations against the enemy in the Republic of Vietnam. On the evenings of 20–21 December 1967, Corporal Smedley led his six-man squad to an ambush site at the mouth of Happy Valley, near Phouc Ninh (2) in Quang Nam Province. Later that night an estimated 100 Viet Cong and North Vietnamese Army Regulars, carrying 122mm rocket launchers and mortars, were observed moving toward Hill 41. Realizing this was a significant enemy move to launch an attack on the vital Danang complex, Corporal Smedley immediately took sound and courageous

Walter K. Singleton

Larry Eugene Smedley

action to stop the enemy threat. After he radioed for a reaction force, he skillfully maneuvered his men to a more advantageous position and led an attack on the numerically superior enemy force. A heavy volume of fire from an enemy machine gun positioned on the left flank of the squad inflicted several casualties on Corporal Smedley's unit. Simultaneously, an enemy rifle grenade exploded nearby wounding him in the right foot and knocking him to the ground. Corporal Smedley disregarded this serious injury and valiantly struggled to his feet, shouting words of encouragement to his men. He fearlessly led a charge against the enemy machine gun emplacement, firing his rifle and throwing grenades, until he was again struck by enemy fire and knocked to the ground. Gravely wounded and weak from loss of blood, he rose and commenced a one-man assault against the enemy position. Although his aggressive and singlehanded attack resulted in the destruction of the machine gun, he was struck in the chest, by enemy fire and fell mortally wounded. Corporal Smedley's inspiring and courageous actions, bold initiative, and selfless devotion to duty in the face of certain death were in keeping with the highest traditions of the Marine Corps and the United States Naval Service. He gallantly gave his life for his country.

*Taylor, Karl Gorman, Sr.** Staff Sergeant, U.S. Marine Corps, Company I, 3rd Battalion, 26th Marine Regiment, 3rd Marine Division (Rein), FMF. *Place and date:* Republic of Vietnam, 8 December 1968. *Entered service at:* Baltimore, MD. *Date and place of birth:* 14 July 1939, Laurel, MD. *Citation.:* For conspicuous gallantry and intrepidity at the risk of his life above and beyond the call of duty while serving as a Company Gunnery Sergeant during Operation MEADE RIVER in the Republic of Vietnam on the night of 8 December 1968. Informed that the commander of the lead platoon had been mortally wounded when his unit was pinned down by a heavy volume of enemy fire, Staff Sergeant Taylor along with another Marine, crawled forward to the beleaguered unit through a hail of hostile fire, shouted encouragement and instructions to the men, and deployed them to covered positions. With his companion, he

Karl Gorman Taylor, Sr.

then repeatedly maneuvered across an open area to rescue those Marines who were too seriously wounded to move by themselves. Upon learning that there were still other seriously wounded men lying in another open area in proximity to an enemy machine gun position, Staff Sergeant Taylor, accompanied by four comrades, led his men forward across the fire-swept terrain in an attempt to rescue the Marines. When his group was halted by devastating fire, he directed his companions to return to the company command post; whereupon he took his grenade launcher and, in full view of the enemy, charged across the open rice paddy toward the machine gun position, firing his weapon as he ran. Although wounded several times, he succeeded in reaching the machine gun bunker and silencing the fire from that sector, moments before he was mortally wounded. Directly instrumental in saving the lives of several of his fellow Marines, Staff Sergeant Taylor, by his indomitable courage, inspiring leadership and selfless dedication, upheld the highest traditions of the Marine Corps and of the United States Naval Service.

Vargas, M. Sando, Jr. Major, U.S. Marine Corps, Company G. 2nd Battalion, 4th Marines, 9th Marine Amphibious Brigade. *Place and date:* Republic of Vietnam, 1 May 1968. *Entered service at:* Quantico, VA. *Date and place of birth:* 29 July 1937, Winslow, AZ. *Citation:* For conspicuous gallantry and intrepidity at the risk of life above and beyond the call of duty while serving as Commanding Officer, Company G, 2nd Battalion, 4th Marines, 9th Marine Amphibious Brigade in action against enemy forces in the Republic of Vietnam from 30 April to 2 May 1968. On 1 May 1968, though suffering from wounds he had incurred while relocating his unit under heavy enemy fire the preceding day, Major (then Captain) Vargas combined Company G with two other companies and led his men in an attack on the fortified village of Dai Do. Exercising expert leadership, he maneuvered his Marines across 700 meters of open rice paddy while

M. Sando Vargas, Jr.

under intense enemy mortar, rocket and artillery fire and obtained a foothold in two hedgerows on the enemy perimeter, only to have elements of his company become pinned down by the intense enemy fire. Leading his reserve platoon to the aid of his beleaguered men, Major Vargas inspired his men to renew their relentless advance, while destroying a number of enemy bunkers. Again wounded by grenade fragments, he refused aid as he moved about the hazardous area reorganizing his unit into a strong defense perimeter at the edge of the village. Shortly after the objective was secured, the enemy commenced a series of counterattacks and probes which lasted throughout the night but were unsuccessful as the gallant defenders of Company G stood firm in their hard-won enclave. Reinforced the following morning, the Marines launched a renewed assault through Dai Do on the village of Dinh To, to which the enemy retaliated with a massive counterattack resulting in hand-to-hand combat. Major Vargas remained in the open, encouraging and rendering assistance to his Marines when he was hit for the third time in the three-day battle. Observing his battalion commander sustain a serious wound he disregarded his excruciating pain, crossed the fire-swept area and carried his commander to a covered position, then resumed supervising and encouraging his men while simultaneously assisting in organizing battalion's perimeter defense. His gallant actions uphold the highest traditions of the Marine Corps and the United States Naval Service. [*Other Navy award: Silver Star. He retired as a colonel.*]

*Weber, Lester W. Lance Corporal, U.S. Marine Corps, Company M, 3rd Battalion, 7th Marines, 1st Marine Division. *Place and date:* Quang Nam Province, Republic of Vietnam, 23 February 1969. *Entered service at:* Chicago, IL. *Date and place of birth:* 30 July 1948, Aurora, IL. Citation: For conspicuous gallantry and intrepidity at the risk of his life above and beyond the call of duty while serving as a Machine gun Squad Leader with Company M, 3rd Battalion, 7th Marines, 1st Marine Division, in action against the enemy in the Republic of Vietnam. On 23 February 1969, the 2nd Platoon of Company M was dispatched to the Bo Ban area of Hieu Duc District in Quang Nam Province to assist a squad from another platoon which had become heavily engaged with a well entrenched enemy battalion. While moving through a rice paddy covered with tall grass Lance Corporal Weber's platoon came under heavy

Lester W. Weber

attack from concealed hostile soldiers. He reacted by plunging into the tall grass, successfully attacking one enemy and forcing eleven others to break contact. Upon encountering a second North Vietnamese Army soldier he overwhelmed him in fierce hand-to-hand combat. Observing two other soldiers firing upon his comrades from behind a dike, Lance Corporal Weber ignored the frenzied firing of the enemy and racing across the hazardous area, dived into their position. He neutralized the position by wrestling weapons from the hands of the two soldiers and overcoming them. Although by now the target for concentrated fire from hostile riflemen, Lance Corporal Weber remained in a dangerously exposed position to shout words of encouragement to his emboldened companions. As he moved forward to attack a fifth enemy soldier, he was mortally wounded. Lance Corporal Weber's indomitable courage, aggressive fighting spirit and unwavering devotion to duty upheld the highest traditions of the Marine Corps and of the United States Naval Service. He gallantly gave his life for his country.

*Wheat, Roy Mitchell. Lance Corporal, U.S. Marine Corps, Company K, 3rd Battalion, 7th Marines, 1st Marine Division. *Place and date:* Republic of Vietnam, 11 August 1967. *Entered service at:* Jackson, MS. *Date and place of birth:* 24 July 1947, Moselle, MS. *Citation:* For conspicuous gallantry and intrepidity at the risk of his life above and beyond the call of duty. On 11 August 1967, Corporal Wheat and two other Marines were assigned the mission of providing security for a Navy construction battalion crane and crew operating along Liberty Road in the vicinity of the

Roy Mitchell Wheat

Dien Ban District, Quang Nam Province. After the Marines had set up security positions in a tree line adjacent to the work site, Corporal Wheat reconnoitered the area to the rear of their location for the possible presence of guerrillas. He then returned to within ten feet of the friendly position, and here unintentionally triggered a well concealed, bounding type, anti-personnel mine: Immediately, a hissing sound was heard which was identified by the three Marines as that of a burning time fuse. Shouting a warning to his comrades, Corporal Wheat in a valiant act of heroism hurled himself upon the mine, absorbing the tremendous impact of the explosion with his own body. The inspirational personal heroism and extraordinary valor of his unselfish action saved his fellow Marines from certain injury and possible death, reflected great credit upon himself, and upheld the highest traditions of the Marine Corps and the United States Naval Service. He gallantly gave his life for his country.

*Williams, Dewayne T. Private First Class, U.S. Marine Corps, Company H, 2nd Battalion, 1st Marines, 1st Marine Division. *Place and date:* Quang Nam Province, Republic of Vietnam, 18 September 1969. *Entered service at:* Detroit, MI. *Date and place of* birth: 18 September 1949, Brown City, MI. *Citation:* For conspicuous gallantry and intrepidity at the risk of his life above and beyond the call of duty while serving as a rifleman with the 1st Platoon, Company H, 2nd Battalion, 1st Marines, 1st Marine Division in action against communist insurgent forces in the Quang Nam Province, Republic of Vietnam. Private First Class Williams was a member of a combat patrol sent out from the platoon with the mission of establishing positions in the company's area of operations, from which it could intercept and destroy enemy sniper teams operating in the area. On the night of 18 September 1968, as the patrol was preparing to move from its daylight position to a preselected night position, it was attacked from ambush by a squad of enemy using small arms and hand grenades. Although severely wounded in the back by the close intense fire, Private First Class Williams, recognizing the danger to the patrol, immediately began to crawl forward toward a good firing position. While he was moving under the continuing intense fire, he heard one of the members of the patrol sound the alert that an enemy grenade had landed in their position. Reacting instantly to the alert, he saw that the grenade had landed close to where he was lying and without hesitation, in a valiant act of heroism, rolled on top of the grenade as it exploded, absorbing the full and tremendous impact of the explosion with his own body. Through his extraordinary initiative and inspiring valor in the face of certain death, he saved the other members of his patrol from serious injury and possible loss of life, and enabled them to successfully defeat the attackers and hold their position until assistance arrived. His personal heroism and devotion to duty upheld the highest traditions of the Marine Corps and the United States Naval Service. He gallantly gave his life for his country.

Alfred M. Wilson

*Wilson, Alfred M. Private First Class, U.S. Marine Corps, Company M, 3rd Battalion, 9th Marines, 3rd Marine Division. *Place and date:* Quang Tri Province, Republic of Vietnam, 3 March 1969. *Entered service at:* Abilene, TX. *Date and place of birth:* 13 January 1948, Olney, IL. *Citation:* For conspicuous gallantry and intrepidity at the risk of his life above and beyond the call of duty while serving as a Rifleman with Company M, 3rd Battalion, 9th Marines, 3rd Marine Division in action against hostile forces in the Republic of Vietnam. On 3 March 1969, while returning from a reconnaissance-in-force mission in the vicinity of Fire Support Base Cunningham in Quang Tri Province, the 1st Platoon of Company M came under intense automatic weapons fire and a grenade attack from a well concealed enemy force. As the center of the column was pinned down, the leading squad moved to outflank the enemy. Private First Class Wilson, acting as Squad Leader of the rear squad, skillfully maneuvered his men to form a base of fire and act as a blocking force. In the ensuing fire fight, both his machine gunner and assistant machine gunner were seriously wounded and unable to operate their weapons. Realizing the urgent need to bring the weapon into operation again, Private First Class Wilson, followed by another Marine and with complete disregard for his own safety, fearlessly dashed across the fire-swept terrain to recover the weapon. As they reached the machine gun, an enemy soldier stepped from behind a tree and threw a grenade toward the two Marines. Observing the grenade fall between himself and the other Marine, Private First Class Wilson, fully realizing the inevitable result of his actions, shouted to his companion and unhesitatingly threw himself on the grenade, absorbing the full force of the explosion with his own body. His heroic actions inspired his platoon members to maximum effort as they aggressively attacked and defeated the enemy. Private First Class Wilson's indomitable courage, inspiring valor and selfless devotion to duty upheld the highest traditions of the Marine Corps and the United States Naval Service. He gallantly gave his life for his country.

*Worley, Kenneth L. Lance Corporal, U.S. Marine Corps, 3rd Battalion, 7th Marines, 1st Marine Division (Rein), FMF. *Place and date:* Republic of Vietnam, 12 August 1968. *Entered service at:* Fresno, CA. *Date and place of birth:* 27 April 1948, Farmington, NM. *Citation:* For conspicuous gallantry and intrepidity at the risk of his life above and beyond the call of duty while serving as a Machine Gunner with Company L, in action against enemy forces in the Republic of Vietnam. After establishing a night ambush position in a house in the Bo Ban Hamlet of Quang Nam Province, security was set up and the remainder of the patrol members retired until their respective watch. During the early morning hours of 12 August 1968, the Marines were abruptly awakened by the platoon leader's warning that "Grenades" had landed in the house. Fully realizing the inevitable result of his actions, Lance Corporal Worley, in a valiant act of heroism, instantly threw himself upon the grenade nearest him and his comrades, absorbing with his own body, the full and tremendous force of the explosion. Through his extraordinary initiative and inspiring valor in the face of almost certain death, he saved his comrades from serious injury and possible loss of life although five of his fel-

Kenneth L. Worley

low Marines incurred minor wounds as the other grenades exploded. Lance Corporal Worley's gallant actions upheld the highest traditions of the Marine Corps and the United States Naval Service. He gallantly gave his life for his country.

Appendix A:
Origins of Recipients

(Includes U.S. Navy Recipients Serving with Marines)

(B. = "Born" *A. =* "Accredited to.")

	B.	A.		B.	A.		B.	A.
Alabama	5	5	Michigan	7	8	Texas	12	15
Alaska	1		Minnesota	6	10	Utah	1	1
Arizona	1	2	Mississippi	3	3	Vermont	1	1
Arkansas	5	4	Missouri	10	7	Virginia	10	9
California	12	26	Montana	1	1	Washington	4	3
Connecticut	4	3	Nebraska	4	4	West Virginia	3	3
Colorado	3	3	Nevada			Wisconsin	5	5
Delaware			New Hampshire	1	1	Wyoming		
Florida	3	6	New Jersey	7	11	District of		
Georgia	7	6	New Mexico	1	1	Columbia	3	9
Hawaii			New York	40	39	Puerto Rico	1	1
Idaho	3	3	North Carolina	3	4	Austria	4	
Illinois	21	19	North Dakota	3	2	Canada	2	
Indiana	6	4	Ohio	15	13	England	2	
Iowa	2	2	Oklahoma	3	3	Germany	4	
Kansas	4	2	Oregon		2	India	1	
Kentucky	7	3	Pennsylvania	37	35	Ireland	15	
Louisiana	2	2	Rhode Island		1	Mexico	1	
Maine		1	South Carolina	5	5	Scotland	2	
Maryland	3	3	South Dakota	1	2	Sweden	1	
Massachusetts	16	22	Tennessee	4	4			

Appendix B:
Numbers of Awards

Numbers of Marines Killed Earning the Medal of Honor in Each War

Boxer Rebellion, of 33 awards, 1 died of wounds.
World War I, of 8 awards, 1 died of gas poisoning.
World War II, of 82 awards, 43 were killed in action or died of wounds.
Korean War Two, of 42 awards, 26 were killed in action or died of wounds.
Vietnam War, of 57 awards, 42 were killed in action or died of wounds, and 1 died of physical abuse.

Numbers of Awards by Regiments from World War I to Vietnam

First Marines	21	Ninth Marines	12	25th Marines	2
Second Marines	1	Tenth Marines	1	26th Marines	7
Third Marines	10	15th Marines	1	27th Marines	6
Fourth Marines	6	18th Marines	1	28th Marines	5
Fifth Marines	28	21st Marines	1	29th Marines	1
Sixth Marines	8	22d Marines	4	3d Reconn Bn	4
Seventh Marines	37	23d Marines	5	4th Tank Bn	1
Eighth Marines	1	24th Marines	5		

Numbers of Regulars and Reservists Awarded Medals

World War II Regulars	39	World War II Reservists	44
Korean War Regulars	29	Korean War Reservists	12
Vietnam War Regulars	56	Vietnam War Reservists	1

World War II Awards to Marines per Engagement

(Plus seven awards to U.S. Navy Corpsmen,
one award to the Coast Guard, 5 killed in action)

Wake Island	1	Tarawa	4	Tinian	2
Midway Island	2	Marshalls:		Guam	4
Makin Island	1	Namur	3	Peleliu	8
Guadalcanal	8	Roi	1	Iwo Jima	22
Solomons (air)	7	Engebi	1	Okinawa	11
Bougainville	3	Saipan	4	TOTAL	82

Korean War Awards

(Five awards to U.S. Navy Corpsmen, 4 killed in action)
TOTAL of 41 awards to Marines.

Vietnam War Awards

(Four awards to U.S. Navy Corpsmen, 2 killed in action, one to U.S. Navy Chaplain, also
killed in action)
TOTAL of 57 awards to Marines.

Appendix C:
Chronology of Awards*

Civil War

1. Mackie, Col John F.
2. Vaughn, Sgt Pinkerton R
3. Nugent, Ord Sgt Christopher
4. Oviatt, Cpl Miles M.
5. Smith, Cpl Willard M.
6. Sprowle, Ord Sgt David
7. Roantree, Sgt James S.
8. Denig, Sgt Henry
9. Hudson, Sgt Michael
10. Martin, Sgt James
11. Miller, Sgt Andrew
12. Binder, Sgt Richard
13. Rannahan, Cpl John
14. Fry, Ord Sgt Issac N.
15. Tomlin, Cpl Andrew J.
16. Thompson, Pvt Henry A.
17. Shivers, Pvt John

First Korean War

18. Brown, Cpl Charles
19. Purvis, Pvt Hugh

20. Coleman, Pvt John
21. Dougherty, Pvt James
22. McNamara, Pvt James
23. Owens, Pvt Michael

Interim

24. Stewart, Cpl James
25. Morris, Cpl John

Spanish-American War

26. Meredith, Pvt James
27. Field, Pvt Oscar
28. Franklin, Pvt Joseph J.
29. Kearney, Pvt Michael
30. Kuchneister, Pvt Hermann W.
31. Scott, Pvt Joseph F.
32. Sullivan, Pvt Edward
33. Campbell, Pvt Daniel K.
34. Hill, Pvt Frank
35. Parker, Pvt Pomeroy
36. West, Pvt Walter Scott

*Marine Corps recipients only. Addition of late award James L. Day in World War II may affect sequence of numbers.

37. Gaughan, Sgt Philip
38. Fitzgerald, Pvt John
39. Quick, Sgt John Henry
40. MacNeal, Pvt Harry L.

Philippine Islands and Samoa

41. Prendergast, Cpl Thomas F.
42. Buckley, Pvt Howard M.
43. Leonard, Pvt Joseph H.
44. Hulbert, Pvt Henry L.
45. Forsterer, Sgt Bruno A.
46. McNally, Sgt Michael J.
47. Harvey, Sgt Harry

Boxer Rebellion

48. Phillips, Cpl Reuben J.
49. Stewart, GySgt Peter
50. Orndoff, Pvt Harry W.
51. Appleton, Cpl Edwin N.
52. Burnes, Pvt James
53. Campbell, Pvt Albert R.
54. Heisch, Pvt Henry W.
55. Hunt, Pvt Martin
56. Dalhgren, Pvt John
57. Young, Pvt Frank A.
58. Fisher, Pvt Harry [1st KIA award]
59. Walker, Sgt Edward A.
60. Foley, Pvt Alexander J.
61. Francis, Pvt Charles R.
62. Kates, Pvt Thomas W.
63. Silva, Pvt France
64. Adriance, Cpl Harry C.
65. Mathias, Pvt Clarence E.
66. Adams, Sgt John M.
67. Sutton, Sgt Clarence E.
68. Davis, Pvt Henry W.
69. Murphy, Pvt John A.
70. Boydston, Pvt Edwin J.
71. Carr, Pvt William L.
72. Cooney, Pvt James
73. Gaienne, Pvt Louis R.
74. Horton, Pvt William M.C.
75. Moore, Pvt Albert

76. Preston, Pvt Herbert I.
77. Scannell, Pvt David J.
78. Upham, Pvt Oscar J.
79. Zion, Pvt William F.
80. Daly, Pvt Daniel J.

Interim

81. Helms, Sgt John
82. Pfeifer, Pvt Louis F.

Philippine Islands

83. Bearss, Capt Hiram I.
84. Porter, Capt David Dixon

Landing at Vera Cruz

85. Dyer, Capt Jesse Farley
86. Fryer, Capt Eli T.
87. Hill, Capt Walter N.
88. Hughes, Capt John A.
89. Neville, LtCol Wendell C.
90. Reid, Maj George G.
91. Berkeley, Maj Randolph C.
92. Butler, Maj Smedley D.
93. Catlin, Maj Albertus W.

Haiti

94. Ostermann, 1stLt Edward A.
95. Upshur, Capt William P.
96. Daly, GySgt Daniel J.
97. Butler, Maj Smedley D.
98. Gross, Pvt Samuel
99. Iams, Sgt Ross L.

Santo Domingo

100. Winans, Sgt Roswell
101. Glowin, Cpl Joseph A.
102. Williams, 1stLt Ernest C.

World War I

103. Hoffman, GySgt Charles F. [double]
       (Also see: Janson, Ernest W.)
104. Stockham, GySgt Fred W.
105. Cukela, Sgt Louis [double]
106. Kelly, Pvt John J. [double]
107. Pruitt, Cpl John H. [double]
108. Kocak, Sgt Matej [double]
109. Talbot, 2dLt Ralph
110. Robinson, GySgt Robert G.

Haiti

111. Hanneken, 2dLt Herman H.
112. Button, Cpl William R.

Interim

113. Smith, Pvt Albert J.

Nicaragua

114. Schilt, 1stLt Christian F.
115. Truesdell, Cpl Donald L.

World War II

116. Cannon, 1stLt George H.
117. Elrod, Capt Henry T.
118. Bauer, LtCol Harold W.
119. Fleming, Capt Richard E.
120. Smith, Maj John L.
121. Vandegrift, MajGen Alexander A.
122. Thomason, Sgt Clyde A.
123. Bailey, Maj Kenneth D.
124. Edson, LtCol Merritt A.
125. Galer, Maj Robert E.
126. Foss, Capt Joseph J.
127. Basilone, Sgt John
128. Paige, Sgt Mitchell
129. Casamento, Cpl Anthony
130. DeBlanc, Capt Jefferson J.

131. Swett, 1stLt James E.
132. Walsh, 1stLt Kenneth A.
133. Boyington, Maj Gregory J.
134. Hanson, 1stLt Robert M.
135. Owens, Sgt Robert A.
136. Thomas, Sgt Herbert A.
137. Gurke, PFC Henry
138. Hawkins, 1stLt William D.
139. Bonnyman, 1stLt Alexander, Jr.
140. Shoup, Col David M.
141. Bordelon, SSgt William J.
142. Power, 1stLt John V.
143. Dyess, LtCol Acquilla J.
144. Anderson, PFC Richard B.
145. Sorenson, Pvt Richard K.
146. D'Amato, Cpl Anthony P.
147. McCard, GySgt Robert H.
148. Epperson, PFC Harold G.
149. Agerholm, PFC Harold C.
150. Timmerman, Sgt Grant F.
151. Skaggs, PFC Luther, Jr.
152. Mason, PFC Leonard F.
153. Witek, PFC Frank P.
154. Wilson, PFC Robert L.
155. Wilson, Capt Louis H., Jr.
156. Ozbourn, Pvt Joseph W.
157. Rouh, 1stLt Carlton R.
158. Bausell, Cpl Lewis K.
159. Pope, Capt Everett P.
160. Jackson, PFC Arthur, Jr.
161. Roan, PFC Charles H.
162. New, PFC John D.
163. Phelps, Pvt Wesley
164. Kraus, PFC Richard E.
165. Stein, Cpl Tony
166. Chambers, LtCol Justice M.
167. Ruhl, PFC Donald J.
168. Cole, Sgt Darrell S.
169. Dunlap, Capt Robert H.
170. Lucas, PFC Jacklyn H.
171. McCarthy, Capt Joseph J.
172. Williams, Cpl Hershel W.
173. Jacobson, PFC Douglas T.
174. Watson, Pvt Wilson D.
175. Walsh, GySgt William D.
176. Gray, Sgt Ross F.
177. Berry, Cpl Charles J.

178. Caddy, PFC William R.
179. Harrell, Sgt William G.
180. Leims, 2dLt John H.
181. Lummus, 1stLt Jack
182. La Belle, PFC James D.
183. Julian, PlSgt Joseph R.
184. Sigler, Pvt Franklin E.
185. Phillips, Pvt George
186. Martin, 1stLt Harry L.
187. Gonsalves, PFC Harold
188. Bush, Cpl Richard E.
189. Kinser, Sgt Elbert H.
190. Foster, PFC William A.
191. Fardy, Cpl John P.
192. Schwab, PFC Albert E.
193. Hansen, Pvt Dale M.
194. Hauge, Cpl Louis J., Jr.
195. Courtney, Maj Henry A., Jr.
[?] Day, Cpl James L. [1998 late award]
196. McTureous, Pvt Robert M., Jr.

Second Korean War

197. Lopez, 1stLt Baldomero
198. Monegan, PFC Walter C., Jr.
199. Commiskey, 2dLt Henry A., Sr.
200. Obregon, PFC Eugene A.
201. Christianson, PFC Stanley R.
202. Van Winkle, SSgt Archie
203. Phillips, Cpl Lee H.
204. Poynter, Sgt James L.
205. Reem, 2dLt Robert D.
206. Mitchell, 1stLt Frank N.
207. Kennemore, SSgt Robert S.
208. Cafferata, Pvt Hector A., Jr.
209. Sitter, Capt Carl L.
210. Myers, Maj Reginald R.
211. Baugh, PFC William E.
212. Davis, LtCol Raymond G.
213. Barber, Capt William E.
214. Windrich, SSgt William G.
215. Johnson, Sgt James E.
216. Littleton, PFC Herbert A.
217. Wilson, TSgt Harold E.
218. Moreland, PFC Whitt L.
219. Abrell, Cpl Charles G.

220. Ramer, 2dLt George H.
221. Mausert, Sgt Frederick W., III
222. Gomez, PFC Edward
223. Vittori, Cpl Joseph
224. Davenport, Cpl Jack A.
225. Dewey, Cpl Duane E.
226. Champagne, Cpl David B.
227. Kelly, Pvt John D.
228. Shuck, SSgt William E., Jr.
229. Simanek, PFC Robert E.
230. McLaughlin, PFC Alford A.
231. Garcia, PFC Fernando L.
232. Kelso, PFC Jack W.
233. Watkins, SSgt Lewis G.
234. Skinner, 2dLt Sherrod E., Jr.
235. O'Brien, 2dLt George H., Jr.
236. Murphy, 2dLt Raymond G.
237. Matthews, Sgt Daniel P.
238. Guillen, SSgt Ambrosio

Vietnam War

239. Cook, Capt Donald G.
240. Reasoner, 1stLt Frank S.
241. O'Malley, Cpl Robert E.
242. Paul, LCpl Joe C.
243. Barnum, 1stLt Harvey C., Jr.
244. Conner, SSgt Peter S.
245. Howard, SSgt Jimmie E.
246. Lee, Capt Howard V.
247. Modrzejewski, Capt Robert J.
248. McGinty, Sgt John J., III
249. Pittman, LCpl Richard A.
250. Anderson, PFC James
251. Singleton, Sgt Walter K.
252. Dickey, PFC Douglas A.
253. Bobo, 2dLt John P.
254. Martini, PFC Gary W.
255. Graham, Capt James A.
256. Newlin, PFC Melvin C.
257. Wheat, LCpl Roy M.
258. Pless, Capt Stephen W.
259. Peters, Sgt Lawrence D.
260. Davis, Sgt Rodney M.
261. Barker, LCpl Jedh C.
262. Perkins, Cpl William T., Jr.

263. Foster, Sgt Paul H.
264. Smedley, Cpl Larry E.
265. Maxam, Cpl Larry L.
266. Gonzalez, Sgt Alfredo
267. Graves, 2dLt Terrence C.
268. Vargas, Capt Jay R.
269. Livingston, Capt James E.
270. Burke, PFC Robert C.
271. Worley, LCpl Kenneth L.
272. Williams, PFC DeWayne T.
273. Taylor, SSgt Karl G., Sr.
274. Noonan, LCpl Thomas P., Jr.
275. Prom, LCpl William R.
276. Creek, LCpl Thomas E.
277. Fox, 1stLt Wesley L.
278. Weber, LCpl Lester W.
279. Austin, PFC Oscar P.

280. Morgan, Cpl William D.
281. Bruce, PFC Daniel D.
282. Wilson, PFC Alfred M.
283. Jenkins, PFC Robert H., Jr.
284. Johnson, PFC Ralph H.
285. Coker, PFC Ronald L.
286. Phipps, PFC Jimmie W.
287. Carter, PFC Bruce W.
288. Anderson, LCpl Richard A.
289. Jimenez, LCpl Jose F.
290. Dias, PFC Ralph C.
291. Clausen, PFC Raymond M., Jr.
292. Kellogg, SSgt Allan J., Jr.
293. De La Garza, LCpl Emilio A., Jr.
294. Howe, LCpl James D.
295. Keith, LCpl Miguel

Bibliography

United States Government Publications

Annual Reports of the Navy Department for the Fiscal Years 1863–2003. Washington, D.C.: U.S. Government Printing Office.

Condit, Kenneth W., and Edwin T. Turnbladh. *Hold High the Torch: A History of the 4th Marines*. Washington, D.C.: Historical Branch, G-3 Division, Headquarters, U.S. Marine Corps, 1960.

Decorations, United States Army: 1862–1926. Washington, D.C.: War Department, Office of the Adjutant General, U.S. Government Printing Office, 1927. (Includes U.S. Marines serving with the U.S. Army in 1918.)

Fuller, Stephen M., and Graham Cosmas. *Marines in the Dominican Republic 1916–1924*. Washington, D.C.: History and Museums Division, Headquarters, U.S. Marine Corps, 1974.

History of U.S. Marine Corps Operations in World War II. 5 vols. Washington, D.C.: U.S. Government Printing Office, n.d. (circa 1958), 1968.

Medal of Honor, 1862–1949, The Navy. Washington, D.C: n.p., n.d (circa 1950).

Medal of Honor Recipients, 1863–1973. Washington, D.C.: Committee on Veterans' Affairs, U.S. Government Printing Office, 1973.

Smith, Julian C., et al. *A Review of the Organization and Operations of the Guardia Nacional de Nicaragua*. By Direction of the Major General Commandant of the United States Marines Corps. Quantico, Va.: n.p., n.d. (circa 1935).

U.S. Marine Corps World War II monograph series (by publishing date):

1947. Heinl, Robert D. *The Defense of Wake*. Historical Section, Division of Public Information, Headquarters, U.S. Marine Corp.

1947. Stockman, James R. *The Battle for Tarawa*. Historical Section, Division of Public Information, Headquarters, U.S. Marine Corps.

1948. Heinl, Robert D. *Marines at Midway*. Historical Section, Division of Public Information, Headquarters, U.S. Marine Corps.

1948. Rentz, John N. *Bougainville and the Northern Solomons*. Historical Section, Division of Public Information, Headquarters, U.S. Marine Corps.

1949. Zimmerman, John L. *The Guadalcanal Campaign*. Historical Division, Headquarters, U.S. Marine Corps.

1950. Hoffman, Carl W. *Saipan: The Beginning of the End*. Historical Division, Headquarters, U.S. Marine Corps.

1950. Hough, Frank O. *The Assault on Peleliu*. Historical Division, Headquarters, U.S. Marine Corps.

1951. Hoffman, Carl W. *The Seizure of Tinian*. Historical Division, Headquarters, U.S. Marine Corps.

1951. Boggs, Charles W., Jr. *Marine Aviation in the Philippines*. Historical Division, Headquarters, U.S. Marine Corps.

1952. Rentz, John N. *Marines in the Central Solomons*. Historical Branch, Headquarters, U.S. Marine Corps.

1952. Hough, Frank O., and John A. Crown. *The Campaign on New Britain.* Historical Branch, Headquarters, U.S. Marine Corps.

1954. Heinl, Robert D., and John A. Crown. *The Marshalls: Increasing the Tempo,* Historical Branch, G-3 Division, Headquarters, U.S. Marine Corps.

1954. Lodge, O.R. *The Recapture of Guam.* Historical Branch, G-3 Division, Headquarters, U.S. Marine Corps.

1954. Bartley, Whitman S. *Iwo Jima: Amphibious Epic.* Historical Branch, G-3 Division, Headquarters, U.S. Marine Corps.

1955. Nichols, Chas. S., Jr., and Henry I Shaw, Jr. *Okinawa: Victory in the Pacific.* Historical Branch, G-3 Division, Headquarters, U.S. Marine Corps.

U.S. Marine Operations in Korea, 1950–1953, 5 vols. Washington, D.C.: Historical Branch, G-3, Headquarters, U.S. Marine Corps, 1954–1972.

U.S. Marines in Vietnam monograph series (by publishing date):

1977. Whitlow, Robert H. *U.S. Marines in Vietnam: The Advisory and Combat Assistance Era, 1954–1964.* Washington, D.C.: History and Museums Division, Headquarters, U.S. Marine Corps.

1978. Shulimson, Jack, and Charles M. Johnson. *U.S. Marines in Vietnam: The Landing and the Buildup, 1965.* Washington, D.C.: History and Museums Division, Headquarters, U.S. Marine Corps.

1982. Shulimson, Jack. *U.S. Marines in Vietnam: An Expanding War, 1966.* Washington, D.C.: History and Museums Division, Headquarters, U.S. Marine Corps.

1984. Tefler, Gary L., and Lane Rogers, and V. Keith Fleming, Jr. *U.S. Marines in Vietnam: Fighting the North Vietnamese, 1967.* Washington, D.C.: History and Museums Division, Headquarters, U.S. Marine Corps.

1986. Cosmas, Graham A., and Terrence P. Murray. *U.S. Marines Vietnam: Vietnamization and Redeployment, 1970–1971.* Washington, D.C.: History and Museums Division, Headquarters, U.S. Marine Corps.

1988. Smith, Charles R. *U.S. Marines in Vietnam: High Mobility and Standdown, 1969.* Washington, D.C.: History and Museums Division, Headquarters, U.S. Marine Corps.

1997. Shulimson, Jack, Leonard A. Blasiol, Charles R. Smith, and David A. Dawson. *U.S. Marines in Vietnam: The Defining Year, 1968.* Washington, D.C.: History and Museums Division, Headquarters, U.S. Marine Corps.

BOOKS

Alexander, Joseph H. *Edson's Raiders: The 1st Marine Raider Battalion in World War II.* Annapolis: Naval Institute Press, 2001.

Arthur, Robert A., Kenneth Kohlmia, and Robert T. Vance. *The Third Marine Division.* Washington, D.C.: Infantry Journal Press, 1948.

Beede, Benjamin R, editor. *The War of 1898 and U.S. Interventions 1898–1934: An Encyclopedia.* New York: Garland, 1994.

Blakeney, Jane. *Heroes, U.S. Marine Corps, 1861–1955. Armed Forces Awards and Flags.* Washington, D.C.: private printing, 1957.

Brown, Ronald J. *A Few Good Men: The Fighting Fifth Marines, a History of the USMC's Most Decorated Regiment.* Novato, CA: Presidio, 2001.

Calder, Bruce J. *The Impact of Intervention: The Dominican Republic During the U.S. Occupation of 1916–1924.* Austin: University of Texas Press, 1984.

Cass, Bevan G. *History of the Sixth Marine Division.* Washington, D.C.: Infantry Journal Press, 1948.

Clark, George B. *Devil Dogs: Fighting Marines of World War I.* Novato, Calif.: Presidio, 1999.

_____. *Legendary Marines of the Old Corps.* Pike, N.H: The Brass Hat, 2002.

_____. *Treading Softly: U.S. Marines in China, 1819–1949.* Westport, Conn.: Praeger, 2001.

_____. *With the Old Corps in Nicaragua.* Novato, Calif.: Presidio, 2001.

Conner, Howard M. *The Spearhead: The World War II History of the 5th Marine Division.* Washington, D.C.: Infantry Journal Press, 1950.

FitzPatrick, Tom. *A Character that Inspired: Major General Charles D Barrett, USMC.* Fairfax, Va.: private printing, 2003.

Heinl, Robert D. *Soldiers of the Sea: The U.S. Marine Corps, 1775–1962.* Annapolis: United States Naval Institute, 1962.

Hoffman, Jon T. *Chesty: The Story of Lieuten-*

ant General Lewis B. Puller, USMC. New York: Random House, 2001.

_____. *Once a Legend: "Red Mike" Edson of the Marine Raiders.* Novato, Calif.: Presidio, 1994.

Johnston, Richard W. *Follow Me! The Story of the Second Marine Division in World War II.* New York: Random House, 1948.

Langley, Lester D. *The Banana Wars: An Inner History of American Empire 1900–1934.* Lexington: University Press of Kentucky, 1983.

McCrocklin, James H., compiler. *Garde d'Haiti, 1915–1934.* Annapolis: The United States Naval Institute, 1956.

McMillan, George. *The Old Breed: A History of the First Marine Division in World War II.* Washington, D.C.: Infantry Journal Press, 1949.

Millett, Allan R. *In Many a Strife: General Gerald C. Thomas and the U.S. Marine Corps, 1917–1956.* Annapolis: Naval Institute Press, 1993.

_____. *Semper Fidelis: The History of the United States Marine Corps.* New York: Macmillan, 1980.

Munro, Dana G. *The United States and the Caribbean Republics, 1921–1933.* Princeton: Princeton University Press, 1974.

Musicant, Ivan. *The Banana Wars: A History of United States Military Intervention in Latin America from the Spanish-American War to the Invasion of Panama.* New York: Macmillan, 1990.

Proehl, Carl W., editor. *The Fourth Marine Division in World War II.* Washington, D.C.: Infantry Journal Press, 1946.

Quirk, Robert E. *An Affair of Honor: Woodrow Wilson and the Occupation of Vera Cruz.* New York: W.W. Norton, 1967.

Schmidt, Hans. *Maverick Marine: General Smedley D. Butler and Contradictions of American Military History.* Lexington: University of Kentucky Press, 1987.

_____. *The United States Occupation of Haiti, 1915–1934.* New Brunswick: Rutgers University Press, 1971.

Schuon, Karl. *U.S. Marine Corps Biographical Dictionary.* New York: Franklin Watts, 1963.

Sherrod, Robert. *History of Marine Corps Aviation in World War II.* Washington, D.C.: Combat Forces Press, 1952.

Sullivan, David M. *The United States Marine Corps in the Civil War.* 4 vols. Shippensburg, PA: White Mane Publishing, 1997–2000.

Thomas, Lowell. *Old Gimlet Eye. Adventures of Smedley D. Butler.* New York: Farrar & Rinehart, 1933.

Venzon, Anne Cipriano, editor. *General Smedley Darlington Butler: The Letters of a Leatherneck, 1898–1931.* New York: Praeger, 1992.

Wise, Frederick M. *A Marine Tells It to You.* New York: J.H. Sears, 1929.

Index

Page numbers in **bold italics** indicate photographs.

197